Wet and Wired

Wet and Wired

A POP CULTURE ENCYCLOPEDIA OF THE PACIFIC NORTHWEST

Randy Hodgins

Steve McLellan

Taylor Publishing Company
Dallas, Texas

Designed by Barbara Werden

Published by Taylor Publishing Company
1550 West Mockingbird Lane
Dallas, Texas 75235
www.taylorpub.com

Library of Congress Cataloging-in-Publication Data
Hodgins, Randy.
    Wet and wired : pop culture encyclopedia of the Pacific
Northwest / Randy Hodgins, Steve McLellan.
        p.   cm.
    Includes index.
    ISBN 0-87833-169-7
    1. Popular culture—Northwest, Pacific—Encyclopedias.
2. Arts, American—Northwest, Pacific—Encyclopedias.
3. Arts, Modern—20th century—Northwest, Pacific—Encyclopedias. 4. Northwest, Pacific—Social life and customs—
20th century—Encyclopedias. I. McLellan, Steve. II. Title.
    F852.3 .H63 2000   99-056833
    979'.003—dc 21

10 9 8 7 6 5 4 3 2 1
Printed in the United States of America

To our families—

*Tina, Alex, Phillip, and
Meagan Hodgins, and
Deb, Daniel, and Matthew
McLellan*

*For once again helping us
follow our muse*

Acknowledgments

We've been gathering the stories, facts, and rumors for this book for years. When it came to actually getting it down on paper (and finding the photographs), many people helped us take what was in our heads and files and put it on the pages you are holding. Many thanks to the staffs of the Tacoma Public Library Northwest Room, the Museum of History and Industry in Seattle, the Vancouver Public Library Special Collections Division, the City of Vancouver Archives, and the University of Washington Special Collections Division for their knowledge and gracious help. A tip of the hat also goes to all the individuals and organizations who allowed us to use photographs and took the time to provide us with special material. We also owe an enormous thanks to our agent, Deidre Knight, who believed in this book and has been a constant source of encouragement and good advice, and to Taylor Publishing Company, which has been a dream to work with. We owe you a pint of IPA at the Fish.

Contents

Introduction

Do you remember the time the Washington State Legislature actually considered making "Louie Louie" the official state song? How about when basketball superstar Bill Walton was the Portland Trail Blazers' organic "mountain man" instead of a glib network television sports commentator? And remember when Vancouver's Bachman-Turner Overdrive were the "heavyweights" of rock music in every sense of the word? If you do, or if you'd like to find out more, welcome!

For the past decade or so, Seattle, Washington; Portland, Oregon; and Vancouver, British Columbia, have been high on the list of the most livable cities in North America. Migration to the Pacific Northwest continues at a record pace and the media is fascinated with all things Northwest, from its entrepreneurial businesses to its coffee and microbrews. Nike, Nirvana, and *The X-Files* have now defined the Pacific Northwest for the world.

But long before this recent international popularity, a vibrant and unique mix of arts, sports, music, politics, business, and literature thrived in relative obscurity in the upper left-hand corner of the continental United States. Remember the famous *New Yorker* poster showing everything west of the Mississippi to be a brain-dead backwoods? We consider those to be the good old days.

Both of us came of age here in the Northwest. Writing our first book, *Seattle on Film*, brought into stark relief just how much things have changed during the past forty years and how much has been lost. For decades, the Northwest lived outside the media, economic, and political spotlights. The world ignored us, so we made our own culture, uniquely suited to our own eccentricities. The discovery of the Northwest by the national media has changed all that. Not to be apocalyptic, but the Northwest is in danger of being turned into a media theme park—"Northwestland"—designed by folks who love the image but have no grounding in the history or reality.

For example, most everyone remembers the grunge music revolution popularized by Nirvana, Pearl Jam, and Soundgarden in the late eighties and early nineties. What they don't remember, though, is the Northwest garage rock scene pioneered by the Wailers, the Kingsmen, and the Sonics in the late fifties and early sixties. In addition, people may know about Northwest restaurant chains Black Angus and Red Robin, but what about legendary eating establishments that never made it out of the region such as Seattle's Dick's Drive-In, Tacoma's Frisko Freeze, and Vancouver's White Spot?

For experts, novitiates, and those of you somewhere in between, let's take a few moments to acquaint you with our little corner of the world.

Washington

Washington State is the center of the Pacific Northwest and home of the region's flagship city Seattle. It has the most people, the hottest economy, and more attitude than you can shake a salmon at. Most people in the state live in cities and towns surrounding Puget Sound—what the late Seattle raconteur Bill Speidel called "the wet side of the mountains." A smaller number of hearty souls live in the arid climate of Eastern Washington, which boasts the Inland Empire centered in Spokane, some of the world's finest wines in the Yakima Valley, the magnificent Grand Coulee Dam, and Washington State University in Pullman (home of keggers and Cougar Gold cheese).

If the Pacific Northwest had a capital city, Seattle would claim the title because of its size and central location. Unfortunately, no one who lives outside the city would ever let that happen because they resent Seattle's insufferable egotism. It was not always that way. Seattle was known in the region for years as the humble and genteel Queen City—the original gateway to riches during the Alaskan Gold Rush and home to a rapidly growing Boeing Company during the war years.

The space-age theme of the Seattle World's Fair in 1962 and general growth in air travel in the sixties led to a new nickname—Jet City. Despite all of this growth, Seattle basically remained a middle-class city. Politics were also fiercely middle-of-the-road. The two most popular politicians in the state were Governor Dan Evans, a liberal Republican, and U.S. Senator Henry "Scoop" Jackson, a conservative Democrat.

During the late seventies and early eighties, however, the culture of the city and the greater Puget Sound area began to change. The growth of Microsoft and the rest of the high-tech industry began to lure highly educated professionals from other parts of the country. Coupled with a plethora of national publications that trumpeted Seattle's livability, the city began to grow in size and complexity.

On the positive side, the city became more cosmopolitan with a surge in the quality of arts, restaurants, sports teams, and more. On the negative side, large national chains began gobbling up longtime local businesses, transforming parts of downtown Seattle into carbon copies of other major North American cities. The influential chamber of commerce succeeded in replacing the Jet City moniker with the nickname Emerald City, much to the chagrin of irascible local observers like longtime newspaper columnist Emmett Watson. The quiet, middle-class outpost had been discovered and conquered by upwardly mobile types from Boston, New York, and Chicago.

Oregon

Oregon is a state of spectacular contrasts. The northern part of the state is heavily urban, but just an hour's drive away is one of the most beautiful coastlines in the world, peppered with a mix of charming art villages and tourist traps. The stretch between Portland and Eugene is lush agricultural land, including some of the region's finest vineyards, while the eastern part of the state has a lot of, well, nothing. Parts of the state are so wet it appears to rain from the ground up;

yet in the Rogue River area near Medford and Ashland, it is sunny nearly three hundred days a year. Whatever your taste in urbanity and climate, Oregon probably has something for you.

The same contrasts apply to Oregon politics. Here's a state popularly known for its environmental commitment, yet periodically the residents elect a legislature slightly to the right of Attila the Hun. If there is a consistent thread in Oregon politics, it seems to be a bit of frisky—or cranky—populism. Voters approved the nation's only assisted suicide law and when church leaders pushed for a revote, they passed it again ("Perhaps you didn't understand us the first time!"). Oregon is also the state where a past governor threatened to erect a "plywood curtain" to keep those pesky Californians out.

Portland is the dominant city in Oregon, though not quite as overwhelming to the rest of the state as Seattle is to Washington. You'll often hear locals say about Portland: "It's like Seattle was twenty years ago." That's meant as a compliment. Known as the Rose City, Portland has used the nation's most aggressive growth management laws to preserve greenspace, reduce sprawl, and protect walkability. Locals are now going through the same grieving process that Seattleites did twenty years ago as their freeways get more congested, their air gets dirtier, and their funky local businesses get squeezed by chains. Housing prices are also on the rise as growth begins to bump up against urban boundaries. Pressure is on for politicians to fudge the boundaries in the name of affordable homes. The next few years promise to be ones of wrenching transition as the Portland area tries to avoid some of the mistakes made by Seattle.

And one more thing: Don't call it "Ory-gun." Ever.

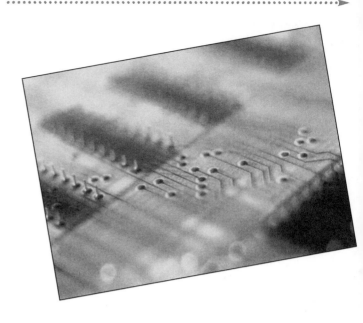

British Columbia

Most Americans don't think of British Columbia as being a part of the Pacific Northwest, but folks who live in Oregon and Washington know better. Robert D. Kaplan's August 1998 *Atlantic Monthly* article on "Travels in America's Future" trained its eye on the Pacific Northwest and envisioned a future in which the dominant culture is international and political units are merely city-state confederations linked by economic loyalties. Kaplan boldly suggested that British Columbia is the one province that would do better if Canada disintegrated. Frankly, he's right.

Actually, not all of British Columbia is part of the Pacific Northwest, only what natives like to call "the lower mainland." The majority of Canada's population lives within one hundred miles of the Canadian-American border, and those geographic measurements are generally used to define the southern portions of B.C. that border Washington State. Anything north of Kelowna is considered the Canadian frontier, populated by bears, moose, and Mounties.

But getting back to Kaplan's point, British Columbia and its flagship city Vancouver are lashed tighter economically to Washington and Oregon than to Ontario and Nova Scotia. Border crossings are routine affairs. Most local rock bands consider Vancouver part of the Northwest circuit. And several Washington and Oregon cable television packages include one or two B.C. channels in their mix. This doesn't mean that British Columbians aren't proud of their Canadian heritage; they would never think of trading their colorful money, better health-care system, or over-the-counter codeine aspirin for a life with Uncle Sam. It's just that B.C., Washington, and Oregon fortunes are inextricably linked.

Vancouver is often referred to as the Terminal City, a reference to the city's role as a port city and, since 1886, the terminus of the Canadian Pacific Railway. "It's the end of the line, the edge of the continent with nowhere further to run." It's also the most cosmopolitan and international of the Northwest's three main cities, boasting the second-largest Chinese population on the West Coast and large concentrations of immigrants from Greece, India, and numerous Asian countries. It's not uncommon to walk the streets of downtown Vancouver and hear several languages being spoken simultaneously.

The city has also been dubbed Hollywood North as a result of the numerous movies, television programs, and commercials shot in the area. Cheaper currency, an experienced film industry workforce, and an anywhere-in-North America look and feel to the city have made Vancouver a viable artistic and economic alternative to Los Angeles. Likewise, the animation industry has a growing presence in the city that boasts several internationally acclaimed animation schools and studios.

As in Oregon and Washington, while one city dominates, there are plentiful charms in the rest of the lower mainland. Victoria, the capital city on nearby Vancouver Island, has maintained a stately, if somewhat touristy, British charm. And the Okanogan region east of Vancouver is sun-drenched and spectacular. And, just as in Oregon and Washington, folks outside the big city look on it with a mix of resentment and envy.

Despite some of the differences between Washington, Oregon, and British Columbia, there are a number of things (other than simple geography) common to the entire Northwest. Casual dress is generally the norm in this part of the world, even when it comes to a night out at the theater or the opera. Historic preservation caught on here before it became fashionable in other parts of the country, with major reclamation activities in Seattle's Pioneer Square and Vancouver's Gastown districts during the late sixties and early seventies. The most popular politicians tend to hug the center of the political spectrum, although Northwest voters will occasionally elect Jesse Ventura-like mavericks such as Washington's Dixy Lee Ray, Oregon's Wayne Morse, and B.C.'s Bill Vander Zalm.

Another thing the whole Pacific Northwest is experiencing is tension between people with a fondness for the past and folks who don't know or care about our shared history. This tension flared up during the debate over the Seattle Mariners' new baseball stadium in 1995. The city and county were bitterly divided over whether to spend public money on a new stadium to keep the team from bolting to another town. Stadium supporters argued that without a better facility, Seattle would earn the distinction of being the only city in history to lose two major league baseball teams. A King County councilwoman who was a vocal opponent of the new stadium reportedly was dumbfounded that Seattle had a major league baseball team before the Mariners. Well, we did. You can find out about it in this book (see "Pilots, Seattle").

That's a brief introduction to where we live. We hope the rest of the book will give you an idea of why we love the Northwest so much. *Wet and Wired: A Pop Culture Encyclopedia of the Pacific Northwest* chronicles and catalogs both current and past Northwest popular culture— what we call the "true Northwest." So, just what does that mean? It means remembering the Seattle Center before they dismantled the Bubbleator. It means remembering that before Starbucks the only place to find good coffee in the Northwest was at Murchies in Vancouver. It means discussing the highlights and lowlights of our college and pro sports teams and chronicling the legends of Northwest broadcasting, music, politics, and business. But mostly, it means sharing our unique Northwest culture—the stuff you just won't find in the typical guidebook or history book.

Who should read this book? Folks who fall into one of the following categories.

- Longtime Northwesterners who want a fun-filled nostalgia trip, remembering events of the past and learning something about other parts of the region where they didn't grow up.
- Newcomers who want to immerse themselves in the popular culture of their adopted home. If you moved to the Northwest within the past decade, you'd probably like to know why longtime locals get misty-eyed when someone mentions Seattle's J. P. Patches, Vancouver's Commodore Ballroom, or Mountain Bars from Tacoma's Brown and Haley candy factory.
- Folks in other parts of North America who have traveled to the Pacific Northwest or would like to visit someday and who appreciate learning more about the region than just the best places to stay or the best places to eat.

Individual encyclopedia entries in the book are organized alphabetically within seven chapters: Arts and Literature; Business and Politics; Food and Drink; Media; Music; Attractions, Places, and Events; and Sports and Recreation. In addition, each chapter contains a couple of brief essays relating to the basic theme of the category, such as top television shows set in the Northwest, the origin of Northwest sports mascots, and field guides to ordering coffee and beer in the Pacific Northwest.

That's enough for starters. We think the best way to really get a feel for our little corner of the world is to dig into the entries and essays that follow. So crack open a microbrew or grab a cup of java, find your favorite reading chair, and enjoy the people, places, products, and events that make the Pacific Northwest "wet and wired."

ARTS AND LITERATURE

▓ Alexie, Sherman

A creative and nontraditional voice in Native American literature, Sherman Alexie was born in 1966 on the Spokane Indian Reservation in Wellpinit, Washington, and is a member of the Spokane/Couer d'Alene tribe. Alexie attended Gonzaga University in Spokane and graduated with a degree in American Studies from Washington State University in Pullman. His first book of poetry, *The Business of Fancydancing*, was a surprise success in 1992 and led to other poetry and short-story books, including the acclaimed *The Lone Ranger and Tonto Fistfight in Heaven*. Alexie's first novel, *Reservation Blues*, resulted in his being named one of the Best Young American Novelists by *Granta* magazine, and his second novel, *Indian Killer*, was named one of the Best of Pages by *People* magazine and a *New York Times* Notable Book. Alexie wrote the screenplay for the 1998 film *Smoke Signals*, which was based on his earlier work. The movie, financed by Seattle's Shadow Catcher Entertainment, is the first major film ever to be written, directed, and produced by Native Americans, and it won two awards at the 1998 Sundance Film Festival. Alexie lives "off the rez" in Seattle with his wife and one child.

▓ Anderson, Guy

Guy Anderson was a member of the Northwest school of mystic artists who were influenced by Eastern philosophy and the natural beauty of the Pacific Northwest. Born in 1907 and raised in the small town of Edmonds, Washington, just north of Seattle, Anderson grew up in an artistic family; the traveling art exhibitions that came to town inspired him to become an artist. A contemporary of Mark Tobey, Morris Graves, and Kenneth Callahan during the 1940s and 1950s, Anderson is considered to be the one least influenced by Tobey and his "white writing" style of painting. Anderson's influences were drawn from his external environment as well as Northwest Coast Native American art. Until his death in 1998, Anderson lived for many years in La Conner, Washington, where he was a friend and neighbor of writer Tom Robbins.

▓ Angel, Rob

Take charades, reduce it to writing, and make a million dollars. That, in a nutshell, is Rob Angel. The creator of the game Pictionary, this Vancouver, B.C., native was living in Spokane in 1981 and working as a waiter when, after work, he and his roommates began to sketch clues to words they had found in the dictionary. After moving to Seattle two years later, Angel found some notes about the game, and the recent success of Trivial Pursuit convinced him to pursue the notion of making Pictionary a reality. He and partners Gary Everson and Terry Langston borrowed thirty-five thousand dollars from Angel's uncle in 1985 to produce their first one thousand games. The three peddled the games to stores throughout Seattle wearing Pictionary sweatshirts and staging small public events to create a stir. Eventually, Pictionary became a hit and was purchased by Milton Bradley. North American sales have topped $35 million and in 1997 a television game show debuted, hosted by Alan Thicke and featuring celebrity players.

▓ Auel, Jean

Portland-area author Jean Auel is the high priestess of Pleistocene potboilers. The best-selling author of the Earth Children series of books, which include *The Clan of the Cave Bear, The Valley of Horses, The Mammoth Hunters,* and *The Plains of Passage,* grew up in the Midwest but relocated to Oregon where she and her husband raised five children. After quitting her job in a Portland electronics firm, Auel got an idea for a short story about a Cro-Magnon girl named Ayla and her interaction with the Neanderthals during the Ice Age. The first draft was more than 450,000 words and fell into six separate parts, and Auel has used this same rough draft as the outline for all of her books. The reclusive Auel is rumored to be hard at work on the fifth book in her Earth Children series.

🎵 Barry, Lynda

A talented comic artist, writer, and the creator of Ernie Pook's Comeek, Lynda Barry was born in Seattle to a Filipino mother and an Irish father and raised in the multiethnic, working-class neighborhood of Beacon Hill. While she loved books, music, writing, and drawing, Barry had no notion of becoming a cartoonist until she attended the Evergreen State College in Olympia (where they offer a doctorate in cartooning—just kidding, we think). It was there she met her "good buddy" Matt Groening, the creator of the *Simpsons* and the comic strip *Life in Hell,* who first published Barry's work in the school paper. Barry's cartoons have been published in several collections over the years and her novel, *The Good Times Are Killing Me,* was performed as an off-Broadway play. Lynda Barry currently lives in Chicago.

🎵 Beyer, Richard

Sculptor Richard Beyer is one of Seattle's best-loved public artists. Born in Washington, D.C., Beyer graduated from Columbia University with a bachelor of arts in English and continued his studies in economics at the University of Washington, where he enrolled in 1957. A former employee of the Boeing Company, Beyer began devoting all his time to sculpting in the mid-sixties. Many of his works rank among Seattle's most popular pieces of public art including the famous *Waiting for the Interurban* statue in the Fremont neighborhood. In 1989, Beyer moved to Pateros, Washington, in the state's Okanogan region.

🎵 Bouton, Jim

Still considered one of the most revealing and landmark works of sports nonfiction, *Ball Four* was written in 1970 by a journeyman baseball pitcher named Jim Bouton. He started his promising career with the New York Yankees, but by 1969 he was struggling to stay in the big leagues with the expansion Seattle Pilots. During that season, Bouton compiled his candid observations about players and managers and set out to shatter the myth of the infallible

Jim Bouton, you're not writing a book, are you?
(Photo from *Seattle Post-Intelligencer* Collection, Museum of History and Industry)

4

major league baseball player. *Ball Four* was published the following year and provoked outcries throughout the sports world, earning Bouton the enmity of the baseball establishment, as well as a truckload of money. Bouton had the last laugh. While the Pilots rank as one of baseball's all-time fiascoes, the New York Public Library recently named *Ball Four* one of the top books of the twentieth century.

Open to the sky, the Oregon Shakespearean Festival's famous outdoor Elizabethan Theatre is the oldest in the western hemisphere.
(Photo by Christopher Briscoe)

⚡ Bowmer, Angus, and the Oregon Shakespearean Festival

During the early thirties, Angus Bowmer was an enthusiastic young teacher at Southern Oregon State College in Ashland. The town had erected a Chautauqua building in 1893 as part of the late nineteenth-century movement to bring culture and entertainment to rural areas. By the late twenties the structure had been torn down and only the cement walls remained. Bowmer was struck by the similarity of the walls to some sketches he had seen of the original Globe Theater in London where Shakespeare's plays were performed. Inspired, he proposed a festival of plays within the walls in conjunction with Ashland's Fourth of July celebration. On July 2, 1935, the Oregon Shakespearean Festival (OSF) was officially born with performances of *Twelfth Night* and *The Merchant of Venice*. Today, the festival is one of the largest and most respected theater companies in North America, presenting an eight-month season of eleven plays to more than 350,000 theatergoers each year. The OSF distinguishes itself by performing all of Shakespeare's plays, even the really boring ones.

⚡ Brautigan, Richard

One of the charter members of the San Francisco "beat movement," writer Richard Brautigan was born and raised in Tacoma. Very little is known about his childhood, although there are rumors it was a troubled one. In 1967, Brautigan published his most famous book, *Trout Fishing in America*, a collection of short stories based on a single theme that became required reading for anyone who claimed to be part of the sixties. Perhaps if Brautigan had experienced a happier childhood in the Northwest, the "trout" in the title would have been changed to a "salmon." We'll never know since the author committed suicide in 1984 at the age of forty-nine.

⚡ Brooks, Terry

Northwest resident Terry Brooks is the best-selling author of the fantasy books known as the Shannara Series. While a law student at Washington and Lee University in 1977, Brooks wrote *Sword of Shannara*, which became the first work of fiction/fantasy to appear on the *New York Times* Trade Paperback Bestseller List. A practicing attorney for many years, Brooks traded pleadings for plots and now writes full time from his homes in Hawaii and near Seattle. He recently penned the best-selling novelization of George Lucas's *Star Wars Episode One: The Phantom Menace*.

⚡ Callahan, John

Shortly after his twenty-first birthday in 1972, Portland cartoonist and writer John Callahan was paralyzed after getting drunk with a buddy and crashing his Volkswagen bug into a Los Angeles billboard. After several understandable years of alcoholism and self-pity, Callahan stopped drinking and began a new life as a quadriplegic cartoonist. Callahan's cartoons are certainly not mainstream—satirist P. J. O'Rourke has said, "When people laugh like hell and say, 'That's not funny,' you can be sure they're talking about John Callahan." Callahan's cartoons appear in more than fifty publications and newspapers like the *San Francisco Chronicle, New York Daily News, Los Angeles Times*, and the *Utne Reader*. The film rights to his autobiography, *Don't Worry He Won't Get Far on Foot: The Autobiography of a Dangerous Man*, were purchased by actor Robin Williams, who plans to play Callahan in the movie.

⚡ Callahan, Kenneth

One of the four artists identified as part of the Northwest mystics school by *Life* magazine in 1953, Kenneth Callahan was born in Spokane in 1906 and studied at the University of Washington, in Mexico, and in Europe. In the early thirties, Callahan served as curator and publicist for the Seattle Art Museum, but left the position in 1953 to concentrate full time on his art. Callahan's subjects were often mountains and horses, and his work is well represented in museums and private collections throughout the United States. After the untimely death of his first wife Margaret, Callahan moved to Long Beach, Washington, where he remarried and lived until his death in 1986.

⚡ Carr, Emily

British Columbia's most renowned artist, Emily Carr, was born in 1871 in Victoria. As a young woman Carr studied in San Francisco, London, and Paris, eventually returning to Vancouver to teach art to children. Although Carr was raised by English parents, she was drawn to the native peoples of British Columbia. She made several trips to native villages and produced a number of paintings and sketches of Native American life and totem art. Unable to support herself as an artist, Carr worked in Victoria as a landlady for many years. In her late fifties, she met the members of the Group of Seven—an influential group of artists from the Toronto area who opposed European traditions in Canadian painting. With their encouragement, Carr returned to her artwork, replacing her Native American subjects with paintings of the great western forests and landscapes of British Columbia. Heart trouble forced Carr to abandon painting in the early 1940s, and she began another career as a writer. Her novel *Klee Wyck* won the Governor General's Award in 1941 (and was the name of the 1994 Commonwealth Games mascot), and other books followed until her death in 1945. Carr's paintings are quintessentially Northwest and the Vancouver Art Museum maintains a large collection of her work.

⚡ Carver, Raymond

Short-story writer and poet Raymond Carver was born in Clatskanie, Oregon, in 1938, and raised in a poor working-class family in Yakima, Washington. He married at nineteen and was the father of two children by the time he was twenty, relocating to various towns in northern California and working a series of menial jobs. Disgracing couch potatoes everywhere, Carver found time after work to write short stories of uncommon power. The *London Times* once said that Carver's work "affirmed the individuality that survives mass-produced goods and look-alike lifestyles." Despite a raging battle with alcoholism, Carver wrote numerous short stories and poems during the sixties and seventies. His writing has been favorably compared to that of master short-story writer Anton Chekhov. In 1977, Carver quit drinking forever. Although his marriage did not survive, he soon met a fellow writer from the Pacific Northwest named Tess Gallagher (a fine author in her own right), who remained his companion until his death in 1988 from cancer. Carver lived the last years of his life in Port Angeles, Washington, and he is buried in the nearby Ocean View Cemetery, overlooking the Strait of Juan de Fuca.

⚡ Chihuly, Dale

America's most enthusiastic ambassador of glass art is Seattle's Dale Chihuly. Born in Tacoma in 1941, Chihuly studied interior design at the University of Washington, graduating with a bachelor of arts in 1965. Numerous trips to Europe to study with glass masters and further degrees in sculpture led to a fifteen-year collaboration with the glass department of the Rhode Island School of Design. In 1971, while teaching in Rhode Island, Chihuly helped to establish the Pilchuck Glass School on a remote tree farm north of Seattle—the first school dedicated solely to glass art. During a visit to England in 1976, Chihuly was involved in a serious automobile accident that cost him the loss of one eye and diminished his ability to work the blowpipe used to shape glass. The accident required him to change his glassblowing methods and hire assistants to do the blowing while he concentrated on creating pieces through sketching and painting. In 1983, Chihuly moved back to Seattle and established a new studio creating even larger pieces, particularly in collaborations with the Seattle Opera. Chihuly has received numerous national and international honors and he continues to create exciting glass art that is showcased throughout the world.

⚡ Cleary, Beverly

If you were read to as a child or have read to a child, you probably know Beverly Cleary's work, if not her name. Born in McMinnville, Oregon, in 1916, Cleary is famous as the author of the Ramona Quimby books, chronicling the lives of Ramona, Henry Huggins, Ribsy the dog, and a host of friends on N.E. Klickitat Street in Portland. After graduating from the University of Washington in 1939 with a degree in librarianship, Cleary decided to write a book for young readers that reminded her of the children with whom she had spent her childhood. Her first book, *Henry Huggins* (1950), was an immediate success and led to a number of others throughout the 1950s. Cleary also wrote a popular series of books about a mouse named Ralph beginning with *The Mouse and the Motorcycle* (1965). She won the Newbery Medal in 1984 for her book *Dear Mr. Henshaw* (1983) about a boy who comes to terms with his parents' divorce. After a fifteen-year hiatus, Cleary recently issued *Ramona's World*, introducing her stories to a new generation. The children's section of the Portland Central Library is named for Cleary, and she also has been honored with a sculpture garden in Portland's Grant Park devoted to her Ramona characters.

⚡ Cornish School

Seattle's internationally recognized Cornish School for the Arts was founded in 1914 by local music teacher Nellie Cornish. During the school's early years, actors, musicians, and dancers such as Merce Cunningham, John Cage, Mark Tobey, and Martha Graham were either students or part of the faculty at Cornish. Nellie Cornish left the school in the late thirties and Cornish began a slow decline in terms of its financial support. In the seventies, a more ambitious board of directors hired a new school director from Buffalo with the goal of transforming Cornish into the "Juilliard of the West." Today, Cornish has an international reputation as one of the finest private arts colleges in North America.

⚡ Coupland, Douglas

North American culture gained a new catchphrase with the publication of Vancouver author Douglas Coupland's 1992 novel *Generation X: Tales for an Accelerated Culture*. Considered the definitive field guide for those born between the mid-sixties and late seventies, the book is a breezy and satirical tale of three twentysomethings drifting through what the authors of *Mondo Canuck* refer to as "post-electronic ennui." The novel was instantly heralded by the media, which was desperate for another identifiable target market and hungry for an alternative to the already overanalyzed baby-boom generation. A former art student, Coupland previously worked on the staff of *Vancouver* magazine. He is also the author of the 1998 book *Girlfriend in a Coma* and the *Microserfs*, a sharp dissection of the computer-programmer life.

⚡ Cunningham, Imogen

An influential twentieth-century photographer, Imogen Cunningham was born in Portland in 1883 and raised in Seattle, where she attended the University of Washington. After college she worked for the Edward Curtis Studio and was awarded a scholarship to study in Europe. Following her marriage and the birth of three sons, Cunningham moved to the San Francisco Bay area where she would spend the rest of her life. There she joined a group founded by legendary shutterbug Ansel Adams called the "Group f/64"—photographers who were dedicated to the honest, sharply defined image. The name of the group referred to the camera's lens opening f/64, which provides the most resolution and depth of field possible. Cunningham divorced in the 1930s but continued with her photography, working on assignment for magazines (particularly *Vanity Fair*), shooting portraiture, and teaching. Cunningham is best remembered for her realistic portraits and close-ups of flowers and plants. She continued to work up until just a few weeks before her death in 1976 at the age of ninety-three.

⚡ Cunningham, Merce

Master choreographer and a leader of the avant-garde movement in American dance, Merce Cunningham was born in 1919 in Centralia, Washington—a small town made famous the same year by a violent clash involving the Industrial Workers of the World (I.W.W. or Wobblies), which became known as the "Centralia Massacre." He studied folk, tap, and ballroom dance in Centralia and later attended the Cornish School in Seattle where he met composer John Cage, with whom he formed a long artistic association. Between 1939 and 1945, Cunningham was a soloist with the Martha Graham Dance Company. In the early fifties, Cunningham founded his own company and since that time has choreographed more than 150 separate works for the group. Merce Cunningham has been the recipient of numerous awards in dance and related fields, and is a Kennedy Center honoree.

Dark Horse Comics

In the early eighties, Bend, Oregon, science fiction bookstore owner Mike Richardson saw an opportunity to offer a line of comic books targeted directly to teenagers and adults. By 1986, Richardson had teamed up with Randy Stradley, and Dark Horse Comics was born. Some of Dark Horse's most successful comics include *Sin City*, *Aliens*, and *Star Wars*, and the company's work has inspired five films to date, including *The Mask*, *Timecop*, *Dr. Giggles*, *Barb Wire*, and *Virus*. Headquarted now in Milwaukie, Oregon, Dark Horse is one of the nation's most popular and successful comic book publishers.

Davis, H. L.

Harold Lenoir Davis may be the most honored writer from the state of Oregon that no one remembers. While Ken Kesey gets most of the attention as Oregon's greatest novelist, it was H. L. Davis who won the Pulitzer Prize in 1936 for his novel *Honey in the Horn*. Born in the small town of Rone's Mill (just north of Roseburg) in 1894, Davis's family eventually moved to The Dalles where his father was a school principal. His crowning achievement—*Honey in the Horn*—was a novel of pioneer life in the state during the first part of the twentieth century, telling the story of a young man searching for the meaning of life as he travels through Oregon. His 1952 novel *Winds of Morning* was also well regarded, telling

Portland's Dark Horse Comics is one of the nation's fastest-growing comic book publishers.
(Dark Horse Comics and the Dark Horse logo are registered trademarks of Dark Horse Comics.)

the story of an Oregon sheriff who investigates a murder with the help of an old pioneer. A private man who rarely granted interviews, Davis wrote numerous other books and articles about Oregon, many of which explored the conflicts between settlers and Native Americans. He died in 1960.

Doig, Ivan

Seattle's Ivan Doig has written several highly acclaimed novels about life in Western Montana. Born in White Sulphur Springs, Montana, in 1939, Doig grew up along the Rocky Mountain front where many of his stories take place. He received his bachelor's and master's degrees in journalism from Northwestern University and a doctorate in history from the University of Washington. A former ranch hand, newspaperman, and magazine editor, Doig's first book, *This House of Sky: Landscapes of a Western Mind*, is his autobiography and was nominated for the National Book Award. He may be best known for his trilogy of books about the fictitious McCaskill family's trials and tribulations in Montana, *Dancing at the Rascal Fair*, *English Creek*, and *Ride with Me, Mariah Montana*.

⑯ Duthie Books

Bill Duthie, who originally hailed from the Canadian province of Ontario, founded Vancouver's premier independent bookstore, Duthie Books, in 1957. Duthie started as a sales representative for Macmillan of Canada and in 1953 became a full-time western representative. Once in Vancouver, Duthie decided to sell books to people who wanted them rather than to reluctant bookstores. He opened the first Duthie Books on Robson Street near the Vancouver Public Library. Today Duthie Books operates several full-service bookstores in the Vancouver area as well as a number of specialty bookstores.

⑯ Elliott Bay Bookstore

Seattle's oldest and best-loved independent bookstore is located in the heart of the city's historic Pioneer Square District. The store was founded in 1973 by Walter Carr and continued to expand throughout the 1970s, adding a basement cafe in 1979. Unable to turn a profit in the face of chains and on-line stores, Carr sold the bookstore to a new local owner in 1999. Thankfully, with more than 150,000 titles set on cedar shelves in the store with exposed-brick walls, wood floors, and numerous nooks and crannies, Elliott Bay Bookstore remains a true booklovers' and browsers' paradise.

⑯ Emerson, Earl

One of the Northwest's most popular mystery writers is a Seattle firefighter. Earl Emerson, who works at the Yesler Way and Twenty-third Avenue fire station in downtown Seattle, is the author of both the Thomas Black and Mac Fontana mystery series. A Shamus Award–winning author, Emerson's muscular prose and witty dialogue have been entertaining mystery fans since the mid-eighties. A Tacoma native who now resides in the Cascade foothill town of North Bend, Emerson admits to being a lot like the teetotaling, bicycle-riding private detective Thomas Black, the main character in his most popular series. Emerson has written eleven Thomas Black novels and five adventures featuring fire investigator Mac Fontana.

⑯ Erickson, Arthur

Vancouver's Arthur Erickson is Canada's best-known and most innovative architect. Erickson has designed such B.C. landmarks as Simon Fraser University in the suburban Vancouver city of Burnaby, Robson Square in downtown Vancouver, and the world-famous Museum

Earl Emerson is Seattle's fire-fighting mystery author.
(Photo by Jeffrey Cantrell)

of Anthropology on the campus of the University of British Columbia in Vancouver. The Robson Square design encompasses several tiers of law courts under an eight-story canopy of glass, with government offices beneath high terraces and waterfalls. He has also designed the San Diego Convention Center and the Canadian Embassy in Washington, D.C. Since 1972, Erickson has been the principal architect in his own firm specializing in large-scale projects in urban settings.

〽 Fulghum, Robert

Western civilization's feel-good philosopher for the nineties is one of Seattle's most famous houseboat residents, Robert Fulghum. A former Unitarian minister, Fulghum's humorous and pointed musings on daily living became the runaway international best-seller *Everything I Always Wanted to Know I Learned in Kindergarten*. Fulghum followed up with two collections of essays, *It Was on Fire When I Lay Down on It* and *Uh Oh/Some Observations from Both Sides of the Refrigerator Door*. A Renaissance man who paints, backpacks around the world, conducts symphonies, and plays the mandocello, Fulghum also maintains homes in Utah and Greece.

〽 Gibson, William

An American-born writer who relocated to Vancouver during the Vietnam War, William Gibson is a pioneer of "cyberpunk" literature and is credited with coining the term "cyberspace." (For our technologically challenged readers, "cyberpunk" is a genre of science fiction writing that portrays a future of technologically saturated societies dominated by large corporations or governments). Gibson's landmark 1984 book *Neuromancer* is considered the first cyberpunk novel and the most important science fiction book of the eighties. *Neuromancer* won the Nebula, Hugo, and Philip K. Dick Awards—

the holy trinity of science-fiction writing trophies. Other works by Gibson include *Burning Chrome* (1986), a collection of short stories that includes "Johnny Mnemonic" (which was made into a 1994 motion picture), *Count Zero* (1986), and *Mona Lisa Overdrive* (1988). Although Gibson never mentions his adopted city in his writing, he recently told *Vancouver* magazine that "every city in my fiction definitely is, in some oddly Borgesian way, Vancouver." His latest book, *All Tomorrow's Parties*, was published in 1999.

〽 Gough, Laurence

Laurence Gough is a British Columbia mystery writer best known for his Vancouver-based detective novels about the team of Alec Willows and Claire Parker. His book, *The Goldfish Bowl*, won the Arthur Ellis Crime Writers of Canada Award for best first novel, and *Hot Shots* won the Ellis Award for best Canadian crime novel. His novel *Killers* opens with a dead body floating in the killer-whale pool of the Vancouver Aquarium (probably not a favorite with the greater Vancouver-area tourist bureau). Gough has written nine Willows and Parker mysteries.

〽 Graves, Morris

One of Seattle's foremost modern artists, Morris Graves was born in Fox Valley, Oregon, in 1910, but in the 1920s he moved to Seattle where he had aspirations of becoming an artist. Graves developed into an award-winning painter and is considered one of the founders of the Northwest mystics school of painting. Along with fellow artists Mark Tobey, Guy Anderson, and Kenneth Callahan, Graves was featured in a *Life* magazine article in 1953 as one of the "mystic painters of the Northwest." His metaphysical paintings of birds, snakes, and flowers are cherished by art lovers the world over. A Seattle fraternal organization called the Mystic Sons of Morris Graves honors the painter's eccentric spirit. Graves lives quietly on an estate in northern California.

⚡ Herbert, Frank

The creator of the enormously popular Dune Chronicles was Tacoma native and Northwest resident Frank Herbert. Born in the "City of Destiny" in 1920 and educated at the University of Washington, Herbert worked most of his career as a reporter and editor for several West Coast newspapers, including the *Seattle Post-Intelligencer* and the *Seattle Star*. Herbert's masterpiece is the 1965 novel *Dune*, an epic ecological story that won the first Nebula Award for Best Science Fiction Novel, shared the Hugo Award, and won the Locus Award for Best All-Time Science Fiction Novel. The idea for *Dune* came to Herbert in the late fifties while doing research for a magazine article about the Florence, Oregon, coastal area where the U.S. Department of Agriculture was conducting a project to control the movement of sand dunes. Several sequels were written by Herbert (including *Dune Messiah* and *Children of Dune*) as well as a number of other works. Herbert lived long enough to see his masterpiece incompetently translated to the screen by David Lynch in 1984, a film which starred University of Washington drama student Kyle MacLachlan (later to star in *Twin Peaks*) in the title role of Paul Atreides. He died of cancer in 1986. Herbert's son Brian recently penned a prequel to the Dune series titled *Dune: House Atreides*.

⚡ Holbrook, Stewart

A high-school dropout who emerged from the logging camps of New England and British Columbia, Stewart Holbrook may have influenced how the rest of the nation saw the Pacific Northwest more than any other regional author.

Born in Vermont in 1893, Holbrook came to the Northwest in 1920 and worked as a logger. In 1923, he moved to Portland where he spent the rest of his life writing about his adopted region. A fast writer who regularly turned out three thousand to five thousand words a day, Holbrook was a regular contributor to the *Oregonian* newspaper as well as the *New Yorker*. He wrote or coauthored more than three dozen books, including *Holy Old Mackinaw: A Natural History of the American Lumberjack*, which made him nationally famous. Holbrook believed in "lowbrow or non-stuffed shirt history" and his stories about the "characters" of the Pacific Northwest endeared him to locals and made him the first person that national editors turned to for perspectives on the region. Holbrook died in 1964.

⚡ Hugo, Richard

Seattle poet and baseball lover Richard Hugo was born and raised in the White Center neighborhood south of the city in 1923—a community "just outside the boundary of the civilized world," he would later write. Hugo attended the University of Washington where he studied creative writing from the legendary poet Theodore Roethke. In 1951, Hugo went to work for the Boeing Company as a technical writer. His first book of poetry titled *A Run of Jacks* was published in 1961, followed by another collection in 1965 called *Death of the Kapowsin Tavern*. Hugo eventually left Boeing to become head of the creative writing program at the University of Montana where he continued to write poetry and short stories until his death in 1982.

Jance, J. A.

Raised in Arizona, popular mystery writer Judith A. Jance now makes her home in Seattle. A former schoolteacher and life insurance agent, Jance's novels usually center around homicide detective Jonas Piedmont (J. P.) Beaumont—a hard-boiled Seattle Police Department veteran who never says no to a pretty woman or a strong drink. Her books are prized by locals for their accurate and witty Seattle references. Jance has launched a second mystery series featuring Joanna Brady, the widowed sheriff of Bisbee, Arizona.

Joffrey, Robert

Robert Joffrey was born in Seattle in 1930, the son of an Afghan father and an Italian mother. As a teenager, he enrolled in a local ballet school founded by Mary Ann Wells who also taught such soon-to-be famous dancers as Merce Cunningham and Joffrey's longtime collaborator Gerald Arpino. In 1954, Joffrey and Arpino founded the Joffrey Ballet School in New York City, and soon the Joffrey Ballet Company was born. Acknowledged as one of the world's leading dance companies, the Joffrey Ballet was known for highly original ballets as well as meticulous recreations of rare ballet classics. When his company became financially strapped during a 1965 European tour, Joffrey returned to Seattle and became the foremost attraction of Seattle's cultural life. During this time, Joffrey premiered his original multimedia ballet "Astarte" and re-created the ballet classic the "Three-Cornered Hat." The Boeing Bust in the early seventies made it difficult to sustain corporate art contributions and Joffrey returned his company to New York. Principal residencies followed in Los Angeles and Chicago, which the company now calls home. Joffrey died in 1988.

Johnson, Charles

The winner of the National Book Award in 1990 for his novel *Middle Passage*, Charles Johnson is a professor of creative writing at the University of Washington in Seattle. Born in Evanston, Illinois, Johnson began his career as a cartoonist and had his work first published when he was just seventeen. His first novel, *Faith and the Good Thing*, was published in 1974 and inspired by his graduate studies at Southern Illinois University in philosophy, African American folktales, and Buddhism. As Johnson studied for his doctorate in philosophy, he wrote screenplays for PBS including *Charlie Smith and the Fritter Tree*, about the oldest living African American cowboy. He was the first African American author to win the National Book Award since 1953 when Ralph Ellison won for *The Invisible Man*. Johnson is a prolific writer of short stories, book reviews, and screenplays. His most recent novel, *Dreamer*, was published in 1998.

Jones, Nard

Longtime Seattle resident Nard Jones wrote prolifically about the Pacific Northwest during his life. Born in Oregon in 1904, Jones penned more than three hundred short stories and twelve novels in a career that also saw him work as a reporter for the *Seattle Post-Intelligencer*. His first book, *Oregon Detour* (1930), was autobiographical, detailing his coming of age in the small wheat-farming town of Weston, Oregon. Other novels followed, drawing on the history of the Northwest, until his death in 1972.

Kesey, Ken

One of the major cultural and literary figures of the 1960s and Oregon's most famous novelist is Ken Kesey—a transgenerational bridge between the Beats of the 1950s and the hippies of the 1960s according to historian Lauren Kessler. Born in 1935 and raised in Springfield, Oregon, Kesey attended the University of Oregon and later Stanford University where he met Ken Babbs, with whom he would form the Merry Pranksters. In 1960, while Babbs did a tour of duty in Vietnam, Kesey volunteered to take LSD for a government study at the nearby Veterans Hospital in Menlo Park. He eventually landed a part-time job at the hospital, and wrote his first novel, *One Flew Over the Cuckoo's Nest*, which was published in 1962 and turned into an Oscar-winning movie in 1975. Kesey returned to Oregon in 1963 to work on his second novel, *Sometimes a Great Notion*—the story of a logging clan's trials and tribulations in the woods of Oregon. After finishing the book, Kesey reunited with Babbs and others to form the Merry Pranksters—the famous troupe of school-bus-riding LSD prophets who were memorialized in Tom Wolfe's 1968 book *The Electric Kood-Aid Acid Test*. After getting busted on a marijuana charge, Kesey settled down in Pleasant Hill, Oregon, to raise his family. He has continued to write books, including his 1994 novel *Last Go Round* about the Pendleton, Oregon, cowboy championships of 1911.

Kinsella, W. P.

The author of *Shoeless Joe Jackson Comes to Iowa* (on which the film *Field of Dreams* was based), W. P. Kinsella lives in White Rock, British Columbia. Much of Kinsella's Midwestern sensibilities were shaped during his childhood in the fifties on an Albertan homestead. Kinsella has also written a number of Native American stories, but it is his baseball novels, such as *Shoeless Joe*, *The Iowa Baseball Confederacy*, and *Box Socials*, which have gained him the most acclaim.

Kizer, Carolyn

The founder of the *Poetry Northwest* journal and the winner of the Pulitzer Prize for poetry in 1985, Carolyn Kizer was born in Spokane in 1925. Kizer founded *Poetry Northwest* in 1959 and served as its editor from 1960 to 1966, when she became director for literature at the National Endowment for the Arts. In 1960, she published her first book of poetry titled *The Ungrateful Garden*. Kizer has authored six additional books of poetry, including *Yin* in 1984 for which she won the Pulitzer Prize the following year. Mentored by Theodore Roethke, Kizer has been the recipient of numerous poetry awards and resides in Sonoma, California, and Paris.

Larson, Gary

The creator of one of the most popular, successful, and twisted comic strips of all time is Tacoma native and Seattle resident Gary Larson. Larson's offbeat comic strip *The Far Side* has been compiled into twenty-two books, each of which has appeared on the *New York Times* Bestseller List. More than thirty million copies have been sold worldwide. Born in 1950, Larson displayed an interest in drawing but never seriously studied art, preferring science, which ultimately found its way into many of the themes in his cartoons. After graduating from Washington State University in 1972, Larson played guitar and banjo and worked in a music store before deciding to concentrate on drawing. For almost a decade and a half until he "retired" at the end of 1994, *The Far Side* appeared in more than nineteen hundred daily newspapers worldwide and was translated into seventeen languages. Larson has received numerous awards for his work, and the voluminous *Far Side* merchandising industry includes greeting cards, calendars, T-shirts, coffee mugs, and more. Although he no longer draws a daily cartoon panel, Larson continues to create, writing and illustrating the children's book *There's a Hair in My Dirt! A Worm's Story*, which was published in 1998.

⚡ Lawrence, Jacob

Jacob Lawrence is a prominent artist whose vivid paintings depict the African American struggle. He was born in New Jersey in 1917 and lived in Pennsylvania before moving to Harlem with his mother when he was thirteen. Influenced at an early age by the writings of W. E. B. Du Bois and other members of the Harlem Renaissance, he studied under painter Charles Alston and later taught at Black Mountain College and the Pratt Institute. Lawrence was appointed full professor at the University of Washington in 1971 and taught there until his retirement in 1983. He continues to live in Seattle and is active in the arts community. Lawrence's paintings appear in the collections of most major American museums. His work has been the subject of at least four major retrospectives, most recently at the University of Washington's Henry Gallery in 1998. He was awarded the Washington State Medal of Merit in 1998.

In his studio in 1994, Jacob Lawrence is Seattle's most famous living artist.
(Photo courtesy of the artist and Francine Seders Gallery)

⚡ LeGuin, Ursula

An award-winning science fiction and fantasy writer from Portland, Ursula LeGuin was born in 1929 in Berkeley, California, the daughter of anthropologist parents. After college at Radcliffe and Columbia University, LeGuin began writing poetry, but was in her mid-thirties before her first novel, *Rocannon's World*, was published. In 1969, LeGuin published the novel *The Left Hand of Darkness*, generally considered to be her masterpiece. The book, which takes place on a planet where winter lasts all year and each inhabitant embodies both male and female genders, won both the Nebula and Hugo Awards. Other award-winning novels by LeGuin include *The Tombs of Atuan* (1971), *The Word for World Is Forest* (1971), *The Farthest Shore* (1972), and *The Dispossessed* (1974). LeGuin has been praised as a feminist whose novels challenge traditional gender roles. She is also a prolific writer of books for children and young adults, having penned the popular Earthsea Trilogy and Catwings stories.

⚡ Lopez, Barry

Internationally famous nature and environment author Barry Lopez hails from Oregon's picturesque Willamette Valley, on the banks of the McKenzie River just outside Eugene. As a young man who grew up in both rural Southern California and Manhattan, Lopez considered becoming a Trappist monk but decided the life was too easy for him. His spirituality is a recurring theme in his writings, which focus on the relationship between humans and nature. His most famous book is *Arctic Dreams* (1986), for which he won the American Book Award. Lopez is also known for a trilogy collection which began in 1976 with *Desert Notes*, followed by *River Notes* in 1979, and concluding in 1994 with *Field Notes*.

⚅ Malamud, Bernard

Although Bernard Malamud lived in the Pacific Northwest for only twelve years, he left a lasting literary legacy. Malamud came west from New York to teach at Oregon State College in 1949. While living in Corvallis, he wrote his first four works of fiction, including the memorable baseball novel *The Natural* (1952) and a collection of short stories titled *The Magic Barrel* (1958), for which Malamud won the National Book Award. Malamud's 1961 novel *A New Life* was a scathing satire about a New York professor's experiences at the fictitious Cascadia College in the Pacific Northwest, and was based in part on his experiences teaching in the Northwest. Malamud wisely scampered off from Oregon State College for Bennington College in Vermont the same year the book was published. He later won the Pulitzer Prize and National Book Award for his 1966 novel *The Fixer*.

⚅ McDonald, Betty

Betty McDonald's 1945 novel *The Egg and I* is one of the most popular books ever written about life in rural Washington State. The heartwarming and hilarious story about the experiences of Betty and her husband, Bob, on a chicken farm in the foothills of the Olympic Mountains was also a runaway national best-

seller. A popular Hollywood movie followed in 1947, starring Fred MacMurray and Claudette Colbert. Two of the supporting characters in the book and film—Ma and Pa Kettle—starred in their own series of films in the 1950s. McDonald also created the classic Mrs. Piggle Wiggle series of children's books. Her battle against tuberculosis at the Pines convalescent center in Seattle was humorously and poignantly chronicled in *The Plague and I*, and her book *Anybody Can Do Anything* is an autobiographical remembrance of life during the depression in Seattle.

⚅ McFarlane, Todd

As a child growing up in California and Calgary, Alberta, Todd McFarlane was a lot like other young boys—he loved playing baseball and he loved drawing comic book characters. Although he showed enough athletic prowess to get the attention of the Seattle Mariners and receive a baseball scholarship from Eastern Washington University, a broken ankle cut short his major league dreams. After graduation, McFarlane was determined to get a job in the comic book industry and after hundreds of rejections, he went to work for Marvel/Epic Comics. Settling in New Westminster, B.C., McFarlane drew comic book characters including the Incredible Hulk, Wolverine, and Spiderman, the latter character taking on renewed appeal under his creative control. In 1992, he helped form Image Comics, and his most famous comic book character, Spawn, was unveiled. The first Spawn issue became the best-selling independent comic book of all time and since then, more than fifty-five million copies have been sold worldwide. A feature-length film was released in 1997. A self-described "sports geek," McFarlane is a minority owner of the Edmonton Oilers National Hockey League franchise, and owns nine home-run balls hit by Mark McGwire and Sammy Sosa during their historic 1998 season home-run battle, including McGwire's seventieth home-run ball.

⧊ McManus, Patrick

America's favorite outdoor humorist hails from Spokane. While teaching at Eastern Washington University in Cheney, Patrick McManus began to hone and submit short stories to various publishers. In 1968, *Field & Stream* bought a humorous offering, leading to an eventual column. A collection of the best *Field & Stream* columns titled *A Fine and Pleasant Misery* was released in 1978. Over time, McManus has become a best-selling author. He has also authored autobiographical plays which are popular throughout the Northwest.

⧊ Montgomery, Elizabeth Rider

See Dick. See Dick run. Run Dick run. Sound familiar? Introduced in the forties, the Dick and Jane books helped millions of American baby boomers learn to read. The woman who wrote the books was a former first-grade schoolteacher from West Seattle named Elizabeth Rider Montgomery. Born in Peru to missionary parents, Montgomery graduated from Washington Normal School (now Western Washington University) in 1925, and taught first grade in Seattle, Aberdeen, and Los Angeles before marrying and retiring from teaching to raise a family. After her marriage, she wrote one hundred books before she finally came to the attention of Scott, Foresman and Company, and a single-syllable empire was launched. In the mid-forties, Montgomery returned to West Seattle and continued to write for the Dick and Jane series until 1963 when she began writing other books, including a biography of Chief Seattle.

⧊ Morgan, Murray

One of the Pacific Northwest's most popular historians is Tacoma native Murray Morgan. After graduating from Columbia University in 1942 with a master's degree in journalism, Morgan returned to his native Northwest despite more prestigious job offers on the East Coast. In 1951, Morgan's most locally famous work was published. Almost half a century later, *Skid Road: An Informal Portrait of Seattle* is still considered the definitive book about the early history of the Northwest's flagship city. Other works by Morgan about Northwest history include *The Dam: Grand Coulee and the Pacific Northwest* (1954), *Puget's Sound: A Narrative of Tacoma and the Southern Sound* (1979), and *The Mill and the Boot* (1982).

⧊ Morris, Mark

Well-known contemporary dancer and choreographer Mark Morris was born in Seattle in 1956 and studied ballet and flamenco with local teachers Verla Flowers and Perry Brunson. In 1976, Morris moved to New York where he danced with a number of companies including Twyla Tharp and Lar Lubovitch. Morris's intolerance of traditional ballet led him to form his own dance company in 1981, and he has created more than ninety works for the group. From 1988 to 1991, Morris and his company were awarded a three-year contract as the official dance company of the Theatre Royal de la Monnaie in Brussels, Belgium. In his final season, Morris staged an irreverent version of *The Nutcracker Suite* retitled *The Hard Nut*, which was set in a 1960s suburb and featured cross-dressing. Morris received a MacArthur Foundation "genius grant" in 1991.

⚡ Newland, Marv

In 1969, British Columbia animator Marv Newland created what Canadian *Maclean's* magazine has called "the definitive 90-second statement about naivete and fate." Yes, *Bambi vs. Godzilla*, perhaps the funniest short film (or the shortest funny film) ever made, has become a certified cult classic over the past three decades. Newland went on to establish International Rocketship Productions in Vancouver, which produces theatrical cartoons, television specials, commercials, and other animated works. Newland's company also produced Gary Larson's "Tales from the Far Side" television special in 1994.

⚡ Olsen, Jack

Called "the dean of true crime authors" by the *Washington Post* and the *New York Daily News*, writer Jack Olsen is a resident of Bainbridge Island near Seattle. The author of thirty books, Olsen is a longtime journalist and former *Time* bureau chief and *Sports Illustrated* editor. His books cover a wide range, including *The Bridge at Chap-*

paquiddick (about Ted Kennedy), *The Night of the Grizzlies* (an ecological thriller), and *Silence on the Monte Sole* (about a Nazi massacre in Italy). Olsen is best known for his true-crime books, some of which are required reading in criminology courses. One of his most popular true-crime stories—*Son: A Psychopath and His Victims*—is about famous Northwest criminal Kevin Coe, Spokane's infamous South Hill rapist. Olsen is considered a national expert on the psychology of criminals and has appeared on a number of television talk shows.

⚡ Pacific Northwest Ballet

The Northwest's premier dance company, Pacific Northwest Ballet (PNB), was founded in Seattle in 1972 and has been under the artistic direction of Kent Stowell and Francia Russell since 1977. One of North America's most highly regarded companies, PNB's repertory is based on original compositions by Stowell; George Balanchine masterpieces staged by Russell (one of the first ballet masters chosen to stage his works); works commissioned for the company; and classics from the ballet to modern dance. Beginning in 1983, PNB began presenting a highly original production of the *Nutcracker* with sets and costume designs by noted illustrator Maurice Sendak. The production is a holiday tradition in Western Washington and was released as a major motion picture in 1986. The PNB has toured extensively throughout the United States and Canada, as

Patricia Barker performs in Pacific Northwest Ballet's *Swan Lake*.
(Photo by Ben Kerns)

well as opening the Melbourne International Festival of the Arts in Australia in 1995 and performing at the Edinburgh Festival in Scotland in 1999.

Powell's Books

Bookstore fans regard it as the best of its kind. Powell's City of Books (the flagship store) takes up an entire Portland city block and has more than one million volumes in stock. From the store's beginnings in the early seventies, Michael Powell and his father Walter pioneered the idea of putting new and used books together on the shelves to broaden their customer's choices. Powell's routinely stocks rare books, out-of-print books, academic books, and a wide variety of foreign language books. While many independent bookstores are closing or downsizing in the face of stiff competition from chain and on-line bookstores, Powell's is significantly expanding the size of its main retail store and Internet site. Soon an even bigger Powell's will exist on Burnside Street to vacuum money from the wallets of book lovers throughout the Pacific Northwest.

Powers, Margaret

In 1964, during a troubled period in her life, a young Margaret Powers wrote "Footprints,"a poem which has touched millions with its poignant expression of God's love and care in the best and worst times of our lives. It's the piece that ends with the line, "When you saw only one set of footprints, it was then that I carried you." For years, the creator of the poem was unknown, but in 1989, Powers emerged as the true author. Her book *Footprints: The Story Behind the Poem That Inspired Millions* chronicles the creation, loss, and legal recovery of the poem, intertwined with her life experiences. As itinerant evangelists, she and her hus-

The flagship store of Powell's Books is the West's largest bookstore, filling an entire city block in Portland.

(Photo courtesy of Powell's Books)

band, Paul, travel throughout the world from their home in British Columbia.

Reid, Bill

One of the Pacific Northwest's most famous First Nations artists, William Ronald Reid was born in Victoria in 1920, the son of a Haida mother and a naturalized Canadian father. Although his first career was in radio broadcasting, Reid's creativity soon led him to the world of native art. His first major carving work was a totem pole at the U.S.–Canadian border at Blaine, Washington. This was followed by restoration of totem pole collections at the University of British Columbia, and during the next three decades, Reid contributed major works to Expo '67 in Montreal, Expo '86 in Vancouver, and Vancouver's Stanley Park. Reid's masterpiece sculpture, *The Spirit of Haida Gwaii*, which is fashioned from black bronze and depicts a canoe full of human and animal travelers based on Haida mythology, resides in the lobby of the Canadian Embassy in Washington, D.C. He also carved the sculpture *The Raven* entirely from yellow cedar; the piece is prominently displayed in Vancouver's Museum of Anthropology. Reid passed away in 1998.

Robbins, Tom

Cosmic, counterculture, and comic author Tom Robbins is a Northwest literary icon for a generation of young fiction writers seeking to find their own unique voice. Robbins' use of madcap metaphors ("the sky is as gruff as a Chinese waiter") and wildly colorful characters (the main subjects in his 1990 novel *Skinny Legs and All* were inanimate objects) instantly identifies his books to readers worldwide. Born in North Carolina and raised in Virginia, Robbins migrated to the Northwest in the early sixties where he attended the University of Washington. Later in the decade, he worked part-time for the *Seattle Post-Intellingencer* as an art critic, as a feature editor for the *Seattle Times*, and contributed to the *Helix* (Seattle's underground newspaper). In 1967, Robbins moved to La Conner, Washington, to work on his first novel, and four years later *Another Roadside Attraction* was published. Robbins, who still lives in La Conner, has written five other books, including *Even Cowgirls Get the Blues* (1976), which was made into a major motion picture by Portland's Gus Van Sant, and *Half Asleep in Frog Pajamas* (1994).

Tom Robbins, captain of the La Conner Fighting Vegetables volleyball team, celebrates with his pregame champagne in 1980.
(Photo courtesy of Tom Robbins)

Roethke, Theodore

Respected and influential twentieth-century poet Theodore Roethke was born in Saginaw, Michigan, in 1908, to German immigrant parents. After graduating from college, Roethke taught at a number of colleges and, while he was popular with the students, his eccentric behavior and hard drinking did not endear him to other faculty or the administration. An eccentric professor who drinks? Perish the thought! In 1935, Roethke had the first of a series of mental breakdowns that would plague him the remainder of his life. After recuperating and a stint teaching at Bennington College, Roethke accepted a position at the University of Washington (UW) in 1947. The following year, his first book of poetry *The Lost Son* was published—much of which dealt with images of Roethke's childhood and plant life associated with his father, who had been a gardener. While at UW, Roethke served as teacher and mentor to a number of successful Northwest poets, including Carolyn Kizer, David Wagoner, and Richard Hugo. In 1954, he was awarded the Pulitzer Prize for a compilation of his poems titled *The Waking*. Further mental breakdowns followed, yet Roethke won the National Book Award for his 1957 work *Words for the Wind*. Roethke died in 1963.

 Rule, Ann

Seattle's Ann Rule is one of America's foremost true-crime writers. The former Seattle police officer and state public assistance caseworker has authored fifteen books (ten of which made the *New York Times* Bestseller List) and numerous articles on real criminal cases. Perhaps her most famous and personal book is *The Stranger Beside Me*, Rule's account of the case of Ted Bundy with whom she once worked at the Seattle Crisis Clinic. Other books by Rule include *Small Sacrifices*, *Dead by Sunset*, and *Bitter Harvest*.

Speidel, Bill

A real Seattle original, Bill Speidel wrote a series of travel, guide, and history books that took a light and irreverent look at the city and the Northwest. For years, Speidel also published the *Seattle Guide*—a directory given to hotel patrons with information about restaurants and tourist attractions. To most people, however, Speidel is probably best known as the originator of the Seattle Underground Tours, which takes patrons on a walk through parts of Pioneer Square that were rebuilt after the disastrous 1889 Seattle fire. Speidel's book *Sons of the Profits* remains a must-read about the wheeler-dealers who built the city during the late 1800s.

Stafford, William

A longtime English professor at Portland's Lewis and Clark College, William Stafford was also one of the nation's most admired poets. Born in Hutchinson, Kansas, in 1914, Stafford was educated at the University of Kansas and Iowa and was a conscientious objector during World War II. His first book of poetry *Down in My Heart* (1947) spoke of his experiences working as a fire lookout in northern California during the war.

He eventually landed in Portland on the faculty of Lewis and Clark College where he taught for more than thirty years. Stafford's verse has been described as simple and plain but leading the reader to a deeper meaning. His 1964 poetry collection *Traveling through the Dark* received the National Book Award. Stafford served as Oregon's poet laureate for several years and was Consultant in Poetry for the Library of Congress. He died in 1993 at the age of seventy-nine.

Steinbrueck, Victor

As a young boy growing up in Seattle, Victor Steinbrueck made numerous shopping trips to the farmer's market on Pike Street. As an adult, he would save his beloved public market and become a Seattle legend. In 1969, the Seattle city

Victor Steinbrueck is known as the savior of the Pike Place Public Market.
(Photo from *Seattle Post-Intelligencer* Collection, Museum of History and Industry)

council adopted a plan to demolish many of the market's historic buildings and build a new parking garage, offices, hotels, and condominiums. But preservation activists, led by now University of Washington architecture professor Steinbrueck (who had formed the "Friends of the Market" organization in 1964), sponsored a successful 1971 initiative to establish the Pike Place Public Market area as a historical district and preserve the market in its original state. Steinbrueck's "Market Sketchbook," which contains detailed drawings of all of the market's nooks and crannies, is considered a Northwest classic. Steinbrueck also was instrumental in the campaign to save the historic Pioneer Square District in Seattle and helped with the design of the Space Needle for the Century 21 Exposition.

Stephenson, Neal

Seattle author Neal Stephenson is one of the growing numbers of science fiction writers making their mark in the world of "cyberpunk" literature. Stephenson's 1993 *Snow Crash* is

Internationally famous avant-garde painter Mark Tobey shops at the Pike Place Public Market in 1963.

(Photo from *Seattle Post-Intelligencer* Collection, Museum of History and Industry)

considered a defining cyberpunk novel in which the United States exists as a patchwork of corporate franchise city-states, a virtual Internet is called the "Metaverse," and a new designer drug called Snow Crash is killing the Metaverse's top personalities. Stephenson was born in Maryland and raised in the Midwest, but his annual summer trips to Seattle to visit relatives persuaded him to move to the city permanently in 1984. Stephenson has written other novels and is currently working on a CD-ROM project (who isn't?) with Seattle's Shadow Catcher Entertainment. His most recent book, *Cryptonomicon*, was published in 1999 and is a massive tale which focuses on code-breaking schemes from World War II to the present.

Tisdale, Sallie

Portland author Sallie Tisdale is a descendent of Pacific Northwest pioneers and explored the magnetic appeal of the region in her 1991 book *Stepping Westward: The Long Search for Home in the Pacific Northwest*. She caused a greater stir with her 1995 publication *Talk Dirty to Me: An Intimate Philosophy of Sex*, which challenges politically correct views of pornography and sexual freedom. Tisdale is also a contributing editor of *Harper's* magazine and a columnist for *Salon* magazine.

Tobey, Mark

The Pacific Northwest's most famous abstract painter, Mark Tobey was born in Wisconsin in 1890 but was living in Seattle by the early twenties. The de facto leader of the Northwest mystics school of art, Tobey's work drew on Asian calligraphy to create what he called "white writing"—intricate white ink lines on a dark background. During the depression, Tobey and colorful Seattle restaurateur Ivar Haglund were friends and would occasionally get together for private musicals, Tobey on the piano and Haglund on the folk guitar. Tobey was also fond of Seattle's Pike Place Public Market and created several paintings of its unique character. He even donated some of his work to raise money to save the market during the early seventies' preservation campaign. His international reputation as an artist grew rapidly during the fifties after he became the first American since Whistler to win a gold medal at the Venice Biennale in 1958. Late in his life, Tobey received the Order of Arts and Letters from the Louvre—the equivalent of the French Legion of Honor for artists. He lived the last years of his life in Switzerland and died in 1976 in the city of Basel.

Tsutakawa, George

University of Washington (UW) School of Art faculty member George Tsutakawa is a well-known sculptor and painter who is best known for creating more than sixty public fountains throughout North America and Japan. Born in Seattle in 1910, Tsutakawa was sent to Japan to live with his grandparents when he was seven, and it was there that he gained an appreciation for Japanese culture and traditions. He returned to the United States in 1927 with aspirations to become an artist. After World War II, Tsutukawa joined the UW faculty, teaching both art and architecture. In 1958, the Seattle Public Library asked him to design a fountain for the plaza of the new downtown main library. The result was Tsutukawa's *Fountain of Wisdom*, the first in a long series of abstract fountains based in part on ritually stacked rock structure called "obos," which are found in the Himalayas.

Wagoner, David

Northwest poet and novelist David Wagoner has been strongly influenced by the geography, climate, and flora and fauna of the region. Born in Ohio in 1926, Wagoner taught at DePauw University and Penn State before accepting a faculty position at the University of Washington in 1954. He became the editor of *Poetry Northwest* in 1966, a position he has held for more than three decades. Today, *Poetry Northwest* is the oldest magazine in the United States that publishes poetry exclusively. Wagoner's own books of poetry include *In Broken Country* (1979), which was nominated for the American Book Award, and *First Light* (1983). He has also written several novels, including *The Escape Artist* (1965), which was directed by Francis Ford Coppola and released in 1982.

Woodcock, George

Canada's most prolific and distinguished travel writer, George Woodcock was born in Canada but raised in England, returning to his native land following the conclusion of World War II. Settling in Vancouver, Woodcock began a series of trips throughout the province which culminated in his first book of travel writing, *Ravens and Prophets*. Numerous travel writings would follow about Canada, China, Mexico, and, most prominently, India. Woodcock also wrote numerous articles about travel for such magazines as *Canadian Forum*, *The Beaver*, and *Western Living*. He was the founding editor of *Canadian Literature*—the first publication devoted exclusively to the study of Canadian writings. Most of Woodcock's 150 books were written on the same black Underwood typewriter in his modest home in Vancouver's Kerrisdale neighborhood. In 1994, Woodcock became the first writer in Vancouver's history to receive the Freedom of the City Award. He died in 1995 at the age of eighty-two.

⚡ Wright, Bagley

Bagley Wright is one of Seattle's major arts benefactors. Together with his wife Virginia, he has been a prominent member of Seattle's art community for more than four decades. Wright was president of Pentagram, the company which built the Space Needle, and a developer of other downtown office buildings. He served as the first president of the Tony Award–winning Seattle Repertory Theater and is a past president of the Seattle Art Museum and a Seattle Symphony trustee. The Wrights have amassed an impressive collection of modern art that was part of a major exhibition at the Seattle Art Museum in 1999. The Seattle Repertory Theater company's performance facility on the grounds of the Seattle Center is named in his honor.

⚡ Yamasaki, Minoru

A world-famous architect whose best-known structure is the World Trade Center in New York City, Minoru Yamasaki was born in Seattle in 1912. His designs combine aesthetic appeal with functional efficiency and tend to employ refined materials like steel and wood instead of brick and concrete. Yamasaki designed the Federal Science Pavilion (now the Pacific Science Center) for the Seattle World's Fair in 1962. The structure is sometimes referred to as "Seattle's Taj Mahal" because of its graceful arches, pools, and interlocking structures. Controversial in architectural circles, Yamasaki died in 1986.

Former Portland Mayor Bud Clark first gained fame as the centerpiece of a now famous poster showing him flashing a statue and imploring viewers to "expose yourself to art." Clark's irreverent attitude and playful twist on a sometimes stuffy subject says a lot about the Northwest attitude toward the sculptures, murals, and fountains that adorn the region's public spaces.

While the most we ever learned about art was by watching the late Bob Ross (the fuzzy haired fella on public television who was always telling us about the furry little creatures in his paintings), we do have some knowledge about what "art" is popular here in the Pacific Northwest. You know, Art Carney, Art Linkletter, Art Fleming . . . sorry, that was cheap. Why don't we pipe down and take a brief look at some of the Northwest's most beloved works of public art in Seattle, Portland, and Vancouver.

Seattle

Downtown Seattle's most prominent sculpture is the recently constructed **Hammering Man** statue. Standing forty-eight feet tall at the entrance of the Seattle Art Museum on First Avenue, *Hammering Man* was completed in 1992 by California artist Jonathan Borofsky. The solid black steel sculpture (which is intended as a tribute to workers) whacks about four times per minute. The sculpture is quite a

step up for First Avenue, which was the original inspiration for *Skid Road*. Less than a generation ago, Seattle's First Avenue was populated by "raincoat men" instead of *Hammering Man*.

Seattle's most famous "musical" artwork is the **Soundgarden** sculpture on the grounds of the National Oceanic and Atmospheric Administration on the shores of Lake Washington in the north part of the city. The piece consists of twelve steel towers topped with weather-vane-shaped structures that contain rotating organ pipes. Musical sounds are created as the wind blows through the different-length pipes, and yes, the Seattle band Soundgarden took its name from the sculpture (listen carefully to the sculpture and you can hear the opening notes of "Black Hole Sun").

Seattle's first significant piece of public art in

the modern era was the **Vertebrae** sculpture located on the plaza of the downtown Seattle-First National Bank Building. Erected in 1971, the building was the Jet City's first modern sky-scraper and at the time, Sea-First Bank set aside the then unheard of sum of three hundred thou-sand dollars for public art for the building. The centerpiece was the sculpture *Vertebrae* by the famous British sculptor Henry Moore. The nine-by-twenty-four-foot bronze work was placed on the concourse outside the main level where it became an instant hit with the public and a source of civic pride. When financial troubles forced Sea-First to sell the building in 1986, the buyers announced plans to dismantle the *Verte-brae* sculpture and move it to Japan. Faced with mounting public outrage, the Seattle Depart-ment of Construction and Land Use issued a stop work order the day the sculpture was to be moved. *Vertebrae* was repurchased and donated to the Seattle Art Museum, and it still guards the entrance to the building.

Just north of downtown Seattle in the city's free-spirited Fremont neighborhood stands **Waiting for the Interurban** by Richard Beyer—the city's best-loved sculpture. The cast aluminum statue features a cluster of life-size working-class people standing under a pergola, patiently waiting for the next streetcar. A dog with a human face peers from behind the legs of the bystanders. (Some claim the face belongs to Armen Stepanian, the one-time honorary mayor of Fremont who opposed the sculpture.) Local residents are fond of decorating the figures with hats, scarves, balloons, and streamers to com-memorate birthdays, graduations, and holidays.

Portland

Portland lumberman and philanthropist Simon Benson donated a number of identical water fountains to the city in 1912, ostensibly as a nonalcoholic alternative for his hard-drinking employees. We doubt if they really dampened

beer consumption, but the fountains, known locally as **Benson Bubblers,** are loved by the public and still bubble invitingly on the city's downtown streets.

Northeast Portland's Grant Park is home to the **Beverly Cleary Sculpture Garden**—three statues representing beloved characters from the local author's children's books. Nestled near the playground you will find life-size statues of Ramona, Henry Huggins, and Ribsy the dog, along with a map of locations from Cleary's sto-ries about life on N.E. Klickitat Street (the real N.E. Klickitat Street is only four blocks away). Portland artist Lee Hunt sculpted the statues of the three Cleary characters in clay, and then had them cast in bronze. There are fountains under Ramona's and Ribsy's feet, perfect for kids to splash in during warm weather. Around the con-crete fountain slab are granite plaques engraved with the titles of the Cleary books that take place in Portland.

The Rose City's most famous lady is a six-ton, thirty-six-foot-tall copper statue known as **Port-landia**. Squatting on her perch downtown atop the avant-garde Portland Building, trident in hand, surveying the crowds below, the statue is one of the most popular symbols of the city. *Portlandia* is based on a figure in Portland's city seal of a woman, dressed in classical clothes, who welcomes traders into the port of the city. *Portlandia* is the second-largest ham-mered copper statue in America (the largest being the Statue of Liberty). Portland Mayor Vera Katz suggested in 1998 that *Portlandia* be moved to a site along the Willamette River, but sculptor Raymond Kaskey was opposed. Presently, the statue remains in its original location.

Skidmore Fountain in Portland's Old Town is the city's oldest commissioned work of public art. The fountain was a bequest from former Portland Commissioner Stephen Skidmore who was taken with the many plazas and fountains of Europe while attending the Paris Exposition 1878. In the tradition of the West, however, Skidmore intended it to be a working fountain where "horses, men, and dogs" could quench their thirst. The fountain's water spills in a curtain around two bronze caryatids (sculpted female figures used as columns) who hold aloft a bowl that fills and overflows. The Skidmore has survived having a traffic sign placed in its bowl during the thirties and an ill-fated attempt at cleaning in the fifties where too much acid was used, resulting in some costly plastic surgery.

Vancouver

Vancouver's Stanley Park, an urban jewel, contains several popular artworks. The **Brockton Oval Totem Poles** were originally placed in the park in 1912 as part of an "Indian village." More poles were purchased over the years and the site is one of the most visited and photographed in the park. Rock star Elvis Costello even used the totems as a backdrop to the music video for his song "What's So Funny about Peace Love and Understanding?"

The giant **Crab Fountain** outside the H. R. Macmillan Planetarium in Vanier Park is a Terminal City favorite. The stainless steel crab that rises out of the fountain, pincers outstretched, is meant to symbolize nature's dominance over man's civilization. The prize-winning work of artist George Norris, the crab is one of the most photographed sculptures in Vancouver. A plaque on the sculpture also conceals a time capsule.

British sculptor Henry Moore (who designed Seattle's *Vertebrae*) also has a famous work in Vancouver. Titled **Knife Edge,** it was the first commemorative sculpture accepted by Vancouver's parks board. It is popular with photographers and with the children who clamber over it. Moore authorized three castings of this work. The other two can be found on Nelson Rockefeller's New York estate and outside the House of Lords in London.

The forty-eight-foot-tall *Hammering Man* sculpture looms over the First Avenue entrance to the Seattle Art Museum.
(Photo by John Farrand)

RANDY'S AND STEVE'S NORTHWEST READING LIST

Now, this sounds like an impossible task. Take the entire spectrum of books written by Northwest authors about the Northwest and pare it down to a list of ten essential works. Sounds really difficult. Come to think of it, too difficult. Never mind.

No, we're going to carry on. While we're not experts on literature, we have read a lot of books by Northwest authors, and we like to hang out in bookstores, so that gives us some limited credentials. To add more heft, we asked the three major independent bookstores in the region—Powell's in Portland, Elliott Bay in Seattle, and Duthie in Vancouver—to give us their suggestions and recommendations.

Now, before you go sending us a nasty e-mail about what's "not" on the list, here are the ground rules for inclusion.

1. The book has to be written by a Northwest author and be about or set in the Northwest.
2. Fiction and nonfiction books only. Collected works of poetry are out. Why? It's boring. And what is this new craze called a "poetry slam"? Some new breakfast at Denny's for literature lovers?
3. No short stories. Sorry Raymond Carver and Thom Jones, but an old professor of ours once said, "Boys, I judge your term paper by weight and volume. Nothing else." A short story sounds like a 2.0 to us, and we can't stand getting bad grades.
4. One book per author, please. We can't have exclusively Northwest writers like Murray Morgan hogging the whole list.
5. Pre-World War II works are excluded. This is a pop culture book after all.

Enough waffling, qualifications, and disclaimers. Here, in chronological order, is Randy's and Steve's Northwest Reading List.

Skid Road: An Informal Portrait of Seattle

(Murray Morgan, 1951)

Murray Morgan is a Northwest historian who knows how to make the past readable and exciting. His 1951 book *Skid Road* is the story of Seattle's first one hundred years as told through the personalities of the city. Here you will find the story of Mercer's Maidens which inspired the TV show *Here Come the Brides*, along with tales of the gamblers, sawdust women, and fancy men who made Seattle's first (and original) *Skid Road* as infamous as San Francisco's Barbary Coast.

A New Life

(Bernard Malamud, 1961)
Although this transplanted New Yorker is more famous for his National Book Award–winning novel *The Fixer* and his beloved baseball book *The Natural*, this story was written about a fictional Northwest college while Malamud taught at Oregon State College (OSC) during the fifties. *A New Life* is a scathing satire of life in a small fictional college town populated by small-minded residents. Malamud left OSC for Bennington College in Vermont the year the book was published—perhaps anticipating the book's local reception. Good thinking, Bernie!

Sometimes A Great Notion

(Ken Kesey, 1964)
Although not as popular as *One Flew Over the Cuckoo's Nest*, Ken Kesey's *Sometimes a Great Notion* is probably a better novel and certainly the best book ever written about rural life in western Oregon. Published in 1964, the book tells the sweeping story of the logging Stamper family's struggle for survival in the Oregon woods. It was made into a 1971 motion picture starring Paul Newman and Henry Fonda. *Sometimes a Great Notion* has been praised for its use of the Northwest landscape as a context for the drama of the book's narrative. A number of literary experts consider it the definitive Northwest novel.

Another Roadside Attraction

(Tom Robbins, 1971)
One of the classic American novels of the past fifty years, *Another Roadside Attraction* is La Conner, Washington, writer Tom Robbins' masterpiece. The improbably strange story (a preview of all future Robbins books) concerns the body of Jesus Christ which has been stolen from the Vatican and taken to Captain Kendrick's Memorial Hot Dog Wildlife Preserve in Washington State's "Magic" Skagit Valley. The book became an instant cult classic and the *Los Angeles Times* proclaimed it was "written with a style and humor that haven't been seen since Mark Twain." High praise indeed.

The Good Rain: Across Time and Terrain in the Pacific Northwest

(Timothy Egan, 1990)

In 1853, Theodore Winthrop traveled through what has now become Washington, Oregon, and British Columbia to experience a land that he believed would change the character of man. In *The Good Rain*, New York Times Seattle correspondent Timothy Egan retraces Winthrop's footsteps to appraise the outcome of his prophecy. Egan explores the challenges and charm of the region in a series of essays that range from salmon fisheries and logging camps, to the used-up "resource towns," to the manicured English gardens of Vancouver.

Disappearing Moon Cafe

(Sky Lee, 1991)
This novel by Vancouver author Sky Lee attempts to do for Asian-Canadian women what Amy Tan (*The Joy Luck Club*) did for her American counterparts: provide context to the experiences of immigration and assimilation of Asian women in the West during the twentieth century. By and large, Lee succeeds masterfully in this debut novel, mixing fact and fiction in the story of three generations of Asian-Canadians that center

around the Disappearing Moon Cafe—the largest Chinese restaurant in Vancouver's Chinatown.

Wildmen, Wobblies and Whistle Punks
(Stewart Holbrook, edited by Brian Booth, 1992)

This is a marvelous posthumous collection of stories written by famed Northwest author Stewart Holbrook. From characters such as Liverpool Liz of the old Portland waterfront to Arthur Boose, the last Wobbly paper boy, these are tales that bring the colorful past of the Pacific Northwest to life. As the Oregonian wrote at the time of Holbrook's death in 1964, "When Stewart Holbrook wrote about a Pacific Northwest logging camp you could fairly smell the smoke from the crooked stove pipe of the cookhouse."

Bachelor Brothers' Bed and Breakfast
(Bill Richardson, 1993)

This is a really fun book that will keep you smiling in that same whimsical way as a Bill Forsyth film. Canadian broadcaster Bill Richardson, who has been called the "Garrison Keillor of Canada," wrote this best-selling and award-winning book in 1993 based on stories originally told on Canadian public radio. The story is about two eccentric twins, Hector and Virgil, who run an unusual bed and breakfast on an island near Vancouver where guests can come and peruse books and enjoy a spot of tea.

Snow Falling on Cedars
(David Guterson, 1994)

Seattle's David Guterson swung on and belted a literary grand salami with this 1994 PEN/Faulkner Award winner, one of the most successful debut novels in recent memory. The story involves a Japanese-American fisherman who stands trial for murder in the shadow of World War II, and the journalist who covers the trial, only to come close once again to his boyhood love—the wife of the accused.

Reservation Blues
(Sherman Alexie, 1995)
Spokane/Couer d'Alene Native American

Sherman Alexie first burst onto the literary scene with his collection of short stories and poems titled The Business of Fancydancing. In his first novel Reservation Blues, recurring character Thomas Builds-the-Fire forms a rock band called Coyote Springs after a miraculous visit from blues legend Robert Johnson. The group, along with friend Victor Joseph, embarks on a magical tour across the country. The familiar Alexie black humor, magic, and lyricism are all in full force in this excellent book.

BUSINESS AND POLITICS

Adams, Brock

When Brock Adams was elected United States Senator from Washington in 1986, it looked to be the capstone to a distinguished public career. A Harvard Law School graduate, Adams served as U.S. Attorney for Western Washington during the Kennedy administration before being elected to the United States House of Representatives in 1964. He left the House in 1977 to become President Jimmy Carter's Secretary of Transportation, but resigned in 1979 over policy differences. Adams was a high-powered Washington lawyer until his successful Senate bid. Almost from the beginning, his Senate term was engulfed in sexual scandal. In 1988, the *Seattle Post-Intelligencer* reported that a House committee staffer named Kari Tupper had charged Adams with drugging and sexually assaulting her. Adams vehemently denied the allegation and no criminal charges were ever brought. Politically, Adams—who was known as a strong supporter of women's rights—was severely wounded, but he still began a reelection campaign. That reelection bid short-circuited in March 1992, when the *Seattle Times* published allegations of sexual improprieties from eight additional, anonymous women. Although he denied wrongdoing, Adams immediately withdrew from the race. Patty Murray, a little-known state senator from Seattle, whose wholesome "mom in tennis shoes" image resonated with a scandal-weary public, won his seat.

Aldus Pagemaker

The brainstorm that launched a thousand badly designed newsletters was invented in Seattle. Paul Brainerd, raised in Medford, Oregon, was a journalist with the *Minneapolis Star and Tribune* when he began to think of ways to merge computers with traditional newspaper production and design functions. He returned to the Northwest in the early eighties and set to work developing a layout program for the then new personal computer. From those roots Aldus Pagemaker was born. Rather than rely on expensive dedicated typesetters, anyone could compose and produce professional-looking documents (or commit serious design crimes, depending on one's talent). Brainerd sold the company in 1995 to Adobe, channeling his energy and money into philanthropy. Even Brainerd's model of giving is novel. His "Social Ventures Partners" gives money to charities but also gets involved with projects, offering planning help, technology upgrades, and accounting advice.

Amazon.com

What product can be easily shipped, doesn't spoil, has an established wholesale distribution system, and a loyal customer base of smart people? Books, you say? Move directly to "Go," issue an IPO, and collect a ton of money. Jeff Bezos answered the question correctly back in 1995 when he started Amazon.com in Seattle, taking advantage of the proximity of big book wholesalers to be able to offer customers quick service and cheap prices while carrying almost no inventory. The Internet book business has gotten a bit more crowded and complex since then, but Amazon.com remains the market leader—despite continually losing money from operations. Following the growth company model, Amazon.com has branched out into auctions, electronics, music, and videos. Whether the company is one of the survivors of the Internet frontier remains to be seen, but its place as an on-line pioneer is secure.

Bardahl, Ole

When he died in 1989 at age eighty-seven, Ole Bardahl was remembered both for his worldwide auto additive business and for the hydroplanes that bore his name. A Norwegian immigrant, Bardahl arrived in Seattle in 1932 and began a contracting business. By 1939, he had purchased a soap company, transforming it into an international manufacturer of oil additives and lubricants. Racing was a natural focus for an oil maker, and Bardahl sponsored Indy-style race cars and racing airplanes. In the late fifties, he discovered hydroplanes and began to sponsor his Miss Bardahl "Green Dragons," which won six national championships, five Gold Cups, and two world titles.

Barrett, Dave

Dave Barrett pulled off a stunning political upset in 1972 when he led his left-wing New Democratic Party (NDP) to victory over long-time British Columbia Premier W. A. C. Bennett. Chaos and controversy racked the free-spending Barrett government. Assailed from the right for being a leftist and from the left for not being leftist enough, Barrett survived just three years before losing to Bill Bennett, son of the former premier. The New Democrats didn't regain power until 1991, when former Vancouver Mayor Mike Harcourt (known as "Moderate Mike") won partly by promising voters he wouldn't be too much like Barrett.

Bauer, Eddie

Unlike Häagen-Dazs and Betty Crocker, there really was an Eddie Bauer who lived right

Eddie Bauer was a real outdoorsman, unlike most of the shoppers at his namesake stores today.
(Photo courtesy of the PEMCO Webster and Stevens Collection, Museum of History and Industry)

here in the Pacific Northwest. The son of Russian immigrants, Bauer was born on Orcas Island in 1900 and moved with his family to Seattle in 1913. Seven years later, he established his first retail store in downtown Seattle called Eddie Bauer's Sport Shop. Bauer pioneered the concept of the "unconditional guarantee," which was a radical retail concept at the time. In 1929, Bauer married Christine "Stine" Heltborg, an accomplished sportswoman who was just as adept as her husband with rifle or fishing rod. She and Eddie were married for fifty-six years, and he affectionately called her "my wilderness companion." Bauer retired in 1968, selling the business to his partner William Niemi and his son. While he probably wouldn't recognize the upscale and chic look of the stores which currently bear his name, he would be happy to know they still sell the quilted down parka which he invented and patented more than sixty years ago. Bauer died in 1986.

Beck, Dave

Born in 1894, Seattleite Dave Beck's first jobs included stints as a laundry truck driver. There he was introduced to the Teamsters, eventually agreeing to become the union's Northwest organizer. By the mid-thirties, Beck had developed a style of cooperation with industry, designed to provide business stability and fund higher wages for workers. Business leaders, while still despising unions, welcomed Beck as an alternative to San Francisco's radical longshore union chief Harry Bridges. Between 1937 and the mid-fifties, Beck increased the Teamsters' western U.S. membership from sixty thousand to nearly four hundred thousand. Beck became national Teamsters' president in 1952, a position he held until 1957 when he was convicted of embezzling nineteen hundred dollars from the sale of a used car owned by a union. He also was convicted of federal tax evasion and served two and one-half years in prison. President Gerald Ford and Washington Governor Albert Rosellini later pardoned Beck. Unlike Jimmy Hoffa, his successor as Teamsters president, Beck didn't mysteriously disappear, living quietly in Seattle until his death in 1993.

Bennett, W. A. C. and Bill

Father W. A. C. and son Bill Bennett led the Social Credit party to thirty years of British Columbia electoral dominance, combining free market philosophy with enormous political skill. William Andrews Cecil Bennett was born in New Brunswick, but moved to British Columbia as a young man, operating a hardware store in Kelowna. He was first elected to the Legislative Assembly in 1941, joining the Social Credit League in 1951.

Bennett assumed leadership of Social Credit in 1952, winning election as premier that same year. Bennett's government was conservative, but still invested heavily in public works, paving the way for economic expansion. Times changed and Bennett's string ran out in 1972 when his government was defeated by the socialist New Democratic Party, led by the fiery Dave Barrett. Barrett's government had a tumultuous three-year reign and B.C. voters quickly returned to the Bennett touch. This time, however, it was son William Richards Bennett who had taken the helm of Social Credit after his father's defeat. Bill Bennett served from 1975 to 1986 before retiring from politics. While Social Credit remained in power, Bennett's replacement, William Vander Zalm, became immersed in scandal, taking the party down with him.

Premier W. A. C. Bennett was a larger-than-life figure on the British Columbia political scene for more than three decades.
(Photo courtesy of the Vancouver Public Library, photo 79794A)

Boeing Company

Over the past fifty years, no company has had as big an impact on the Washington State economy as Seattle-based Boeing—not even Microsoft. To some, Boeing is the definition of the military-industrial complex. To local wags, it's the "Lazy B"—home of overpaid and underworked union members. To labor activists, it's the home of family wage jobs, fueling the Puget Sound middle class. After making a fortune trading forestlands near Grays Harbor, founder William Boeing moved to Seattle and eventually undertook to build a seaplane. In 1916, he formed the Pacific Aero Products Company (renamed Boeing a year later). World War I Navy seaplane orders gave the company its first shot of growth and World War II led to a virtual employment explosion. The wartime boom, however, led to a peacetime bust as the company laid off seventy thousand people. Boeing then began to diversify, adding commercial passenger aircraft and rockets to its product lines, and the company thrived in the sixties. In the early seventies, however, things again turned bleak. The wind-down of NASA's Apollo project and recession in the airline industry caused Boeing finances to go into the tank. The famous "Boeing Bust" was on and the workforce shrank by 60 percent. Improvement in the airline industry, acceptance of the 747 airplane, and another diversification effort slowly brought Boeing out of its slump, but the Puget Sound economy had been deeply scarred by the Boeing boom and bust cycles. In the nineties, Boeing purchased leading competitors McDonnell Douglas in the commercial sector and Rockwell in the military sector. Recently, production problems and the Asian economic crisis have again mired the company in financial difficulties, causing the company first to ramp up production and then call for significant layoffs. Some things never change.

During the sixties, it seemed like everyone in Puget Sound worked at the Lazy B.

(Photo courtesy of the Special Collections Division, University of Washington Libraries, photo UW10704)

Boldt Decision

Salmon has been a bone of contention between Washington Native American tribes and state officials since a series of treaties were signed in the late 1800s. Tribes claimed rights to fish at their "usual and accustomed places" while the state claimed rights to manage all fish harvest. The battles escalated in the 1960s as tribal members, led by Billy Frank of the Nisquallys, engaged in a series of highly publicized confrontations with state game wardens. Celebrities such as Marlon Brando and Jane Fonda came for "fish-ins" while the state responded with tear gas and arrests. In 1970, the federal government sued the state on behalf of the tribes and the case was assigned to U.S. District Court Judge

George Boldt. After a complex three-year trial, Boldt issued a landmark decision in February 1974. The Boldt decision said tribes were entitled to 50 percent of the state's harvestable salmon catch and had rights to protect habitat, making them comanagers of the fish resource. Despite virulent protests from non-Native American fishermen and endless appeals by then Washington State Attorney General (now U.S. Senator) Slade Gorton, the Boldt decision prevailed, radically changing the power structure of Washington State politics. In the years following Boldt, Native American fishing rights were extended to include shellfish and game.

Bottle Bill

Saving the environment one bottle at a time, Oregon adopted deposits on beer and soft drink containers back in 1971. While grocers moaned, the public loved the law which significantly reduced roadside litter and spurred early versions of recycling fever, not to mention the following joke: "A Texan, a Californian, and an Oregonian were sitting around, bragging up their respective states. The Texan pulled out a bottle of the finest Tequila, drank one shot, tossed the bottle into the air, pulled his pistol, and blew it to pieces. To the horrified looks of the Californian and the Oregonian the Texan merely smirked and said, 'Hell, we got more of that than we know what to do with.' The Californian went next, uncorking a fine Cabernet, taking a swallow, tossing the bottle in the air, pulling a gun, and blasting it to bits. The Californian took his turn to smirk and say, 'Hell, we got more of that than we know what to do with.' The Oregonian went last. He took out a superb microbrew, took a swallow, threw it into the air, drew his gun, shot the Californian, and caught the bottle. Turning to the Texan, he said, 'Hell, we got more Californians than we know what to do with and, besides, we get back five cents apiece for these.'" Efforts to adopt a similar deposit in Washington State have failed miserably, no doubt because the joke was already taken.

Canwell Committee

Washington State Senator Albert Canwell was a low-budget version of Joe McCarthy. In 1948, Canwell's "Joint Legislative Fact-Finding Committee on Un-American Activities" began hearings on alleged subversive activities at the University of Washington. Among the persecuted was Professor Melvin Rader who wrote a comprehensive account of his efforts to clear his name ("False Witness"). Despite his high profile, Canwell lost his seat in the 1948 elections. Later investigations showed irregularities in committee records and spending. Canwell failed in his 1950 bid for the U.S. Senate and in 1952 and 1954 races for Congress. While he never again held public office, Canwell remained active in right-wing causes, establishing the "American Intelligence Service" (AIS) which began a smear campaign against John Goldmark, a state legislator from Okanogan County. Goldmark sued Canwell and a number of associates and prevailed at trial, though the verdict was later overturned on constitutional grounds. William Dwyer, who would later go on to become a respected federal judge, represented Goldmark at trial. Dwyer wrote a book about the events titled *The Goldmark Case*. In a tragic twist, the Goldmark story came to the attention of a mentally unstable drifter who believed that Goldmark's son was a Communist, murdering him and his family in their Seattle home on Christmas Eve in 1985.

Chow, Ruby

Longtime King County Councilwoman Ruby Chow was the driving force in the Seattle Chinese political community for decades. Seen as opening the way for future generations of Chinese politicians, including current Washington State Governor Gary Locke and her daughter Cheryl Chow, Ruby Chow first gained fame as a restaurateur, employing at one time a then-unknown Bruce Lee. In the 1950s, Chow organized women to join the board of directors of the influential Chong Wa Benevolent Association. She continued her community service and won a seat on the King County Council in 1973, which she held until her retirement from politics in 1985. Throughout her career—both in food and politics—Chow was noted for her spectacular, gravity-defying pompadour.

Clark, Bud

Portland's colorful mayor from 1985 to 1993, Bud Clark provoked strong reactions from friends and foes. A tavern owner who once posed flashing a statue (for a popular poster titled "Expose Yourself to Art"), Clark had a flowing white beard and wore a rose in his lapel. He frequently paddled his canoe up and down the Willamette River and could be seen biking through town emitting a jubilant "whoop whoop." Critics conceded Clark's charm, but railed at his inexperience and chaotic governing style. In Clark's first term, he went through four police chiefs, provoking chaos in the ranks. His plain-spoken style also could land Clark in hot water—he once offered to get a tan to better understand the problems of African Americans. Clark supporters pointed to his successful effort to build a convention center and his innovative plans for helping the homeless as marks of his effectiveness. Clark upset incumbent Mayor Frank Ivancie to gain office, and surprised critics by winning reelection despite his political problems. Clark decided not to run for a third term, citing recently enacted spending limits and a desire to leave office still perceived as a "citizen mayor." Clark remains the proprietor of Portland's popular Goose Hollow Inn.

Don't Let Spot Die!

This was a heart-tugging slogan used by groups opposed to an early seventies Washington State ballot initiative that would have legalized the sport of greyhound racing. For the uninitiated, the "sport" consists of betting on which emaciated pooch can chase a mechanical rabbit fastest around the track. Newspaper editorials alleging corruption in the industry and commercials featuring the skinny greyhounds together with tales of abuse and mistreatment killed the measure at the polls.

Douglas, William O.

One of the most controversial Supreme Court justices in U.S. history, William O. Douglas was a fiery civil libertarian who was raised in Yakima, Washington. He suffered infantile polio and climbed mountains to help his rehabilitation. He would later be as famous for his lyrical love of the outdoors as for his sharply worded opinions (and attempts by conservatives to impeach him). Douglas graduated from Columbia law school and taught law at Columbia and Yale before being appointed to the Securities and Exchange Commission in 1934. In 1939, President Franklin Roosevelt appointed him to the U.S. Supreme Court. Douglas frequently returned to his home at Goose Prairie, Washington, though the conservative local establishment was never very comfortable with their liberal neighbor. He wrote a two-volume autobiography titled *Go East Young Man* and *The Court Years*, and a passionate tribute to the great outdoors titled *Of Men and Mountains*. Douglas's thirty-nine years of service remains a Supreme Court record. He died in 1980.

Ehrlichman, John

Born in Tacoma in 1925, John Ehrlichman was a partner in a Seattle law firm before he was tapped by President Richard Nixon to become his domestic policy advisor. In retrospect, he has been praised as a creative, pragmatic policy leader on issues such as school desegregation and welfare reform. But that legacy has been far overshadowed by his role in the Watergate scandal that ultimately toppled Nixon. Together with Chief of Staff H. R. Haldeman, Ehrlichman was part of the inner circle that was implicated in the cover-up by John Dean. Nixon forced Ehrlichman's resignation (along with Haldeman and Attorney General Richard Kleindienst) in a ploy to stop the political damage. During the scandal, Ehrlichman uttered a phrase that has now become standard political jargon, advising Nixon to leave acting FBI director L. Patrick Gray "twisting slowly in the wind." Eventually, Ehrlichman was convicted of conspiracy, perjury, and obstructing justice in connection with false Senate testimony and the break-in at the office of Daniel Ellsberg's psychiatrist. After serving his time, friends spoke of a changed Ehrlichman. He softened his image, grew a beard, lived in Santa Fe, and wrote well-received political novels. Ultimately, Ehrlichman moved to Atlanta, where he died in 1999, still dogged by his Watergate past.

Evans, Dan

Arguably the most popular and influential politician in Washington State history, Dan Evans has been a state legislator, three-term governor, U.S. Senator, and college president. His style of fiscal prudence and social liberalism was reduced to the shorthand "Evans Republican" (though in recent years Democrats have adopted the style more often). Born October 16, 1925, Daniel Jackson Evans was trained as an engineer. He became involved in politics as a volunteer, and was persuaded to run for the legislature in 1956. There he rose to the top of a talented class of young Republican House members, including future U.S. Senator Slade Gorton and future Congressman Joel Pritchard. Evans was elected governor in 1964, winning reelection in 1968 and 1972—the only Washington governor to serve three terms. While Evans maintained his "straight-arrow" reputation, he surrounded himself with crafty political operatives who could play serious hardball, and his campaigns were often rough-and-tumble affairs, leading former Washington House Speaker Len Sawyer to say, "Nobody ever ran against Dan Evans who didn't get muddied up a bit." After leaving the governor's office in 1977, Evans took on the presidency of the Evergreen State College, an avowedly alternative institution located in Olympia. Evans was preparing to leave the Evergreen presidency in 1983 when Senator Henry Jackson died suddenly. He was appointed to the vacant seat by Governor John Spellman, but had a surprisingly difficult time with fiery Seattle Congressman (and future Governor) Mike Lowry in the subsequent special election. By all accounts, Evans found the Senate frustrating, as his executive skills and tendencies clashed with the Senate's fondness for arcane procedure and gridlock. After one frustrating term, Evans retired to Seattle, where he remains a visible commentator on political and policy issues.

Foley, Tom

Spokane's Tom Foley first came to the U.S. House of Representatives in 1965. Over the years he earned a reputation as a decent, civil, and creative legislator, serving as majority leader for the Democrats and ultimately Speaker of the House. A longtime *Washington Post* political reporter described Foley as "on everyone's list of the five best legislators in Congress and the three best television performers in American politics." His long tenure and consummate insider status ultimately proved his undoing as Newt Gingrich's Republicans made Foley one of the poster children for the evils of big Democrat government in 1994. Foley, who had grown out of touch with an increasingly conservative district, was swept out in the Republicans' "Contract with America" tidal wave. Polls showed that some voters thought that Foley's replacement, political novice George Nethercutt, would simply replace Foley as Speaker. But there are no "do-overs" in elections (or evidently civics classes in Spokane), and Foley retired from elective politics. Foley has since served in diplomatic capacities for the Clinton administration.

Frank Jr., Billy

A Nisqually tribe member, Billy Frank Jr. was a symbol for Native American activism in the 1960s and 1970s. From his base at Frank's Landing, north of Olympia, Washington, Frank was a tireless and fearless champion of Native American fishing rights. He was branded a "renegade" by state officials for his confrontational style, which saw him arrested more than forty times. After the Boldt decision in 1974 validated Native American treaty claims, Frank began the transition into a respected political leader. He has been awarded the Albert Schweitzer Prize for Humanitarianism and is now a key player in discussions over how to restore wild salmon runs throughout the Northwest.

Frederick and Nelson

A homegrown Seattle department store that defined local elegance before a protracted demise, Frederick and Nelson dates back to 1891. Nels Nelson and Donald Frederick were partners in a used-furniture store that gradually branched into a department store. Chicago's Marshall Field Company eventually purchased the store and Frederick and Nelson began a long and affectionate association with Western Washingtonians. A series of ownership changes in the eighties and early nineties slowly bled the store dry, and the chain unceremoniously closed in 1992. While in operation, Frederick's was known for its "Santa breakfasts" where kids could dine with Kris Kringle; cafes full of "ladies who lunch"; and decadent Frango candies. In fact, when Frederick's finally folded, locals were most upset by the potential loss of Frangos (not to worry, the Bon Marché took over the line).

Gamscam

In 1980, a federal sting operation targeted Washington State House Speaker John Bagnariol, Senate Democratic Majority Leader Gordon Walgren, and lobbyist Patrick Gallagher, trying to tie them to efforts to expand gambling in Washington State. At the time, Bagnariol was planning a gubernatorial run and Walgren was looking at the state's attorney general post, so when they were indicted the political landscape was turned upside down. Despite a vigorous defense and holes in the evidence, all three were ultimately convicted on the basis of secret FBI tapes, many with the chatty Gallagher who said on one tape, "I have a very practical sense of politics. There ain't no point in being in it unless you can profit from it." Walgren's convictions were later overturned.

🎶 Gardner, Booth

Enormously popular with voters, former Washington State Governor Booth Gardner managed to evoke the common touch even though he belonged to one of the region's wealthiest families. Early in life, Gardner's mother divorced his father and married Weyerhaeuser bigwig and real estate tycoon Norton Clapp. During the sixties, Gardner moved from one project to another, including a term in the state senate and teaching assignments at the University of Puget Sound in Tacoma. In the early seventies, Gardner headed the family-owned Laird Norton Company, owners of a regional building-supply chain. Gardner eventually reignited his political spark and was elected Pierce County Executive. In 1984, he ran for governor, defeating incumbent John Spellman, and in 1988 easily won reelection. Upon taking office, Gardner quickly established his signature style—here was a scion of great wealth who enjoyed eating burgers at Tacoma's Frisko Freeze drive-in and who spent days walking around state agencies seeking the views of front-line workers. His political caution frustrated Democrats wanting a bolder agenda, but Gardner was hugely popular with the public. After leaving office in 1989, Gardner served as a special trade representative and an executive with a national women's soccer organization. Recently diagnosed with Parkinson's disease, he now stays out of the public eye.

🎶 Goldschmidt, Neil

Over a long career, Neil Goldschmidt has moved from charismatic "Young Turk" to established power broker, continuing to shape the face of Portland along the way. Goldschmidt was just thirty-two years old when he was elected Portland mayor in 1972. During his term, he laid the groundwork for the Rose City's current reputation for livability. The seeds of the Max light rail were sewn during

Portland Mayor and Oregon Governor Neil Goldschmidt is credited with ensuring the livability of the Rose City.
(Photo published with permission of the Oregon State Library)

Goldschmidt's tenure, as were a number of the key planning and growth restrictions designed to keep Portland livable. Hailed by progressives, Goldschmidt became President Jimmy Carter's Secretary of Transportation in 1978. When Carter lost his reelection bid, Goldschmidt returned to Oregon, and worked for his friend Phil Knight at Nike. Coming out of "retirement" in 1986, Goldschmidt was elected Oregon governor, serving until 1990 when he left politics and became a private consultant. Since then, in the words of Portland's *Willamette Week* newspaper, "Goldschmidt, the private citizen, is quietly exercising enormous clout, leaving fingerprints all over the city, state, and nation."

⚡ Greenpeace

The granddaddy of "in-your-face" environmental groups was founded in Vancouver in 1969. The catalyst was a U.S. nuclear bomb test on Amchitka Island in the Alaskan Aleutian chain. Local Vancouver peace activists met with environmentalists to protest another planned Amchitka test. The environmentalists wanted to broaden the agenda to include other environmental threats—calling for a "green peace." While weather made the protest unsuccessful, the name stuck and the Greenpeace foundation was formed. Over the next twenty years, Greenpeace launched a series of highly visible campaigns against nuclear testing, whaling, and seal hunting, often taking to the water in small "zodiac" boats to harass opponents. In 1985, the Greenpeace ship *Rainbow Warrior* was blown up by the French secret service, but the organization continued to grow (as did its staff and budget, causing friction in the environmental community). By the mid-nineties Greenpeace itself was taking on water. Hard-core environmentalists complained the organization had gone corporate and lost its confrontational edge. Donations were drying up and the organization no longer could automatically generate headlines for its activities. Although Greenpeace's future appears uncertain, its legacy of launching a harder-edged environmental movement is secure.

Early Greenpeace fund-raisers were low-budget affairs.
(Photo courtesy of the Vancouver Public Library, photo 80323A)

⚡ Group Health Cooperative

Progressive doctors seeking to provide inexpensive, quality health care for working families formed the Group Health Cooperative in Seattle in 1945. An early model of the health maintenance organization (HMO), Group Health members paid dues instead of fees for service to be covered for their health-care needs. By the end of 1946, the "co-op" had nearly four hundred members—that number would grow steadily over the years, despite frequent battles with the medical establishment. Whereas in the early years Group Health members (who paid into a capital account and could vote on co-op affairs) outnumbered group enrollees, that ratio reversed as Group Health went on a growth spurt, reaching nearly four hundred thousand enrollees by 1990. In the early nineties, changes in health-care economics began to take their toll on Group Health, which laid off employees and formed an alliance with Seattle's Virginia Mason Hospital. By 1998, Group Health had merged with Kaiser Permanente, another pioneering health plan from California. While the co-op structure remained in part, most observers marked the merger as final transition of Group Health from pioneering social experiment to standard (though still liberal) HMO.

⚡ Hamilton Farms Billboard

For years, drivers on Interstate 5 near Chehalis, Washington, have been treated to right-wing one-liners as they motor north and south on the freeway. Just off the side of the road, a double-sided billboard featuring the likeness of Uncle Sam himself has been dispensing conservative viewpoints that occasionally tickle the funny bone. When Hamilton Farms was sold several years ago, the billboard was redone and moved across the freeway where it continues to drive liberals crazy to this day.

Hatfield, Mark

The longest-serving senator in Oregon history, Mark Hatfield personified a politics that was independent, moderate, and civil. Hatfield was a political science professor at Salem's Willamette University when he was first elected to the Oregon state legislature in 1950. In 1956, he became the youngest secretary of state in Oregon history at the age of thirty-four. In 1958, he was elected governor, winning reelection in 1962. From there, Hatfield was elected to the U.S. Senate in 1966, serving until his retirement in 1996. Hatfield was a dove, opposing the Vietnam War and working for nuclear disarmament. At the same time, he was skilled at bringing home the bacon for Oregon, securing funding for major public works programs such as the Portland Max light rail system and numerous college facilities. A skilled campaigner and legislator, Hatfield earned bipartisan respect for his ability to bridge party lines in the pursuit of solutions. The voters of Oregon must have agreed with his approach—Hatfield never lost an election.

Hunthausen, Raymond

During the 1970s and 1980s, Seattle's liberal Catholic Archbishop Raymond Hunthausen was a lightning rod for political controversy. To protest the nuclear arms race, Hunthausen participated in demonstrations outside the Bangor Navy Base (near Bremerton), held mass for jailed protestors, and refused to pay part of his federal income tax. Hunthausen also endorsed the Equal Rights Amendment and held liberal

views on issues such as gay rights, causing enough consternation for the Vatican to investigate and, in 1986, limit his powers as archbishop (they were ultimately restored). Hunthausen served as archbishop until his retirement in 1991.

Jackson, Henry "Scoop"

Born in 1912, Everett's Henry Jackson became one of Washington State's most popular politicians and one of the nation's most powerful leaders. Nicknamed "Scoop" after a newspaper cartoon character, Jackson served six terms in Congress and five in the U.S. Senate, routinely racking up more than 70 percent of the vote. Jackson ran twice for president (1972 and 1976), failing to catch on with the national electorate, but he remained a powerful national figure, often mentioned as a vice presidential candidate. Nationally, Jackson came off as a mix of social dove, foreign policy hawk, and fiscal con-

Henry "Scoop" Jackson was one of the Evergreen State's most beloved political figures.
(Photo courtesy of the Tacoma Public Library, Richards Collection, photo D163000-48c)

servative. The mix led to some odd policy contradictions. For example, Jackson was a key architect of the 1970 National Environmental Policy Act, yet a decade later his skepticism about energy conservation helped lead to the WPPSS debacle. Ultimately, enduring political success is often less about national issues and more about taking care of the home folks. Here Jackson excelled. His reserved persona was a perfect balance for the more flamboyant Warren Magnuson. Jackson was also a master politician. His memory for names, faces, and political favors is legendary, and he maintained a robust network of contacts throughout the state. Jackson also never lost touch with his hometown of Everett, maintaining an elegant, though not ostentatious, home in the north end. It was there that he died unexpectedly of a heart attack in 1983.

Jantzen

Founded in 1910 as the Portland Knitting Company, the Jantzen company first produced wool sweaters, socks, and gloves. It stumbled into its signature swimwear business when a Portland rowing club asked the company to make swim trunks warm enough to wear for their morning practices. Jantzen responded with the world's first stretch swimsuits in 1913. The suits became casually known as "Jantzens" after cofounder Carl Jantzen, though the formal name of the company wasn't changed until 1918. The company adopted its famous "diving girl" trademark in 1921. Considered a bit risqué for the time, some cities banned stickers featuring the logo, citing a safety hazard. People knew what they liked—during the twenties more than four million stickers and auto ornaments were in circulation.

K2 Corporation

From a base on tranquil Vashon Island (located in Puget Sound between Tacoma and Seattle), the K2 Corporation invented and marketed the first successful fiberglass snow skis in

1965. After the skis were used to win a 1968 World Cup gold medal, sales took off. Named for the founding Kirschner brothers (Bill and Don) as well as the mountain, K2 evolved from a company that made animal cages and metal splints for veterinarians. The fiberglass skis were the brainchild of Bill Kirschner who wanted to avoid paying top dollar for competitor Head's metal skis. The brothers have long since sold K2, but the company still retains offices and manufacturing facilities on Vashon Island.

In 1947, Marilyn Monroe (known at the time as Norma Jean Baker) models this Jantzen swimsuit "Double Dare" for the wholesale catalog.
(Photo courtesy of Jantzen, Inc.)

◪ Krogh, Egil "Bud"

Now a respected Seattle lawyer, Bud Krogh has two claims to pop culture fame. First, he was a deputy counsel in the Nixon White House, playing a role in the infamous Watergate cover-up. More importantly, he arranged one of the most surreal meetings of the century—when an obviously drugged Elvis Presley met with President Nixon, receiving an FBI narcotics bureau badge. Unfortunately, the meeting took place before the White House taping system had been installed, but Krogh has recounted the event in his book *The Day Elvis Met Nixon*.

◪ Landes, Bertha

Bertha Landes, Seattle's only female mayor, rode a reform wave into office in 1926. Landes had been active in Seattle women's clubs and the war relief effort. Friends persuaded her to run for city council, and she eventually rose to council president. A strong proponent of public power and a corruption fighter, Landes frequently tangled with then Mayor Edwin Brown and the police department, which was under suspicion. Landes took on Brown in the 1926 election, winning a stunning upset. Although her term is generally given good marks, Landes also continued to do battle with public power foes. In the 1928 election, civil service workers (who did not care for Landes's anticorruption themes) and private power interests coalesced behind Frank Edwards, a political unknown, who unseated Landes.

◪ Lesser Seattle

Lesser Seattle is an informal organization started by former *Seattle Post-Intelligencer* columnist Emmett Watson to rail against the sins of excessive growth in the Seattle area. The name is a play on the pro-growth "Greater Seattle" association that was active in the fifties. Lesser Seattleites looked askance at all plans to gentrify, yuppify, and generally turn Seattle into a "festival marketplace." By the late nineties, the forces of Lesser Seattle had been routed, with downtown being invaded by Planet Hollywood, Niketown, Wolfgang Puck, and all manner of upscale chain retailers.

◪ Luke, Wing

The son of a Chinese immigrant laundryman, Wing Luke became the Pacific Northwest's first Asian American elected official when he won a seat on the Seattle City Council in 1962. Only three years later, Luke was tragically killed in a plane crash. In his honor, the community established a multicultural Asian American museum in Seattle to preserve the history, art, and culture of Asian Pacific Americans.

◪ Mabon, Lon

The force behind a series of antigay and antiabortion initiatives, Lon Mabon formed the Oregon Citizens Alliance (OCA) in the late eighties. Mabon and the OCA hit their high-water mark in 1994 when they almost succeeded in passing "Measure 13," which would have prohibited any state agency, including schools, from representing homosexuality as an acceptable lifestyle. After that, support for the OCA began to ebb and it failed to get subsequent measures to the ballot. Mabon, however, remains active, plotting a return to prominence. When *Monk Magazine*, a gay-oriented travel 'zine, published its Portland issue, it referred to Mabon as "the mabonic plague."

◪ MacMillan Bloedel

A giant of the British Columbia timber industry, MacMillan Bloedel is the outcome of the merger of three forest products companies in 1951 and 1959. The components were the Powell River Company, founded in 1908; Bloedel, Stewart and Welch, founded in 1911; and the H. R.

MacMillan Export Company, founded in 1919. The company suffered in the timber industry downturns of the nineties and has refocused on its core building materials business, selling off its papermaking operations. The imprint of the company can be found in the cultural life of Vancouver as well. The H. R. MacMillan Planetarium in Vanier Park is a local favorite and the VanDusen Botanical Gardens (W. J. VanDusen was H. R. MacMillan's business partner) are the city's largest. VanDusen Botanical Gardens also houses MacMillan Bloedel Place. In Queen Elizabeth Park, one can find the Bloedel Conservatory, a domed compound filled with jungle and desert settings. In 1999, Weyerhaeuser Company announced its acquisition of MacMillan Bloedel.

For half a century, Warren "Maggie" Magnuson brought home the pork for Washington voters.
(Photo courtesy of the Tacoma Public Library, Richards Collection, photo D99212-3)

Magnuson, Warren

Over a political career spanning fifty years, Washington State's beloved Warren "Maggie" Magnuson was the embodiment of the joyful politician. While his early reputation was that of a fun-loving playboy (try to get away with that nowadays), Maggie ultimately became known as the consumer's friend in D.C. Legislation with the Maggie imprint include truth-in-advertising laws, the Consumer Product Safety Commission, Amtrak, the National Science Foundation, and the National Cancer Institute. Maggie took on and squashed Washington Governor Dixy Lee Ray, rolling through federal legislation banning supertankers in Puget Sound. He also was a master of bringing the pork back home, including key funding for the University of Washington Medical School and Hospital (now named for Magnuson). The specific accomplishments of Magnuson are a sizable legacy, but a perhaps more enduring one is the network of former Maggie staff members now occupying key political and business positions throughout the Northwest. Magnuson was ultimately defeated for reelection in 1980 by Washington State Attor-

ney General Slade Gorton, who himself had developed a proconsumer image (although few would argue he has maintained that reputation over the past twenty years). Maggie retired to Seattle, where he lived until his death in 1989.

Manning, Harvey

The grandfather of Washington State's environmental movement, Harvey Manning is the hirsute author of numerous mountaineering and hiking guidebooks and a longtime advocate for wilderness preservation. During the sixties, Manning was a major force behind the establishment of the North Cascades National Park, and he led the effort to preserve the Issaquah Alps in the mid-seventies. Some of Manning's classic books include

46

Mountaineering: Freedom of the Hills, Back-packing One Step at a Time, and the popular *101 Hikes* and *Footsore* series.

McCall, Tom

Governor of Oregon from 1967 to 1975, Tom McCall left a legacy of environmental protection and progressive policies. McCall started his career as a journalist, eventually landing as a news commentator at Portland's KEX radio. In 1964, McCall entered politics, successfully running for secretary of state. Two years later he won the governorship and began building his record as a premier environmental politician. He pursued initiatives to clean up the Willamette River, find cleaner energy sources, and discourage "dirty" industries from locating in Oregon. McCall also tried to manage and limit growth—at one point he counseled outsiders to "visit Oregon but don't stay," a sentiment heartily embraced by many Oregonians who wanted to avoid the "Californication" of their state. McCall left office in 1974, returning to Portland to teach and become a broadcast commentator. He died in 1982.

McCaw, Craig

Craig McCaw's father was a pioneer in Northwest radio, television, and cable services. He proved not to be as skilled at estate planning, and when he died most of his holdings were liquidated to pay debts and taxes. The sole remaining asset was a small cable system in Centralia, Washington, which McCaw's four sons took over. A gifted business visionary, Craig McCaw took charge, rapidly expanding the cable system. In 1981, he became convinced that the cellular telephone market would be an eventual gold mine, and that permits were undervalued. He soon began building a cell phone empire—and the prototype for a technology growth company. McCaw sold the cable business in the mid-eighties to concentrate solely on wireless telephony, taking on huge chunks of debt to knit together a nationwide network. In 1994, McCaw sold out to AT&T for more than $11 billion, but he was far from retired. Since then, he has launched Nextlink, another highly successful wireless company, and Teledesic, which plans to provide high-speed data transmission via satellite. In his spare time, McCaw—an ardent environmentalist—found time to push for the return of Keiko the whale to a natural habitat, presumably with a cell phone mounted in his blowhole.

Oregon Governor Tom McCall was an environmentalist and fought the "Californication" of the state.
(Photo published with permission of the Oregon State Library)

Meier and Frank

Portland's retail institution began in 1857 when Bavarian immigrant Aaron Meier opened a small general store on Front Street. In the 1870s, Sigmund Frank married Meier's daughter and became a partner in the business. Now known as Meier and Frank, the enterprise expanded, becoming a full-service department store. During the 1930s, company president Julius Meier was elected Oregon's first (and still only) independent governor. The company remained in family hands until 1965, when it was sold to the national May Company department store chain. For years, Meier and Frank was known nationally for its "Friday Surprise" sales—special goods were obtained and marked down for one day only. No goods were advertised in advance—you had to show up to find the deals.

⚜ Meyer, Fred

Born in Brooklyn in 1886, Fred Meyer came west to seek his fortune in the early 1900s, landing in Portland. There he began a retail empire of "one-stop shopping centers" that pepper the Northwest. Meyer's business career began inauspiciously with a "route selling" business that brought coffee and tea to loggers in camps outside of town. He refined his ideas and by 1917, Meyer had opened his first full grocery store in downtown Portland. Meyer was a retail innovator, introducing prepackaged foods and "cash and carry" service instead of delivery. He used the savings to lower prices and attract more business. By the 1930s, cars were proliferating and Meyer noticed that many customers were commuting to downtown from suburban Portland. Capitalizing on the trend, Meyer opened his first "suburban" one-stop store in Portland's Hollywood District, beginning three decades of steady, measured expansion. After the death of his wife, Eva, in 1960, Fred Meyer took his company public and began to expand throughout the Northwest. Fred Meyer died in 1978, using his will to establish the Fred Meyer Memorial Trust that has become a major philanthropic force in the Pacific Northwest.

⚜ Microsoft

In 1968, the mother's club at Seattle's private Lakeside School paid to put a computer terminal in the school. It proved to be the bargain of the century, because two students named Bill Gates and Paul Allen soon found the terminal and each other. Over the next several years, Gates and Allen became thoroughly hooked by computing, working after school debugging programs and starting their first company to sell a traffic-counting program (Traf-o-Data). In 1973, Gates left for Harvard and persuaded Allen to move East as well. There, Allen discovered an article on the MITS Altair personal computer. Then they both made a gazillion dollars. Okay, there were a few steps in between, but not as many as you might think (or hope). In 1974, Allen and Gates developed a version of the BASIC programming language that could work on the Altair—making it usable to casual users. They pitched the program to MITS, which offered Allen a job in Albuquerque. Once there, Allen and Gates set up shop—calling themselves Micro-Soft (though they didn't actually incorporate the company until 1981). By 1979, Apple had wiped out the MITS, and Gates and Allen relocated to Seattle. A year later, the company had grown to thirty-five employees, with Steve Ballmer (now Microsoft CEO) having been hired to "manage things." IBM soon came calling, seeking an operating system for its new personal computer project. At the same time, Allen was purchasing a new operating system called Q-Dos from a small Seattle computer company. This product—renamed MS-Dos—would become the cash engine that drove the first wave of Microsoft growth. All seemed well until 1982 when Paul Allen was diagnosed with Hodgkin's disease. He left Microsoft to facilitate his recovery and decided not to come back. Since then, Allen (who still owns a huge share in Microsoft and remains on the board of directors) has pursued a vision of a "wired world"—purchasing multimedia firms, sports teams, and becoming a major arts and health-care benefactor. Gates stayed lashed to the Microsoft wheel, becoming the world's richest man and dominating his industry in a way not seen since the days of Carnegie and Rockefeller. Microsoft's influence on Northwest pop culture is profound. It changed the way the region is viewed nationally and created enormous wealth, particularly for the "Microsoft Millionaires"—initial employees who turned stock options into early retirement. It spawned a round-the-clock work ethic that clashed with the region's legendary laid-back style. Revenge of the nerds indeed.

Morse, Wayne

Oregon Senator Wayne Morse was the definition of a political maverick. In 1944, he ran for U.S. Senate as a Republican, defeating the isolationist incumbent Rufus Holman. In 1952, Morse shocked the political world by leaving the Republican Party and declared himself an independent. After remaining independent for three years, Morse joined with the Democrats in 1955, winning reelection to the Senate in 1956. Morse embarked on a failed campaign for the Democratic presidential nomination in 1960, but his most remembered stand was yet to come. In 1964, Congress passed the Tonkin Gulf resolution, which was used to justify continued American involvement in Vietnam. The House of Representatives passed the resolution unanimously. In the Senate, only Morse and Alaska Senator Ernest Gruening voted no. Morse continued to oppose the war and earned a bitter (and crafty) enemy in President Johnson, who decided to target Morse for defeat

by asking him to arbitrate two nasty union disputes. Johnson correctly surmised that Morse's Democratic base would be split and Morse narrowly lost the election to Bob Packwood. He undertook a rematch in 1974, but died during the campaign.

Newman, Peter

Canada's premier business and political columnist, Vancouver's Peter Newman was editor of Maclean's magazine from 1971 to 1982 (he remains a senior contributing editor and columnist). Newman, who has won numerous journalistic awards, is also known for a number of books on the Canadian political and business scene, including *The Canadian Revolution* and *The Canadian Establishment*.

Nike

With a "swoosh" and a motto of "Just Do It," Portland's Nike rode to the top of American business in the nineties before being sidetracked by charges of labor exploitation and a softening market. Nike was born in Eugene in 1957 when then-student Phil Knight met legendary University of Oregon track coach Bill Bowerman. Knight had a mind for business and went to Stanford for an MBA after graduating. Bowerman stayed at Eugene and continued to tinker with ideas for high-performance athletic gear. While in college Knight wrote a research paper showing there was an opportunity to import high-quality athletic shoes from Japan. In partnership with Bowerman, Knight began a company called Blue Ribbon Sports to import and sell Japanese shoes. As Bowerman tinkered with shoe designs and Knight handled the business, Blue Ribbon Sports began to grow. In 1972, the company broke with its original supplier and renamed itself Nike, debuting its products at the

1972 Olympic Trials in Eugene. Using Knight's innovative business model, Nike grew to capture 50 percent of the U.S. running market by 1979, going public in 1980. During the eighties, Nike became a global brand, signing endorsement contracts with stars such as Michael Jordan and establishing its logo and slogan in the national consciousness. A serious threat emerged in the late nineties, however, as human rights activists targeted Nike, contrasting the differences between wages and working conditions for those making the shoes (in Third World countries) with the extravagant salaries and endorsement fees of Nike officials and spokespeople. Sales began to decline and layoffs ensued. The company has recently taken steps to improve factory conditions and pay, and appears to be regaining its market popularity.

Nintendo of America

The Seattle suburb of Redmond is the Western Hemisphere's home to Mario, Donkey Kong, and Pokémon. Nintendo's roots are in Japan, where the company began by manufacturing playing cards. In the 1970s, Nintendo began working on video games in earnest, consolidating its American operations in Redmond in 1982. In recent years, the company has seen stiff competition from Sony, which got its high-resolution Play Station to market a year ahead of the Nintendo 64. Nintendo's president is the major investor in the consortium that purchased the Seattle Mariners in 1992 to keep the team from moving to Tampa Bay. (And, naturally, one of Nintendo's most popular sports games features Mariners superstar Ken Griffey Jr.) In recent years, one of the plum jobs for Eastside high school students has been to staff Nintendo's game answer line for the days after Christmas. "You mean I get to play games, talk about games incessantly, learn every cheat code ever invented, AND I get paid? Gee, I don't know."

Nordstrom

From the polished wood floors, to the grand pianos near the escalators, to the elegant and pricey merchandise, Nordstrom stores have come to define quality. The beginnings of this Seattle-based retail giant, however, were a bit more humble. John Nordstrom came to New York from Sweden in 1887. After a decade of laboring in mines and logging camps, he ended up in Seattle and joined the hordes going north to Alaska in search of gold. He returned with thirteen thousand dollars which he used to open (with partner Carl Wallin) the Wallin & Nordstrom shoe store in downtown Seattle in 1901. Nordstorm retired in 1928, selling his share of the company to his sons. Wallin retired the next year and also sold to the Nordstrom boys. Over the next three decades, the Nordstroms built their stores into the largest independent shoe chain in the United States. Looking to expand, the company purchased the Best Apparel clothing store in 1963. The business continued to grow. When the brothers retired in 1968, a third generation of Nordstroms took the helm. This

ownership group took Nordstrom's public in 1971. Carefully planned expansions followed, with the company entering the California market in 1978, and the East Coast in 1988. For years, Nordstrom was famous for taking back any merchandise, in any condition, no questions asked (alas, changing times have made the company tighten up a bit). The only misstep the Nordstrom family has made was selling their beloved Seattle Seahawks to California (that should have been a clue!) real estate developer (another clue!) Ken Behring, who proceeded to run the team into the ground.

Norris, Leonard

Longtime cartoonist for the *Vancouver Sun* Leonard Norris was widely respected for his talented artwork and sharp wit. From 1950 to 1988, his cartoons appeared on the editorial pages of the *Sun* featuring politicians in swallowtail coats, horse-faced bureaucrats "who are just following orders Ma'am," and occupants of the easy chairs in the Victoria Conservative Club harrumphing at events beyond their control. Norris's attention to detail, artwork, and social commentary led Walt Kelly, the creator of Pogo, to call him "the greatest in the business." Norris, a longtime resident of West Vancouver (Amblesnide and Tiddlycove in his cartoons), died in 1997 at the age of eighty-three.

Owl Party

The brainchild of Tacoma jazzman Red Kelly, the fondly remembered Owl party took flight from his Tumwater Conservatory restaurant in 1976. Putting up a slate of candidates such as "Bunco" Bob Kelly for attorney general, Archie "Whiplash" Breslin for insurance commissioner, and "Fast Lucie" Griswold for secretary of state, the Owls let the air out of political pretension. For example, lieutenant governor candidate Jack "The Ripoff" Lemon declared that his platform was a four-cornered triangle. State treasurer candidate (and Kelly's pianist) Jack Perciful vowed to charge all state expenses on a really big credit card. The Owls (which stood for Out with Logic, On with Lunacy) were always good for a quote. Kelly proclaimed, "We started out tongue-in-cheek, but the tongue gradually came more toward the front of the mouth." None of the Owls came close to winning, but they surfaced periodically in future races until restrictions on filings by minor party candidates took the fun out of it.

Packwood, Bob

A Republican senator from Oregon, Bob Packwood was first elected in 1968, narrowly defeating legendary maverick Wayne Morse. During his Senate career, Packwood was known for his fierce commitment to women's issues. Perhaps that's why the reaction was so strong when it came out shortly after the 1994 election that Packwood was also a world-class groper. Packwood denied the allegations, but eventually resigned after the Senate Ethics Committee recommended he be expelled for sexual misconduct, soliciting jobs from lobbyists for his ex-wife (to reduce his financial obligations), and altering his diaries to obstruct the Senate probe. Proving that Washington, D.C., has a long memory for power and a short one for scandal, Packwood has successfully reemerged as a top lobbyist.

Pendleton

Classic Northwest style is wearing your Pendleton wool cap and shirt to a football game on a crisp fall afternoon, taking care to wrap your lap in a genuine Pendleton blanket. Pendleton Woolen Mills traces back to 1893, when a wool scouring plant was built in the railhead city of Pendleton, Oregon. The plant served regional sheep growers and was converted into a full woolen mill specializing in blankets and robes. The venture failed and the plant went idle until 1909 when it was purchased by the Bishop family who resumed production of Indian blankets. By 1924, the company managed to find some virgin sheep and began to make virgin wool shirts for men, over time expanding into a full line of clothes. A very successful line of women's clothing was added in 1949. Eventually, the company began to make non-wool clothing for spring and summer wear, but classically styled woolen garments remain Pendleton's signature.

⚡ Ray, Dixy Lee

When Dixy Lee Ray was elected Washington's governor in 1976, you could almost hear the smugness—"We've got a woman governor and you don't." Within the first few months of her term that sentiment largely changed to, "What were we thinking?" An academic, Ray had never run for office before she was elected governor. She was a professor of animal zoology at the University of Washington and best known to the public as the director of Seattle's Pacific Science Center. Despite her controversial views supporting nuclear power and allowing oil supertankers in Puget Sound, Ray won a three-way primary battle with Seattle Mayor Wes Uhlman and environmental attorney Marvin Durning. She went on to handily defeat King County Executive John Spellman in the final election. Ray's outspoken and uncompromising ways immediately landed her in hot water with the Capitol press corps. She took the unusual steps of canceling press conferences, demanding that questions be submitted in advance and naming pigs on her Fox Island farm for members of the press. Relations did not improve. Ray's governing style was mercurial and erratic, leading veteran political reporter Shelby Scates to note, "Her four year performance was cited by statehouse professionals as evidence that state government could run itself through its established bureaucracy with or without a steady hand in the governor's office." Ray also blew through a sizable state surplus, leading to lower bond ratings for the state and planting the seeds for a serious financial crisis. She ran for reelection in 1980, but was defeated in the primary by state senator Jim McDermott (who would later go on to be a congressman from Seattle). Ray retired to Fox Island, occasionally writing books and making appearances criticizing the environmental movement. She died in 1994.

⚡ Real Networks

Seattle's Real Networks is a perfect example of the power of the Internet to change the way we live (and make a lot of people rich along the way). Founded by former Microsoft executive Rob Glaser in 1994, Real Networks makes software to allow audio and video to be "streamed" over the Internet, avoiding the need for huge files and lengthy downloads. The company's Real Player is one of the most-used pieces of software in the world, with more than seventy million users. The company maintains a family of Web sites that provide thousands of hours of live broadcasts each week. Real Networks has drawn its share of challengers—including Microsoft itself—but the company appears poised to remain one of the major players as more television and radio signals move through the Internet.

Dixy Lee Ray: What were the voters thinking?
(Photo courtesy of the Tacoma Public Library, Richards Collection, photo D168504-1)

Reed, John

Portland-born John Reed gained fame as an international adventurer and journalist. His best-known work, *Ten Days That Shook the World*, chronicles the 1917 Russian Revolution. Prior to that, Reed had covered Pancho Villa's insurgency in Mexico and World War I. His leftist sympathies led to charges of sedition. Reed died of typhus in Russia in 1920 when he was just thirty-three years old and is the only American buried in the Kremlin. The last years of Reed's life are chronicled in Warren Beatty's 1981 film *Reds*.

REI

For years "having a low REI co-op number" was proof of real Northwest credentials. Recreational Equipment, Incorporated began in 1938 when Seattleites Lloyd and Mary Anderson called together a small group of dedicated mountain-climbing enthusiasts. Frustrated by their inability to secure quality equipment at an affordable price, the small band formed the Recreational Equipment Cooperative. Membership entitled one to purchase goods and to receive a rebate at the end of the year if a profit was earned. Growth was steady and sure, accelerating in the seventies under new CEO (and legendary mountaineer) Jim Whittaker. Today's Seattle-based REI is still a cooperative (members still receive patronage rebates), though it operates on a mass retail scale with more than 1.4 million members and stores throughout the country.

Rosellini, Albert

When Albert "Rosy" Rosellini was elected Washington's governor in 1956, he became only the second Italian American governor in the nation's history, and the first Catholic governor of a state west of the Mississippi. Born

Albert Rosellini was the first Catholic elected governor west of the Mississippi.
(Photo courtesy of the Tacoma Public Library, Richards Collection, photo D142309-3)

in 1910, Rosellini is part of an influential extended family that includes Hugh, a former state supreme court justice, and Seattle restaurant legend Victor. Albert was the politician of the family, winning election to the state senate in 1938 before his successful run for governor. A progressive Democrat, Rosellini was reelected in 1960 but defeated by Dan Evans in a 1964 bid for an unprecedented third term. He was then defeated in a bid for King County Executive in 1968, and most political observers wrote him off. But in 1972, Rosellini reemerged to mount a strong challenge to Governor Dan Evans as he tried for a third term. Even though he was dogged by whispers of financial scandals, Rosellini appeared a strong bet to win until a miscue in a televised debate—calling the governor "Danny Boy"—sapped his support. In recent years, a still spry Rosellini has been back in the spotlight as an elder statesman for Democrats. Northwest pop culture fans are forever indebted to Rosellini for persuading Elvis Presley to come to Seattle to film a movie at the 1962 World's Fair (*It Happened at the World's Fair*).

⚡ Satiacum, Bob

During the 1960s and 1970s, as chairman of the Puyallup Tribe (located near Tacoma), Bob Satiacum was a controversial Native American activist, leading demonstrations that ultimately led to the Boldt decision, which guaranteed tribal fishing rights. As a businessman, Satiacum was equally aggressive, running gambling, liquor, cigarette, and liquor sales operations that netted him millions. In the early eighties, Satiacum's luck turned sour as he was ousted as Puyallup chairman and indicted on federal racketeering charges. Satiacum was convicted in 1982 and fled to Canada. He was arrested by the RCMP in 1983, but avoided extradition by claiming political refugee status, which was granted four years later. In 1988, Satiacum was charged with molesting a Richmond, B.C., girl. He was convicted the next year, his political refugee status was revoked, and he was ordered deported. Once again, Satiacum fled before being jailed. He was captured on March 19, 1991, in Chase, B.C., and died of a heart attack six days later.

⚡ Schwab, Les

In 1952, Les Schwab bought a small tire manufacturer called the O.K. Rubber Welders in Prineville, Oregon. Over the next forty-five years he built that single location into one of the nation's largest chains of tire stores, with nearly three hundred locations throughout the Northwest. A straight-talking cowboy, Schwab built his reputation with innovative profit-sharing plans for employees, a flawless reputation for customer service, and unusual promotions such as giving away free beef with a set of tires.

⚡ Smith, Sam

Longtime state legislator and Seattle city councilman, Sam Smith was the premier African American politician of his era. During the early 1960s, Smith pushed the state legislature to pass open housing and antidiscrimination laws. He was elected to the Seattle City Council in 1967 where he served for twenty-four years, including four terms as council president. Not a knee-jerk liberal, Smith was known for being tough on crime and fighting for lower taxes and utility rates. While Smith was easily reelected five times, by the early nineties his health was in decline and he appeared politically vulnerable. Smith was defeated in 1994 by Sherry Harris, an African American lesbian who siphoned off some of his traditional election allies and mobilized the gay community. He died in 1995.

⚡ SST

In 1966, Seattle was both atwitter and divided over Boeing's successful bid to build America's first supersonic transport plane. Boosters saw it as a feather in the cap of Boeing, which needed to keep up with the Europeans in the air technology race. Even the city's new National Basketball Assocation (NBA) franchise adopted the name in 1967. But environmentalists—both at home and nationally—worried about environmental damage from the plane and the sonic booms that would emanate when it broke the sound barrier. Eventually, the project dried up, helping contribute to the famous "Boeing Bust" of the early seventies.

⚡ Taxes

Although big thinkers proclaim that Oregon, Washington, and British Columbia are really one big economic region (Cascadia), there are some differences that make life fun. For example, Oregon and Washington are blessed (or cursed) with unusual state tax structures. Washington is one of a handful of states without a state income tax; Oregon has no sales tax. Whereas politicians and economists argue that adding the missing link(s) would make for a fairer, more stable tax system, voters consistently rout such proposals at the polls. One effect of the structure is that many Washingtonians, particularly those living close to Oregon, shop across the border to avoid sales tax (a practice frowned on mightily by Washington State authorities). Voters in the two states have also taken to the ballot to enact significant property tax limits (in Oregon) and spending limits (in Washington). In B.C., people are taxed on just about everything, plus the economy is relatively weak, so shoppers routinely flood across the border in search of bargains.

United Parcel Service (UPS)

In 1907, when Jim Casey established the American Messenger Service in a basement near Seattle's Pioneer Square, he probably had no idea of the potential scope of his operation. Using a slogan of "Best Service—Lowest Prices," the company found a niche in department store package deliveries. By 1919, the company expanded to California and adopted the name United Parcel Service. The headquarters moved to New York in 1930, but the original site, at the corner of Second and Main, has been turned into a lovely waterfall garden with a plaque commemorating the roots of UPS.

Vander Zalm, Bill

Former British Columbia Premier Mike Harcourt describes Bill Vander Zalm as "the political equivalent of a neutron bomb—he destroys political parties but leaves the buildings still standing." Vander Zalm was B.C. premier from 1986 to 1991, succeeding popular Social Credit leader Bill Bennett. In just five years, Vander Zalm's administration dissolved in scandal and dissension, taking the party down with it. A native of the Netherlands, Vander Zalm came to B.C. with his parents during World War II. He was elected to parliament in 1975 and became known for political grandstanding and blunt talk. He retired in 1983 to run his "Fantasy Garden World" biblical theme park, but returned to capture the party and the premiership in 1986 when Bill Bennett retired. Ineptitude and the whiff of scandal followed. Eleven cabinet ministers resigned during Vander Zalm's tenure, either because of conflicts of interest or an inability to get along with their leader. Vander Zalm himself was investigated twice on ethics charges, though he was ultimately cleared. The mounting scandals forced Vander Zalm to resign in 1991, and his handpicked successor was crushed at the polls. Social Credit hasn't been a factor since.

Weyerhaeuser

In 1900, a group of Midwestern timber capitalists (including the Clapp and Laird families) purchased nearly one million acres of the Northern Pacific Railroad's Northwest land grant. The group was led by Frederick Weyerhaeuser, and the purchase was the beginning of the Tacoma-based forest-products giant that bears his name. Over the years, the company established sawmills and pulp mills, becoming a perennial resident of the Fortune 500. The company has also branched out into real estate, developing numerous business and residential properties. Weyerhaeuser found itself struggling in the nineties, beset by environmental concerns that made corporate logging practices, including clear cuts, unpopular. Over the company's one-hundred-year history it has remained very much a family affair. Until 1988, all of Weyerhaeuser's presidents had been a member of the founding family, and until 1997, all had come up through

A Weyerhaeuser meeting: Wonder if spotted owl was on the menu?
(Photo courtesy of the Tacoma Public Library, Richards Collection, photo D155701-35R)

the corporate ranks. In the thirties, the Weyerhaeuser family made news when young George Weyerhaeuser was kidnapped. He was returned unharmed after a ransom was paid, but the experience shook the Northwest business community. In 1984, the extended Weyerhaeuser network was again in the news when Booth Gardner, stepson of longtime company president Norton Clapp, was elected Washington governor.

Woodward's

Until its financial collapse in 1992, Vancouver-based Woodward's was one of Canada's premier retail chains. Founded as a clothing and shoe store in 1892 by Charles Woodward, the chain grew to be a full-service department store with dozens of outlets across Canada. By the late eighties, however, shoppers were staying away in droves, preferring specialty stores or department stores with a hipper image. Woodward's fell into a financial hole and declared bankruptcy; the rival Hudson's Bay Company purchased many of its assets.

WTO Conference

To Seattle city leaders it seemed like a great idea at the time—celebrate Seattle's emergence as a center of international commerce by hosting the late November 1999 meeting of the World Trade Organization (WTO). Composed of trade ministers from around the globe, the WTO negotiates ground rules for international trade. Its single-minded focus on free trade has earned the ire of environmental groups, labor unions, and others who geared up for "The Battle in Seattle," a massive protest on a scale not seen since the Vietnam War. Most of the protest was peaceful, including a labor-sponsored march on November 30 with an estimated 40,000 participants. But not everyone was so polite—a group of self-proclaimed "anarchists" from Eugene launched a melee of property damage in downtown Seattle. The police responded with tear gas and pepper spray, and the next day the police response was even stronger as much of the downtown was turned into a "no-protest" zone, forcing the confrontation into the Capitol Hill neighborhood, just to the east. By the time the riot chemicals had dispersed, the political toll was becoming clear: Police Chief Norm Stamper had resigned, the City Council had launched a full investigation, Mayor Paul Schell was hunkering down amidst calls for his resignation, lawsuits were multiplying, and local pundits were huffing about "Seattle's loss of innocence." As we said— it *seemed* like a good idea at the time.

Ask a native Northwestener—he's the over-fifty "graybeard" with the REI parka—about the big dogs of the regional economy and odds are he'll say "planes and trees." Since World War II, Boeing and the big timber companies have been the money pumps in the Northwest economy. In the fifties and sixties, it seemed that every family had or knew someone who owed their paycheck to aircraft or logs. The money fueled a comfortable, middle-class lifestyle.

Now ask the same question to the corner barista standing on Seattle's Capitol Hill—she's the one with the lime green hair, nose stud, tongue stud, eyebrow ring, and three tattoos who just moved here from the Midwest—and you'll likely hear "java and Microsoft." High-tech talent is in hot demand, with salaries to match. Business magazines talk about the new "Generation Equity" that job hops in search of stock options (and the hoped for subsequent stock market windfalls).

The difference in perception is partly a generational gap. The fact that both descriptions are at least partly right illustrates how much the Northwest economy has changed over the past thirty years. We're still big on riveting planes together and cutting down trees, but robust high-tech, service, and financial sectors have joined those economic mainstays. Northwest firms such as Amazon.com are Wall Street darlings, radically altering the distribution chain that gets products from manufacturers to consumers. Northwest investors, such as Paul Allen, have the financial resources to reshape entire industries (and buy our sports teams). Northwest brands, such as Starbucks and Nike, are market leaders in their industries. Instead of a sleepy region on the edge of nowhere, the world now looks at the Northwest as a symbol of the new economy (albeit still with a laid-back, green lifestyle).

How much of this change is real and how much is hype? One simple way to track the changes in the Northwest economy is through the Fortune 500 rankings of the largest U.S. companies.

In 1969, Washington and Oregon had just five entries on the Fortune 500 list, led by Boeing, Weyerhaeuser, and Georgia-Pacific. In 1999, Boeing and Weyerhaeuser still make the list, but they've been joined by such superstars of the new economy as Microsoft, Costco, Nike, Washington

Mutual Bank, and Nordstrom. Fourteen of the Fortune 500 now call the Northwest home. Similar changes have taken place in British Columbia. The *Greater Vancouver Book* notes, "Real estate, tourism, financial services, technology, and higher education have been added to the city's backbone of mining, fishing and lumber. They have fleshed out an economy once hostage to international resource prices."

Moreover, the growth in the Northwest economy is coming from the upstarts. The *Seattle Times* calculates a ranking of more than one hundred top Northwest firms based on their projected growth. In the 1999 rankings, not a single timber firm made the *Times'* list and Boeing came in at number ninety-eight. That doesn't mean the old-timers still aren't healthy, just that their growth rates will be modest compared to newcomers such as Real Networks and Amazon.com.

Make no mistake—the new Northwest business elite hasn't made Boeing and Weyerhaeuser irrelevant to the health of the Northwest economy. And most of them employ comparatively few people. For example, based on 1999 figures, Boeing still employs more workers than Microsoft, Nike, Costco, Safeco, and Nordstrom—combined. No wonder local economists still go into a full-on frothing and lathering panic when the commercial airplane market takes a dive.

As the economy has heated up, the value of the top Northwest companies and the wealth of their key owners have increased as well. When Microsoft went public in 1986, its market value was $519 million. Now its market value, based on stock price, floats around half a trillion. Real Networks, the maker of the Real Audio sound player for personal computers, has gone from zero to $2 billion in less than five years.

To quote Garrett Morris's Chico Escuela character from *Saturday Night Live*, the bull market

has "been berra berra good" to people packing stock options. Microsoft founders Bill Gates and Paul Allen as well as Microsoft President Steve Ballmer routinely top the Forbes list of the world's richest people. Seattle is loaded with "Microsoft millionaires" who retire at age thirty-five on the proceeds from their company-provided stock options. Sure they worked twenty-two hours a day for five years to get there, but hey, what's a life when there are millions to be made and all that good coffee to keep you awake?

And suppose you had the foresight to pop for one hundred shares of Microsoft stock back in 1986 instead of buying that bitching new stereo for your dorm room? How much money would you have now, assuming you did nothing but hold on to your shares? Trust us, you don't want to know. It would only depress you. Especially since the stereo fizzled out in less then a year when your drunken roommate spilled a beer on it. Okay, we'll tell you, but you have to promise not to cry. In 1986, your one hundred shares would have cost you twenty-one hundred dollars. Right now, you would have more than fourteen thousand shares worth more than $1.4 million. We told you that you didn't want to know.

The South had voting rights to fight over, the Northeast had its school bussing battles—out here we've got birds and fish. Visitors to the Northwest see a green paradise, full of trees, streams, and animal life. Environmentalists see rampant development that threatens wildlife habitat and the quality of life. That tension has provided the setting for some of the most ferocious natural resource battles ever waged.

In the beginning was the spotted owl, a rare species that exists in the old-growth forests (aka "very tall trees") of the Northwest. Eric Forsman was an Oregon State University student in the late sixties when he happened upon one of the birds in the Willamette National Forest. Forsman brought his discovery to the attention of state and federal forest managers, who were thrilled to have an owl sighting. The story might have ended there, but in 1973, the federal Endangered Species Act (ESA) was passed, guaranteeing protection for threatened species and their habitat. By the late seventies, Forsman's discovery and the ESA would combine to set off a nasty and ongoing fight about Pacific Northwest natural resources.

In the early eighties, federal officials declined to formally list the spotted owl as threatened or endangered.

At the same time, state agencies were pushing ahead with plans to set aside habitat for the owl, which is considered an "indicator" species that gauges the health of a forest system. Repeated petitions by environmental groups to list the owl under the ESA were rejected. The groups appealed and ultimately a federal judge rejected the decision not to list as flawed. Faced with the court ruling, the feds reconsidered and proposed the owl for an ESA listing.

The resulting process of developing a habitat plan for the owls provoked bitter splits between environmental groups and timber interests. The economy of timber communities suffered, as the harvest was restricted. Many observers blamed other factors, such as the practice of shipping raw logs to Asia, for the economic woes of loggers. But for the public at large, and for the timber workers most directly affected, the owl was the reason for the pain. If you went to a small timber town during the height of the owl wars you would likely find a "spotted owl burger" on the menu at the local cafe and bumper stickers reading "If it's hootin' I'm shootin'" on the trucks in the parking lot.

For the "greenest-green" urban dwellers, the owl was easy to love. You could save old-growth forests and the economic pain was concentrated in faraway towns you'd never visit filled with people you'd never care to meet. It won't be the same as efforts to save wild salmon ramp up.

In March 1999, several species of wild salmon were listed as threatened or endangered under the ESA. There are five basic types of salmon: chinook, coho, sockeye, chum, and pink. Because salmon return to the same spawning grounds, genetic differences have emerged over time. That means each type on each stream system counts as a separate species—there could be hundreds of salmon species in the Northwest. The potential effects of the listing are mind-boggling—the Puget Sound chinook's habitat encompasses the entire Seattle metropolitan area with more than three million people.

Why have the salmon declined? It's a combination of factors ranging from dams that wipe out salmon habitat, to urban growth that encroaches on creeks, to pesticide runoff from lawns. Salmon recovery efforts have been going on for years, with billions spent on the Columbia River system to help fish survive. Turbines have been revamped, predators have been killed, and salmon have even been barged around dams. These expensive rescue efforts haven't worked and the number of wild salmon has continued to decline.

But wait, you say. When I go to the grocery stores there are heaping piles of salmon and it's always on sale. And restaurants keep serving salmon dinners. And those guys at the Pike Place Public Market keep tossing salmon over the heads of gawking tourists. Is that all going to end? Hardly. Most of the salmon served in the world is farm raised, or caught in other regions such as Alaska or the Atlantic. Analysts say that even if all the wild salmon in the Northwest disappeared, there would hardly be a blip in the supply or price.

To those most directly affected the salmon debate has serious implications beyond what appears on your plate for dinner. For Northwest tribes, salmon is a matter of culture and economics. Commercial and sports fishing interests are fighting to preserve catch that is vital to their industries. Developers are concerned that growth restrictions designed to protect streams will drive up development costs. Politicians worry about striking the balance between a response strong enough to keep federal officials from taking over recovery efforts, while not alienating voters. Environmentalists see an opportunity to reshape growth and energy policies, while ESA foes think the pain of salmon recovery will be enough to fuel a repeal effort. Recent polls show that the public is willing to take individual steps to save salmon, such as reducing the use of lawn pesticides, but isn't willing to pay higher taxes.

So what's going to happen? In the short term, governments are ramping up spending on salmon recovery efforts, adopting modest growth restrictions, limiting water draws in some areas, and holding lots and lots of meetings. No one really knows how far the federal government is willing to clamp down on growth in the urban Northwest to save salmon. And even if massive changes are made in conditions beyond our control—ocean temperatures or fishing by other countries could negate the gains, and the salmon could be wiped out despite the government's best efforts.

Oh well. At least we've got plenty of owls now.

FOOD AND DRINK FOOD AND DRINK FOOD AND DRINK

Alar Scare

In 1989, *60 Minutes* broadcast a segment on Alar, a chemical sprayed on apples to keep them red for a longer period of time. The segment claimed that Alar was a potent carcinogen and, subsequently, Washington State apple sales plummeted. Growers tried to make the case that Alar was safe, but the public—led by celebrities such as Meryl Streep—voted with their dollars and Alar use was discontinued. Washington apple growers tried to sue *60 Minutes* for lost profits, but their case was dismissed. Just how dangerous Alar was remains controversial. As a result of the Alar incident, a number of agricultural states have adopted "food libel laws" that try to make it illegal to disparage the safety or quality of food products.

Alpenrose

The Alpenrose dairy is the lone survivor of Portland's early dairy industry, which spread across pastures west of town. Founded by Swiss immigrants in 1891, Alpenrose is named after a mountain flower that blooms in the Alps. After a fire in 1943, the dairy relocated to a fifty-two-acre, parklike campus near Beaverton. The Alpenrose "park" is open to the public and has baseball fields, a velodrome, an opera house with pipe organ, and "Dairyville"—a replica of a western frontier town.

Anderson, Stuart (Black Angus)

The Northwest's Baron of Beef, Stuart Anderson is the founder and namesake of the Black Angus steakhouse chain. Anderson got his start in post-World War II Seattle, leasing the now defunct Caledonia Hotel and Grill. A disastrous experiment with a French menu sent Anderson scrambling for a replacement dish to bring in the crowds. Reasonably priced steak dinners were the ticket, and the seeds of an empire were planted. Knowing he had a winner, Anderson sought to expand. The first stand-alone Black Angus opened April Fools' Day 1964 in Seattle. The chain ultimately expanded to more than one hundred locations, reaching back

Stuart Anderson is known as the Northwest's Baron of Beef.
(Photo courtesy of Stuart Anderson)

to the Midwest, though in some locations they were known as Stuart Anderson's Cattle Company because of trademark concerns. In the 1970s, Black Angus restaurants were ground zero of the singles' scene, featuring large bars, dance floors, and live music in addition to steak. Anderson was also a master of promotion. His Black Angus Ranch, located just off Interstate 90 near Ellensburg, was a visual landmark for travelers for years. He starred in a series of highly successful commercials, serving as a prototype of the company founder as chief spokesman. Anderson also experimented with upscale restaurants, opening Stuart's at Shilshole on the Seattle waterfront in the 1980s. Now retired, Anderson travels extensively, promoting his memoir *My Story of Beef*, a combination of Black Angus history and an ardent defense of beef.

Apples are the Evergreen State's signature crop.
(Photo courtesy of the Tacoma Public Library, Richards Collection, photo D30160)

▥ Aplets and Cotlets

Love them or hate them, there's no mistaking an Aplet or Cotlet. Armenian immigrants Armen Tertsagian and Mark Balaban created the unique confection in the 1920s. The friends had moved from Seattle to an orchard in Cashmere, Washington, and were looking for additional uses for their fruit. They hit on creating a variation of a traditional Near Eastern candy called Rahat Locoum, using fruit puree, walnuts, and powdered sugar. Marketing of the candy puttered along for years, until the Seattle World's Fair put the confection on the national map. In 1974, the company (now known as Liberty Orchards) created Grapelets as a promotional treat for the Spokane World's Fair. We're still waiting for the "Beerlet."

▥ Apples

Apples are Washington's signature crop, as well as the state's top commodity. Washington State orchards supply more than half the apples grown in the nation for fresh eating, and

growers sell in all fifty states and more than forty foreign nations. Annual sales of apples approach one billion dollars. Apple orchards are concentrated in Central Washington and in the eastern foothills of the Cascade mountain range. The lava- and ash-rich soil, coupled with abundant sunshine, is ideal for raising a variety of apples. Washington apples would remain a seasonal treat if not for the development of controlled atmosphere storage. Originally discovered in England, "CA" facilities control temperature, oxygen levels, carbon dioxide, and humidity. Generally, apples sold in the early fall and winter are fresh harvest. Those sold between January and September are usually from CA facilities.

▥ Barber, James

Vancouver's "Urban Peasant," James Beard, is known throughout Canada as a witty and charming advocate for "snob-free"

Wet & Wired

gourmet cooking. Not that Barber is without opinion. In an early guidebook to the Vancouver restaurant scene, Barber wrote, "Restaurant reviewers in general are a self-opinionated and pompous lot, frequently venal and self-serving, seldom to be trusted. I am as self-opinionated and pompous as the rest of them, maybe even more so. BUT I KNOW WHAT I AM TALKING ABOUT." Barber has authored eleven cookbooks, hosted a popular CBC television-cooking program, and penned numerous columns and articles for the Canadian press. Among Barber's practical rules for choosing a good restaurant are "the bigger the sign, the worse the food" and "beware of too much accent." An accomplished actor, Barber has also starred in theater productions as well as the CBC series *The Beachcombers*.

a concept from a New York restaurant that he admired, Bishop concocted a space that he describes as having "all the trappings of a wonderful French restaurant, but no stuffiness." Bishop calls his style "international new food" and features local fresh ingredients, simply prepared but in eclectic, inventive combinations. So the next time you go to a restaurant and are told the special tonight is "grilled fresh salmon layered with lemon, walnut-dilled chutney, and assorted fragrant wildflowers, then brushed with a chipotle tomato reduction," you'll know who to thank or blame. Bishop's is a perennial favorite in regional guidebooks, and John Bishop has been elected to the *Vancouver* Magazine Restaurant Hall of Fame.

Beard, James

Born in Portland in 1903, James Beard became one of the most respected and well-known American chefs. He championed the use of fresh, local American ingredients—a by-product of youthful summers spent at Gearhart on the Oregon Coast. After a brief stint at Reed College, Beard hit the road to find fame in the theater. Luckily for gourmets the world over, his relative lack of theatrical success forced him to open a catering business. In his later years, Beard split his time between New York and the Oregon Coast, where he ran a cooking school and praised fine coastal restaurants such as the Ark on Washington's Long Beach peninsula. He also authored a series of still-influential cookbooks as well as the memoir *Delights and Prejudices*, which chronicles his Northwest childhood.

Bishop, John

John Bishop revolutionized Vancouver cuisine when he opened his small Kitsilano District restaurant, Bishop's, in 1985. Borrowing

Blue Moon Tavern

Founded in 1934, the Blue Moon is Seattle's Bohemian hangout, hosting Beats in the 1950s, radicals in the 1960s, Deadheads in the 1970s, and itinerant poets, writers, and philosophers throughout its existence. The Blue Moon was a place where the odd was commonplace. For example, in 1970 author Tom Robbins—a Blue Moon regular—reported in the *Helix* (a local underground paper) of his attempt to contact Pablo Picasso on the tavern's pay telephone. Robbins actually got through, but Picasso declined the charges. A smoky dive, the Moon resides on the edge of the University District—a result of an old law that required alcohol to be kept a mile from campus. It nearly met the wrecking ball in 1990, but a determined preservation effort by its patrons, such as local author Walt Crowley, kept the Moon alive.

Brown and Haley

Since 1912, family-owned Brown and Haley has been Tacoma's citadel of chocolate, creating nationally famous confections such as Almond Roca and "they're only ugly until you taste them" Mountain Bars. Harry Brown and J. C. Haley were wholesale candy merchants who decided to enter the manufacturing business. The Mountain Bar was born in 1915 as the Mount Tacoma Bar, a vanilla center buried in a misshapen (though vaguely mountainous) glob of rich chocolate. After realizing that Mount Tacoma had lost out to Rainier as the name of Washington's signature mountain, the current name was adopted. Almond Roca, a toffee and nut log, followed in 1927, and the familiar gold foil wrapped candy has since gained international popularity. Brown and Haley's seasonal warehouse sales have become "must-attend" events for sugar addicts throughout the Puget Sound region.

Canlis

One of Seattle's premier (and most expensive) restaurants, the Canlis is the victim of an unfortunate piece of enduring urban folklore. Opened in 1950 by Peter Canlis, the visually stunning restaurant sits north of downtown on a promontory overlooking Lake Union. Guests were greeted by kimono-clad waitresses and dined on thick steaks, Northwest seafood, and strong drinks. For years, the rumor circulated about a dinner party—often alleged to be young prom revelers—who failed to spend enough to suit the restaurant. According to the story, these guests received a small, discreet card asking them not to return. The story has never been confirmed, but its persistence is a mark of the restaurant's exclusive reputation, and of the fact that it continues to be mentioned in books like this.

Carnation

The Carnation dairy empire had humble beginnings as the Pacific Coast Condensed Milk Company in 1899. As sales picked up, company founder E. A. Stuart wanted a more memorable name. During a walk through downtown Seattle, he spied a window display of cigars with the name Carnation. In 1907, the company introduced the "contented cow" symbol, which it used for decades, even sponsoring a national radio broadcast known as "The Contented Hour." More recently, the Nestle food conglomerate purchased Carnation, although it continues to maintain farms and facilities near the city of Carnation in rural King County.

Lucy and Ethel would have had fun with the Brown and Haley production line.

(Photo courtesy of the Tacoma Public Library, Richards Collection, photo A77890-1)

Chateau Ste. Michelle

Washington's oldest winery, Chateau Ste. Michelle, dates back to 1934. You won't find it on the corporate Web site, but the winery's ancestors were Pommerelle and National Wine Company, which specialized in cheap, sugary vino (the kind best served in brown paper bags). The company got serious about better wine in the 1960s, adopting the Ste. Michelle name in 1967. By 1974, Ste. Michelle wines were upsetting California wines in tastings, announcing to the world that Washington wine had arrived. The winery is also famous for its spectacular location on the grounds of the former summer home of Seattle timber baron Frederick Stimson. Opened in 1976, the "Chateau" Ste. Michelle is a major tourist attraction and home to an excellent outdoor summer concert series. In 1993, Ste. Michelle opened an Eastern Washington winery overlooking the Columbia River near the Tri-Cities.

Clore, Dr. Walter

Known as the "father of the Washington wine industry," Walter Clore was lead horticulturist for the Irrigated Agriculture Research and Extension Center near Prosser, Washington. In 1964, he embarked on research that proved Eastern Washington was ideal for growing premium wine grapes. Local farmers, such as the Hogue family, added grapes to their crops based on the research, eventually founding highly successful wineries.

Cloud Room

In 1955, Seattle tour master and bon vivant Bill Speidel said this of the city's Cloud Room: "High above the mundane streets is the Cloud Room . . . our answer to the St. Regis Roof in New York and the Top of the Mark in San Francisco. Imbued with elegance, it was the first restaurant of our new trend . . . the first to provide the diner with a sky scraper view of the scenery which is one of the Pacific Northwest's great natural assets." Located atop the Camlin Hotel, the Cloud Room made the full circle from new sensation, to aging warhorse, to retro favorite. Fine cuisine and liquor mingled with piano bar luxury as the Cloud Room played host to Seattle movers and shakers for four decades.

Cougar Gold

Another love-it or hate-it food (we have a lot of them up here), Cougar Gold is a beyond-sharp cheddar made at the Washington State University (WSU) creamery in Pullman. As an agriculture college, WSU has long maintained a dairy herd. In the 1940s, the college became involved in research sponsored by the U.S. Government and the American Can Company, designed to develop a canned cheese product that did not develop gas causing cans to bulge. Cougar Gold was a by-product of this research, and it has been in continuous production ever since. The WSU creamery produces more than 160,000 cans of cheese a year, 75 percent of which is Cougar Gold. A local's tip—order your cheese directly from the University because regional merchants tend to charge an exorbitant markup.

Darigold

This distinctive brand of milk, cheese, yogurt, and other dairy products traces back to 1918, when five Puget Sound cooperatives formed the United Dairymen's Association. The name Darigold was adopted in 1920. Today, the Seattle-based company embraces a milk marketing cooperative owned by more than nine hundred dairy farmer members, a processing arm, and a retail farm store business.

Dick's

Seattle's venerable purveyor of burgers, shakes, and hand-cut french fries, Dick's opened in 1954 with a single outlet on Forty-fifth Street in Wallingford. Four others have joined that first location—now the oldest fast-food restaurant in Washington State, though Dick's has never franchised. Dick's received a modicum of national notice when Seattle rapper Sir Mix-a-Lot featured the Capitol Hill location in his song and video "Posse on Broadway." While Mix-a-Lot venerated Dick's as the place "where the cool hang out," the simple truth is that everyone eats at Dick's. Business people crowd the window at lunch, high-schoolers in the afternoon, families at dinnertime, and college students looking for something to soak up the beer in their system after midnight. The secret to Dick's success lies in simplicity—you can't find a fish sandwich or chicken strips on the menu—just burgers, shakes, and fries. The company remains family owned with son Jim Spady taking over for his father, company founder Dick Spady.

Doebeli, Erwin

Since the early sixties, Erwin Doebeli has been the dean of Vancouver restaurateurs, presiding over his William Tell restaurants and earning continuous rave reviews. In 1988, the *Best Places* guidebook raved, "If the city has a finer continental spot to dine, we haven't found it. Owner Doebeli is the consummate restaurateur, greeting arrivals at the door with enthusiasm, dispensing bread from a large wicker tray like one of the busboys, or whipping up a Café Diablo with a flamboyance that alone makes the expensive tab a small price to pay." In 1998, Doebeli was inducted into the *Vancouver* Magazine Restaurant Hall of Fame.

Dog House

Twenty-four hours a day, from the thirties to the early nineties, Seattle's Dog House restaurant served up belly-filling sandwiches, burgers, and breakfasts to the denizens of the Denny Regrade neighborhood. Locals came to the Dog House lounge for sing-alongs with organist Dick Dickerson, and local mystery writer J. A. Jance used the restaurant as a frequent locale for her Seattle-based mysteries. When the Dog House closed in 1993, people worried about what would happen to the kitschy neon sign featuring a dog proclaiming it was always "time to eat." Not to worry—according to the *Seattle Times*, the sign is safe in the collection of a local museum.

E-coli

In 1993, more than six hundred people, mostly in Washington State, became sick after eating Jack in the Box hamburgers tainted with the e-coli bacteria. Three children died, and a number had serious complications including kidney failure. The incident led to new cooking standards for ground beef and calls for revised food inspection programs. While Jack in the Box's owners would not disclose the total cost of lawsuits stemming from the outbreak of e-coli, observers speculate the total cost to the company and its meat suppliers was well over $100 million. In 1998, a smaller breakout of e-coli struck the Western Washington State Fair in Puyallup, though the precise source was unclear.

Farrell's

During the 1960s and 1970s, a Northwest kid hadn't arrived until he or she had a birthday party at Farrell's. Founded in Portland by restaurateur Bob Farrell in 1963, the parlor evoked a "Gay-90s" theme, with straw-hat-wearing waitresses, an old-fashioned candy store up front, a player piano, and a selection of enormous ice-cream treats with names such as the "Pig Trough" and the "Zoo." The delivery of the largest sundaes would become a production, with staff members beating drums and setting off sirens as they paraded the treat around the parlor before delivering it to the table. A visit to Farrell's was always good for gaining two pounds, a fact that ultimately led to the chain's decline after its purchase by the Marriott corporation in 1972. For those wanting to sample the Farrell's vibe, the Original Portland Ice Cream Parlor near Lloyd Center has kept the basic motif and menu. Bob Farrell remains active as a restaurant consultant and motivational speaker.

Fisher Scones

Fresh, hot, and loaded with fruit preserves, Fisher scones are as much a part of local fairs as cows and pigs (but they smell a whole lot better). The scones are the product of Fisher Mills, founded in Seattle in 1911. While the Fisher Company sells a scone mix in local grocery stores, purists insist they don't taste as good as their fair brethren. The Fisher Company has expanded to include broadcasting (KATU-TV in Portland, KOMO-TV in Seattle, and numerous radio stations), fiber-optic and satellite services, and extensive real estate holdings.

Frangos

For years, Frangos were the signature holiday candy sold by Seattle's Frederick and Nelson department store chain. The rectangular, rich chocolate mints were created by Seattle candymakers Ray Clarence Alden and Joseph Vinikow. When Frederick's finally met its financial demise in 1992, the question most asked by the press was, "What will happen to Frangos?" You can't keep a good candy down—the Bon Marché picked up the distribution and the Northwest holiday tradition continues. Other stores, such as Nord-

strom, have accorded Frangos the highest honor by commissioning knockoff products.

Frisko Freeze

A much-loved Tacoma drive-in, the "Freeze" is best known as one of the guilty pleasures of former Washington State Governor Booth Gardner, before his doctor cracked down on his hypoglycemia. An abortive franchising plan proved disastrous, but the original Frisko Freeze, which is located at 1201 Sixth Avenue and Division Street, has survived. No indoor seating, no drive-thru, just hot and juicy "beefburgers," fries, and shakes. It's the kind of food you just know isn't good for you, but you can't help yourself. Aaaaaahhhh!

Genoa

Credited with sparking a revolution in the Portland food scene, Genoa has been serving decadent seven-course Northern Italian dinners since the early 1970s. Founder Michael Vidor proved that Portland had its share of gourmands, while keeping the atmosphere Northwest casual. A succession of owners has tinkered around the edges (smaller meals are available on weekdays), but generally maintained the restaurant's four-star reputation.

Geoduck

Geoducks (pronounced "gooeyducks") are one of the most common clams in the Northwest. They certainly are the most distinctive, provoking an almost universal cry of "that looks obscene!" The giant clam is the world's largest burrowing bivalve, often weighing in at more than ten pounds. Unlike most clams that are fully enclosed within their shell, the geoduck is notable for its large protuberance which—well, let's just say that it really does look obscene. Aficionados enjoy the geoduck chopped up in chowder, or long geoduck steaks, pounded thin, lightly coated with a batter and sautéed. Something of a cult has grown up around the geoduck. The Evergreen State College has adopted the bulky bivalve as its mascot, with a fight song that features the lines, "Siphon high, squirt it out, swivel all about, let it all hang out."

Grant, Bert

In 1981, Bert Grant retreated to his Yakima, Washington, basement and brewed his first batches of Scottish Ale and Imperial Stout. His friends raved, and by 1983, Grant had opened his first brew pub in a building that had once been the Yakima Opera House. Grant's beers were big and aggressively hoppy—the very definition of today's Northwest microbrews. In 1989, Grant moved shop across the street to the former Yakima railroad depot and shortly thereafter built a larger brewery on the outskirts of town. The company was sold in 1995, though Grant remains an active and visible front man. Grant has written his memoirs of a life in beermaking titled *The Ale Master: How I Pioneered America's Craft Brewing Industry, Opened the First Brew Pub, Bucked Trends, and Enjoyed Every Minute of It*. Kind of says it all, doesn't it?

Granville Island Market

Granville Island was dredged out of Vancouver's False Creek in 1913, becoming an industrial site. It remained a dank, charmless place until the mid-seventies when the Canadian government set about turning the island into an urban village and tourist destination. The island's centerpiece is a large, eclectic public market, filled with fresh vegetables, meats, and gourmet products. The market, opened in 1979, has spurred more development, and now Granville Island has a unique collection of shops, parks, restaurants, art galleries, and lodgings.

Haglund, Ivar

A promoter without peer, Ivar Haglund transcended the restaurant business to become one of Seattle's favorite sons. Born in 1905, Haglund began his waterfront empire after a visit to a cousin's aquarium in Seaside, Oregon. Impressed by the potential profits, he returned to Seattle and established a small aquarium of his own on Seattle's waterfront. At first, business was poor. In an effort to create some excitement, he began to sing funny sea songs on the sidewalk in front of the aquarium. Haglund eventually took his songs to the schools and to radio, gaining more fame with each step. In 1946, he decided to enter

Ivar Haglund "kept clam" when pancake syrup once spilled outside his restaurant.

(Photo from *Seattle Post-Intelligencer* Collection, Museum of History and Industry)

70   **Wet & Wired**

the restaurant business, establishing his flagship Acres of Clams restaurant on the Seattle waterfront. Haglund proved a master of promotion, hiring wrestler Tony Galento to wrestle an octopus, sponsoring clam-eating contests, and appearing on the local *Captain Puget* kids' television show. When a truck carrying pancake syrup spilled its load in front of his restaurant, Haglund called the newspapers, whipped up a batch of flapjacks, and scored some instant publicity. All the while he kept adding restaurants, including the high-end Captain's Table, the Native American-themed Ivar's Salmon House, and a chain of fast-food fish and chips eateries. Later in life, Haglund bought Seattle's famous Smith Tower, boldly flying a salmon wind sock from the top. In 1983, to the surprise of everyone (including Haglund), he was elected to the Seattle Port Commission. His health began to fail, however, leading to some criticism of his effectiveness as a Port commissioner. True to form, Haglund spotted a publicity opportunity, serving clam chowder at a mea culpa session with the press and asking everyone to "keep clam." Seattle became a little less colorful when Haglund died in 1985.

Harry and David

If you have a mailbox, you probably know Harry and David. The Medford, Oregon, fruit vendor is one of the world's largest mail-order operations, sending millions of catalogs a year around the world. The company dates back to the early 1900s, when Sam Rosenberg bought 240 acres of pear orchards on Bear Creek, near Medford. (In a bit of Northwest cross-pollination, Rosenberg bought the orchards after selling Seattle's classic Sorrento Hotel, which he built in 1909). After Sam died in 1914, his sons—Harry and David—developed a luxury hotel market for their Comice pears. After the Great Depression took a chunk out of their sales, the brothers hit on the notion

of selling fruit by mail order. To give the humble fruit more cachet, the pears were rechristened "Royal Rivieras" and the Fruit of the Month Club was born. The company—now known as Bear Creek Corporation—branched into nursery products in 1966, purchasing Jackson & Perkins. More recently, Bear Creek has launched Harry and David retail stores and a clothing catalog.

Henry Weinhard's Private Reserve Beer

Portland's Blitz Weinhard brewery touched off a minor revolution in the Northwest when it produced the first batch of "Henry's" in 1976. Named to celebrate the transfer of brewery ownership to the founder's great grandsons, the beer carved out a premium niche with better ingredients and packaging than the standard lager or pilsner available at the time. Production was limited and early runs sold out, creating even more demand. The national advertising campaign was likewise unique and memorable, establishing Henry's as the iconoclastic beverage of the old West. Local analysts point to Henry's as the first proof that American beer drinkers were willing to pay more for a better beer—a fact not lost on the embryonic craft brewing industry fermenting in Portland garages. Henry Weinhard was a German immigrant who founded his first brewery in Vancouver, Washington, in 1856, moving operations to Portland in 1862. While the company is now owned by the Miller Brewing conglomerate, it is expected to continue to produce the Henry Weinhard recipes, but the brewery, located in Portland's trendy Pearl District, will probably be demolished to make room for more upscale development.

Horse Brass Pub

Don Younger's Horse Brass Pub, which opened in 1976, is revered among Portland hopheads as one of the birthplaces of the Northwest "real beer" movement. Located on Southeast Portland's Belmont Street, the Horse Brass models itself on a British pub and has always featured fine British beers along with a British-style pub menu. When Northwest brewers began crafting their own thick, hoppy brews, Younger offered tap space, allowing the newcomers to get a toehold in the market. Oregon's Rogue Brewing has twice honored Younger by brewing special beers, the most recent called "Brutal Bitter," on the pub's twentieth anniversary.

Hy's Encore

A quintessential old-line Vancouver steak house, Hy's Encore is a gathering place for the city's lawyers, bankers, and grand high poobahs. In 1985, Vancouver's premier restaurant critic James Barber described Hy's as a place that "understands the ritual of steak. Steak is an expensive indulgence for prehistoric intelligences. You don't find non-smoking areas in steak houses, and you don't find liberated waitresses, but you do find comfortable sit-back-and-talk-about-the-market chairs, thick carpets, and a nice red glow over everything, including, if you do it often enough, your own nose." Ouch.

Johnny's Dock

Tacoma's old-line purveyor of "surf and turf," Johnny's Dock is located at the end of Pier 3 on Tacoma's waterfront. When confronted with a lease that would force him to move within twenty-four hours in the event of war, owner Johnny Meaker came up with an unusual solution. He commissioned a building that could be lifted by crane and set on a barge to be floated away to a new location. Johnny's also spawned a locally popular brand of salad dressings and seasonings.

Keg Restaurants

A highly successful "casual steak house" chain, the Keg was started in 1971 in North Vancouver. Vancouver entrepreneur George Tidball, who had built Canada's first McDonald's franchise, saw a niche for a steak restaurant placed firmly between the cheap chains and the elegant downtown establishments. Over the years, the chain has grown to more than eighty locations throughout Canada and in Washington and Oregon.

Kerr, Graham (Galloping Gourmet)

Charming chef Graham Kerr first found fame in Australia, then worldwide as the Galloping Gourmet during the late 1960s. A bon vivant who would slosh down copious quantities of wine as he dashed about his kitchen, Kerr finally hit the wall as his lifestyle and a near-fatal car wreck took their toll. Kerr found spirituality,

Graham Kerr, television's "Galloping Gourmet," reinvented himself in the Northwest.

(Photo courtesy of Graham Kerr)

sold his assets, and disappeared from public view for the better part of a decade. In 1981, he landed in Tacoma, running a small ministry devoted to simple living. Ironically, Kerr's offices were just a few blocks from the deli owned by the man who would soon become the new celebrity chef sensation, Frugal Gourmet Jeff Smith. After his wife suffered a heart attack in the mid-eighties, Kerr began to reemerge, teaching his "mini-max" gourmet cooking—emphasizing minimum risk and maximum flavor by replacing fats with spices. Highly successful cooking shows and cookbooks followed and Kerr's return to the public eye was complete. Kerr today makes his home in Mount Vernon, Washington, devoting his time to both culinary and charitable activities.

Latteland

Popularized by *Seattle Times* columnist Jean Godden, the phrase "latteland" captures the Northwest's addiction to espresso and thick drip coffee. The Northwest coffee revolution is often traced to the original Starbucks opened in Seattle's Pike Place Public Market in 1971 by Gortle's Pike Place Public Market in 1971 by Gordon Bowker, Jerry Baldwin, and Zev Siegl. Still, the espresso explosion, which often saw an espresso stand on every key downtown corner, didn't fully hit until the mid-eighties. Other key players in the Northwest coffee market are Portland's Coffee People and Kobos, Seattle's SBC and Tully's, and Olympia's Batdorf and Bronson. Starbucks received the ultimate pop culture salute when the 1999 blockbuster movie *Austin Powers: The Spy Who Shagged Me* identified the chain as a key part of the villainous Dr. Evil's plan for world domination.

Loaf You Save May Be Your Own, The

This mid-sixties slogan of Gai's Bakery adorned company delivery trucks exhorting drivers to be careful. The

Gai's brand dates back to 1932, when an immigrant baker named Giglio Gai founded a bakery to serve Seattle's Italian community. Gai's took over the Seattle French Baking Company from the DeLaurenti family in 1941. By the eighties, the Gai's enterprise employed more than fourteen hundred people and turned out more than one million loaves of bread a year. The bakery was purchased by out-of-state interests in 1992, but returned to Northwest ownership when it was sold to Portland-based U.S. Bakery in 1997.

Marionberries

No, the former mayor of Washington, D.C., didn't move to the Northwest. Marionberries are a special type of blackberry that is less seedy, making them ideal for pies and jams. They are among the bounty of Oregon's Willamette Valley, where warm days and cool nights lead to a sweet result for berry lovers. Strawberries are the Northwest's largest berry crop, with the marionberry and blueberry also grown in large commercial quantities.

McMenamin's

Portland's Brian and Mike McMenamin are the reigning emperors of Northwest brew pubs. Starting in 1974 with Southeast Portland's Produce Row Cafe (later sold), the brothers have turned their taste for good beer and love of funky architecture into a formidable chain. Each location features a similar menu and a core set of beers (including the signature Terminator Stout and Hammerhead), though some local specials and variations exist. The McMenamins have never sold their beer in stores, avoiding the expense of running a bottling operation and helping to immunize them from the shakeout in the craft brewing industry. Instead of bottling, the brothers have put their time and effort into real estate. The McMenamins began restoring architecturally significant properties on a grand scale in the late eighties when they converted an old evangelical mission into a theater/pub, renovated Portland's Baghdad Theater, and opened their sprawling Edgefield complex on the old Multnomah County poor farm. Later projects restored Portland's historic Crystal Ballroom, converted Portland's Kennedy School into a bed and breakfast, restored Centralia's venerable Olympic Club, and reopened McMinnville's Hotel Oregon.

Menghi, Umberto

Umberto Menghi's name is synonymous with gourmet Italian food to a generation of British Columbians. Menghi was born in the Tuscany region of Italy (before it became trendy), and came to Canada in 1967. After a stint working in the kitchen of the Hotel Vancouver, he became co-owner of a delicatessen and coffee shop near the University of British Columbia and then catering manager at the University Club. With money made by selling sweaters on consignment to Woodward's department store, Menghi opened his first restaurant in 1973 in a little yellow house on the corner of Hornby and Pacific. He has since opened additional restaurants in Vancouver, Whistler, Seattle, and San Francisco. In 1995, Menghi established the Villa Delia cooking school in his native Tuscany as a tribute to his mother.

Microbrews

People around the country have an image of Northwesterners as perpetually walking around in the rain with an IV drip of coffee going into one arm, balanced by a drip of microbrews going into the other. That's not true, though if someone invented such a rig they would make a million dollars. While the American craft brewing industry is generally acknowledged to have started in California, the Northwest represents the place where it first gained critical mass. In the 1970s, beer lovers and brewers in search of flavor

began making batches of heavily hopped beer in garages and basements. By the early eighties, a few began to market commercially, including Seattle's Red Hook, Yakima's Bert Grant, Portland Brewing Company, Hales from Colville, Washington, Pyramid from Kalama, Washington, and Vancouver's Granville Island and Bowen Island breweries. These new brews were generally sold on tap, though many eventually appeared in bottled form. Another development in the craft brewing movement was the proliferation of brew pubs where pub owners brewed house beers on the premises. The McMenamin's chain, stretching across Oregon and Washington, is the most visible, though virtually every medium-size city and above has its own local favorite. Despite all the media buzz about microbrews, the national market share for the distinctive and more expensive beers has never climbed above 10 percent. Microbrew fans knew the industry had really arrived when Portland-based advertising firm Weiden and Kennedy began a faux backlash on behalf of Miller Beer, claiming that it was time "for a good old macrobrew."

Mo's

Chowderheads of the world unite—your shrine is in Newport, Oregon, where in 1944 Mo Neimi founded this Oregon coastal restaurant empire that bears her name. According to the *Portland Oregonian*, "Mo's is a classic because it's inevitable: a spot, a joint, a gathering place for locals and visitors alike, as emblematic of its surroundings as a seagull dropping clams on the rocks and as stubbornly rooted to its culture as a barnacle to the piling of a pier." There are other Mo's outposts in Cannon Beach and Florence, but aficionados swear by the Newport original. A bowl of steaming chowder, a pint of brew, and a hot hunk of bread—simplicity and perfection.

Murchies

When Scotsman John Murchie came to Vancouver in the late 1800s, he brought with him a love of fine tea. In 1894, Murchie started a tea import business (later adding coffee) that continues to thrive today. Before Starbucks and the Northwest coffee revolution, you had to visit Murchies if your palate craved something more than canned coffee or tea from a flow-through bag. Murchies is known for their "blend book," which was begun in 1920 to document the specific tea preferences of customers. The blend book now contains the special brews of more than ten thousand customers.

Nalley's

Marcus Nalley, a Tacoma hotel chef, founded the company that bears his name in 1918 when he began retail sales of "Saratoga Chips"—crispy fried potato chips popular with restaurant and hotel patrons. Using the distribution system he built for his potato chip business, Nalley expanded into table syrup and salad dressings. To meet increasing demand, he purchased a twenty-acre site in an industrial area on Tacoma's outskirts for his factory. The area was dubbed "Nalley Valley," a moniker that sticks to this day. Marcus Nalley died in 1962, and the company is now owned by the national food processor Agrilink. Other Northwest brands that have been acquired by Nalley include Adams Peanut Butter and Farman's Pickles.

Nick's Italian Cafe

Every industry seems to have its informal meeting place—in the Oregon wine country it's Nick's Italian Cafe. Nick

Peirano has been offering his multicourse, fixed-price menu in downtown McMinnville since the late seventies. Nick's drew attention almost immediately, with the *Best Places* guide noting, "The unwary traveler who thinks that this is just another red-sauce spaghetti factory will discover to his or her delight that Nick's is a real northern Italian trattoria: informal, good-humored, noisy, no decor to speak of—and deadly serious about its food."

Marcus Nalley's food products have been a staple in Northwest kitchens for seventy years.
(Photo courtesy of the Tacoma Public Library, Richards Collection, photo D35153-1)

Oberto's

Constantin and Antionetta Oberto founded this Seattle sausage and jerky company in 1918. They settled in an Italian part of Seattle's Rainier Valley known locally (if not politically correctly) as "Garlic Gulch." The business really took off in the mid-fifties under the leadership of son Art Oberto, a man with a gift for promotion. Using the slogan "Oh Boy, Oberto!" Art Oberto was everywhere. His 1957 Lincoln was painted with company colors and dubbed "the Jerkymobile." He sponsored the Oh Boy, Oberto!

Unlimited hydroplane. At Christmas he roamed the city in his mobile home, passing out snacks. His presence was so pervasive the company merited a special exhibit at Seattle's Museum of History and Industry. Even today, the "Oh Boy" slogan is piped through Seattle's Safeco Field loudspeakers after an extraordinary play by the Mariners. Oberto's remains a family-owned company and has become the second-largest producer of meat snacks in the nation.

Olympia Beer

The prototype Northwest "macrobrew" was first produced in 1896, using pure artesian water from Tumwater, Washington. Brewery owner Leopold Schmidt bought a number of Northwest breweries in the early 1900s, but would brew Olympia only at his Tumwater facility because of the water. To promote its purity, Olympia Beer adopted the slogan "It's the Water" (though critics would say "It's all Water"). Prohibition led to a temporary shutdown, but the brewery was revived in 1933. For years, "Oly" dueled with Rainier for the loyalty of Puget Sound beer drinkers, often engaging in a bit of promotional tit-for-tat. For example, when Rainier scored heavily with a series of witty ads, Olympia countered (less successfully) with tales of whimsical creatures known as the "Artesians." Consolidation in the brewing industry led to the sale of the Olympia Brewing Company to Pabst in 1983. The next decade saw the slow decline of Olympia from a well-advertised premier label to a cheap second-tier brand. Although the brewery's flagship brand faded, modernization of the company's Tumwater brewery allowed it to survive by using excess capacity to brew a number of different beers under contract. Most recently, the brewery facility was purchased by Miller and, in more than a bit of irony, will likely be used to brew former arch-rival Rainier.

Olympia Oysters

Feasted on by Lewis and Clark and praised by chefs the world over, the tiny Olympia oyster is the true native oyster of the West Coast. The oysters take at least three years to grow to the size of a fifty-cent piece. True aficionados prefer their Olympia oysters, raw on the half shell, perhaps with a dash of pepper sauce and fresh-squeezed lemon.

Pang, Mary

With her husband, Harry, Mary Pang built an empire on frozen Chinese food. Originally, the Pangs owned a small grocery store in Seattle, but sold out to go into the Chinese food business with Mary Pang's sister, restaurateur, and local politician Ruby Chow. Chow and Pang eventually fell out, with Chow leaving the business. By the mid-eighties, Mary Pang Food Products was a million-dollar business, operating from a warehouse in Seattle's International District. Stiff competition, however, set the business back, and by the early nineties, Mary Pang's company was in financial trouble. So was her son Martin, which led to tragic consequences when he torched the company warehouse in a January 1995 insurance scam. Four Seattle firefighters died trying to put out the blaze. Martin Pang fled the country, setting off an international manhunt. He was eventually located in Brazil and brought back to face trial after a lengthy extradition battle. The Mary Pang company never recovered and the brand has disappeared from the shelves.

Pelligrini, Angelo

A longtime professor at the University of Washington, Angelo Pellegrini is best known for a series of books celebrating good food, good wine, and good company. Winner of a Guggenheim Fellowship, Pellegrini preached that "bread and wine are twins; that either without the other is but half itself." Now there's a sentiment you can live by. Pelligrini's best-known books are *The Unprejudiced Palate* and *The Food Lover's Garden.*

Pence, Caprial

One of the new wave of Northwest chefs, Caprial Pence earned special note as the chef at Fullers Restaurant in the Seattle Sheraton, challenging stereotypes about hotel food by earning constant four-star reviews. In 1990, she earned the James Beard Award for best Northwest chef. In 1992, she took her talent to Portland, opening a bistro in the comfortable, funky old Westmoreland neighborhood. Pence has also launched a series of cookbooks and television cooking shows.

Pike Place Public Market

Opened in 1907, the Pike Place Public Market may be Seattle's second most recognizable tourist attraction (after the Space Needle). Fish-throwing barkers rub elbows with vegetable merchants, crafters, bakers, and souvenir vendors. The maze-like market structure has survived a number of close calls. None were more serious than in the late sixties and early seventies when the market buildings were crumbling, leading many business-types to call for tearing it down. Local architect and University of Washington professor Victor Steinbrueck rallied the citizenry to save the market. The city eventually formed a development authority to revive the market's flagging economic fortunes and crumbling buildings. The second challenge came a decade later, when out-of-state developers wanted to turn the market into an urban shopping wonderland. Local color prevailed and the market remains a cranky, eccentric, and popular spot. Current struggles at the market center around whether preference should be given to food vendors or craft and flower peddlers. A bit of cinematic glory came in the 1993 date-movie classic *Sleepless in Seattle* when Rob Reiner and Tom Hanks strolled down to the market for a clams and beer repast at the Athenian restaurant, located in the center of the main market building.

Local producers remain the backbone of Seattle's Pike Place Public Market.
(Photo by John Farrand)

Poodle Dog

A beloved Northwest diner located in Fife, Washington, on Old Highway 99, the Poodle Dog has sated the hunger of travelers since 1933. Founded by Rocco "Mac" Manza and E. J. "Jimmy" Zarelli, the Dog serves up roadhouse favorites—"fat boy" burgers, chicken, and cream waffles. Zarelli and Manza also opened the now-closed Century Ballroom next to the Poodle Dog in 1934, hosting the likes of Louis Armstrong and Duke Ellington. They also formed a lucrative contracting company that was a main builder of the Villa Plaza shopping center (later turned into the Lakewood Mall), and the Tacoma Dome.

Rainier Beer

Before microbrews became the rage, Rainier was Seattle's beer. Texans had their Lone Star, and Pittsburghers had Iron City—if you were from Seattle you drank "Vitamin R." (If you were really hardcore, you drank the green-bottled, high-alcohol Rainier Ale—known locally as "Green Death"). The Rainier brewery, located on Seattle's Airport Way, dates back to 1878. The brewery went dark in 1916 when the state went dry, four years ahead of Prohibition. After the repeal of Prohibition in 1933, Fritz and Emil Sick purchased the brewery and reclaimed the rights to the Rainier name. To promote the beer, Emil Sick purchased a minor league baseball team, renamed them the Rainiers, and set them up in Sick's Stadium, which also served as the Seattle Pilots' home for their one lamentable season. Sick also put a large lighted "R" on top of the brewery, which is located next to

Poodle Dog, a classic roadhouse diner, is still going strong near Tacoma after sixty years.

(Photo courtesy of the Tacoma Public Library, Richards Collection, photo A57476-3)

Interstate 5 just south of Seattle's downtown, creating a local landmark. Rainier is perhaps best remembered for a series of funny, innovative commercials in the 1970s. Dreamed up by local adman Terry Heckler, the ads featured bottle-shaped creatures known as the Rainiers, frogs that croaked the brand name, and motorcycles that roared RRRRAAAIIIINNNIIIEEEERRR. Humor-impaired new owners eventually killed the ads, beginning a long decline for the Rainier brand and triggering a series of ownership changes, culminating with a buyout by Miller Brewing. By the summer of 1999, the Rainier plant had been shuttered, with brewing of the Rainier brand likely transferred to (gasp!) the Olympia brewery in Tumwater.

Red Robin

Once a small hangout near the University of Washington (UW) famous for its cheeseburgers, Seattle's Red Robin currently has restaurants in sixteen states and Canada. Founded in 1969 on the corner of Eastlake and Canal Streets near UW, Red Robin was an instant hit with students for its adventurous "gourmet" burgers, thick steak fries, and copious quantities of beer. Much more upscale and calculating today than in its humble college beginnings, Red Robin Burger and Spirits is nonetheless one of the Northwest's most successful dining exports.

Redhook Beer

Seattle's Gordon Bowker deserves special mention for his role in the Northwest's favorite fluids. Bowker was a founding partner in Starbucks. After selling the chain, he helped found the Redhook brewery in 1982. Redhook wasn't the first Northwest microbrew, and its first batch had a bizarre banana aftertaste, but it deserves credit for pushing microbrews into wider distribution. In 1994, Redhook sold an equity stake to brewing giant Anheuser-Busch in exchange for national distribution of its beers. Microbrew purists decried the new alliance as "Budhook," but the increased demand allowed the company to build

Vitamin R, Rainier Beer, was the beverage of choice for most Seattleites until the microbrew revolution.
(Photo courtesy of the Tacoma Public Library, Richards Collection, photo D83881-2)

expanded breweries in Woodinville, Washington, and Portsmouth, New Hampshire. In recent years, Redhook has suffered along with other craft brewers from a slowing in demand growth. Still, with Redhook's loyal following and powerful partner, most analysts expect the company to be one of the long-term survivors of the "real beer" movement.

Ringside

In the immortal words of Space Ghost's sidekick Brak, "Sometimes you just have to have a big ol' piece of beef." In Portland, when the mood hits, you go to the Ringside. Opened in 1944, the Ringside exudes "steak house"—all wood and leather and stiff drinks. The restaurant's famous Walla Walla sweet onion rings are a signature item as is the authentic southern fried chicken. A more recent Eastside location matches the food, but can't duplicate the 1950s decadence of the Burnside original.

⚡ Rosellini, Victor

For decades the name Victor Rosellini was synonymous with the best in Seattle dining. After a stint in San Francisco, Rosellini returned to Seattle and opened his first restaurant in 1950. Despite a move from downtown to the Denny Regrade, Rosellini's signature 410 restaurant remained a favorite of movers and shakers, where drinks were strong, food was rich, and service was impeccable. Rosellini is the first cousin of former Governor Albert Rosellini and served as one of his informal advisors; the connection made Victor's restaurants required stops for the political establishment. Rosellini's mother, Fine Gasparetti, also was a restaurateur, operating the very popular Gasparetti's Roma Cafe. Although the 410 closed in the 1980s, and Rosellini has retired from the restaurant business, he continues to surface at charity functions, particular the local Teamsters annual Saint Patrick's Day lunch.

You knew you had made it in the Jet City when you could afford dinner at Victor Rosellini's 410 Restaurant.

(Photo from *Seattle Post-Intelligencer* Collection, Museum of History and Industry)

⚡ Rose's

Under the ownership of Rose Naftalin and later Max Birnbach (former food service manager at the Benson Hotel), Rose's was Portland's premier Jewish deli during its heyday in the sixties and seventies. "Deli" really doesn't do Rose's justice—the full-service restaurant featured huge sandwiches, specialties such as borscht and gefilte fish, and desserts that would blow your yearly calorie budget in a single sitting. Rose's main location in Northwest Portland eventually fell victim by the early nineties to gentrification and changing tastes. A remaining location in Northeast Portland continues to keep the flame alive.

⚡ Smith, Jeff (Frugal Gourmet)

An ordained Methodist minister, Jeff Smith was the chaplain at the University of Puget Sound in Tacoma when he established a small gourmet deli in the city's historic Stadium District known as the Chaplain's Pantry. From there Smith began a low-key cooking show on the local public television station. These humble beginnings begat the

Frugal Gourmet, a cooking sensation who ruled the cookbook and cooking-show world from the mid-eighties to the early nineties. Smith was engaging, extolling the virtues of good food and good wine with style and wit. His empire crumbled in 1997 when a number of men filed lawsuits claiming Smith had sexually molested them between 1973 and 1981 when they worked at the Chaplain's Pantry. Smith maintained his innocence but future cooking shows were canceled and cookbooks put on hold. In January 1999, Smith settled with seven plaintiffs, admitting no wrongdoing but agreeing to pay nearly $5 million in damages. The court papers also revealed a 1991 agreement to pay $1.5 million to a former employee in exchange for not pursuing sexual assault claims.

Sokol Blosser

One of the earliest of the Oregon wineries, Sokol Blossor established its vineyard in 1971 and first produced wine in 1977. Famed primarily for its excellent Pinot Noir, the winery has become one of Oregon's best known. Other pioneers of the Oregon wine industry include Roseberg's Hillcrest (established in 1959), Eyrie (1966), and Erath (1972). Most of the state's wineries are concentrated in the Willamette Valley, though Southern Oregon's Rogue and Umpqua Valleys also have a fair share.

Spar, The

Since the thirties, the Olympia, Washington, downtown Spar restaurant has been serving basic cafe food with an occasional flourish. The Spar is notable for preserving its original look and feel, with a long J-shaped counter, wood cigar cases, and funky neon. The basic food and lack of pretense has drawn an odd mix of politicos, state workers, Greeners, and tourists. The Spar was a favorite hangout of former Washington State Attorney General Smith Troy, credited with saving Olympia by blocking the movement of state offices to Seattle.

Starbucks

From its 1971 origins as a funky coffee shop in the Pike Place Public Market, Starbucks has grown to define the gourmet coffee revolution. Starbucks was founded by Jerry Baldwin, Zev Siegl, and Gordon Bowker (who would later play a role in founding Redhook and the *Seattle Weekly*). Baldwin had been exposed to the Peet's Coffee store in the Bay Area and wanted to bring the pleasures of

strong, fresh coffee to Seattle. The partners pooled their money, working with local designer Terry Heckler to come up with the name and the distinctive mermaid logo. (Seattle old-timers still mourn the day the corporate Starbucks decided to cover the mermaid's breasts as the official tri-

Espresso shot 'round the world: Starbucks first made its wet-and-wired impact in Seattle. Shown is the Queen Anne location in Seattle.
(Photo courtesy of Starbucks)

umph of political correctness). For a decade, the company puttered along, desiring little more than to satisfy the growing gourmet coffee tastes of local drinkers. That changed in 1982 when Howard Schultz joined the company as director of retail operations and marketing. After a visit to Italy, Schultz convinced Starbucks founders to test a coffee bar location in downtown Seattle. By 1987, Schultz had bought the assets of the original Starbucks, and by 1992, the company had opened 165 locations and gone public. Over the next five years, Starbucks went into hyperdrive, growing to more than one thousand locations worldwide. Even Starbucks' detractors concede the company is masterful at marketing and seizing opportunities. While some local wags have suggested that the company's heavily roasted coffee should be renamed "Charbucks" (the company has recently introduced a milder alternative), Starbucks has become the shorthand for better coffee everywhere.

Sunny Jim

For years the face of "Sunny Jim" beamed benignly on Seattle I-5 freeway drivers from an oversized sign in the industrial area. The symbol for a regionally popular brand of peanut butter, Sunny Jim was a rosy cheeked cherubic boy. Along with the still-active Adams brand (the kind you have to stir), Sunny Jim dominated the regional peanut butter market into the 1970s when major brands took over. Although the brand has been inactive for years, the factory sign remained intact until 1997 when a fire destroyed the old manufacturing facility.

Oregon's Tillamook Cheese factory has been cooking up cheddar for decades.
(Photo Courtesy of the Tacoma Public Library, Richards Collection, photo A67477-90)

Tillamook Cheese

It rains a lot in Tillamook County, located on the Oregon coast. That makes for some gloomy days for people, but fabulous conditions for cows. The county boasts almost two hundred dairy farms, populated by twenty-five thousand cows—more than the human population. And the milk that comes from these cows often goes to the Tillamook County Creamery Association. Founded in 1909, the Association has established the Tillamook brand nationally for milk, cheese, and ice cream. The Tillamook factory (located in Tillamook) is Oregon's largest cheese factory and one of the top tourist attractions in the state, producing more than forty million pounds of cheese a year.

Tree Top

A sizable apple-growing cooperative based in Selah, Washington, Tree Top has approximately twenty-five hundred apple growers located in Washington, Oregon, and Idaho. Tree Top markets its own brand of apple juice and sauces, but also produces apple-based ingredients for other food processing companies. Always looking for new ways to sell apples, the company in recent years has experimented with new juice blends and packaging.

Walla Walla Sweet Onions

Washington State's entry for national sweet onion bragging rights (take that, Vidalia) traces back to the late 1800s when a French soldier named Peter Pieri brought a sweet onion seed from Corsica to Walla Walla. The new plant was adopted by the immigrant farming community (mostly Italian), who longed for foods that were reminiscent of home. The farmers soon found the sweet onion was well suited to the arid climate. Over the years, the crop has been perfected and local farmers—realizing that an onion people could actually take a chomp out of was a good thing—have organized a sophisticated marketing effort.

Wheat

Drive through the dry parts of Eastern Washington and you'll see gently rippling fields of wheat, as far as the eye can see. Washington is the fifth-largest producer of wheat in the nation, with annual revenues well over half a billion dollars. In addition to being a key part of the Washington economy, wheat farming has also stimulated groundbreaking agricultural research. A key discovery came in 1961 when Washington State University researchers developed a strain known as "Gaines wheat." The wheat was designed to stand up to spring rains, allowing earlier planting and bigger yields. "Gaines wheat" played a role in the "green" revolution, which helped developing countries improve agricultural self-sufficiency. Dr. Orville Vogel, the developer of "Gaines wheat," was awarded a National Medal of Science in 1976.

White Spot

When Nat Bailey turned his 1918 Model T truck into a traveling lunch counter in the early twenties, he hardly knew he was launching a British Columbia restaurant empire. In 1924, inspired by patrons who didn't want to walk to the truck, he began to employ "carhops" to deliver the food. Bailey carried the concept forward in 1928 when he started the first White Spot Drive-In at Sixty-seventh Avenue and Granville Street in Vancouver. Over the years, Bailey built the White Spot chain and expanded

into luxury restaurants, hotels, and even farming. On the side, he indulged his love for baseball by becoming part owner of the Vancouver Mounties franchise of the Pacific Coast League. (The minor league baseball stadium in Vancouver is named Nat Bailey Stadium.) In 1968, Bailey sold the chain to General Foods, though it returned to B.C. ownership in 1982. Nat Bailey died in 1978.

A White Spot "Triple O burger" and shake is, ah, heaven!
(Photo courtesy of the Vancouver Public Library, photo 80304B)

When Gordon Bowker, Jerry Baldwin, and Zev Siegl opened the first Starbucks coffee store in Seattle's Pike Place Public Market back in 1971, they probably didn't know the effect they would have on Northwest culture. Strong and flavorful coffee plays as much a role in the Northwest's "wired" reputation as high-tech companies and high-achieving entrepreneurs, and it tastes a whole lot better than the stuff your parents used to drink. Understanding the fundamentals of our coffee etiquette is essential to establishing one's credibility as a true Northwesterner.

Let's start with the basics. In the Northwest, coffee for home or office use never comes in a can. Coffee comes in small bags with little built-in wire closures that work perfectly at the coffee store but never work when you are closing the bag at home. Also, real coffee is never percolated or run through a flat-bottomed Mr. Coffee. It should be freshly ground (using a sleek European grinder) and then prepared with a cone-shaped drip machine, an espresso machine, or a French press. The more technology and steps, the better—nothing is too good or complex for your cup of Joe. It's no fair

buying cheap coffee and then putting it into a gourmet brand bag before guests arrive—they'll know, trust us.

What about ordering coffee out? Just remember that there are basically three choices you'll have to make—how many shots of espresso, what you want added to the espresso, and how you want it topped.

First, decide how many shots you want. A standard shot is one fluid ounce of espresso. Espresso is simply a concentrated coffee that comes from "pulling" pressurized hot water through very finely ground coffee. Gourmets value the "crema," which is the caramel-colored foam that lingers for a few seconds on the top of a freshly pulled shot. One shot is standard for small drinks (say eight ounces), while larger ones usually require two. If you are standing behind someone who orders a "quad," be sure you keep a prudent distance. You can always order decaf (or half-and-half), but what's the fun if you don't instantly achieve your target heart rate for the day?

Next, decide what you want mixed with your

shots. Lattes have steamed milk; cappuccinos have foamed whole milk. A drink ordered with nonfat milk is called a "skinny." If you want to clog your arteries with pure half-and-half, order it "breve." Of course, you can also order a shot of flavored syrup in your drink. Or perhaps you'll have a mocha, essentially hot cocoa for grown-ups, where a little dark chocolate is mixed in with the basic latte.

Finally, decide how you want your drink topped. To finish the drink, your barista (the trendy Italian name for the guy with the nose bone ring working the espresso machine behind the counter) can top it with some extra foam, some whipped cream, or a sprinkle of chocolate shavings or nutmeg.

To see if you've got it, try to decode this order (actually overheard at the Dancing Goats coffee house in Olympia): "Give me a double-tall half-caf hazelnut extra hot and a decaf single skinny mocha no whip" (also known as a "what's the point"). You should receive something resembling a twelve-ounce whole milk latte with two shots of espresso, a shot of hazelnut syrup, and a float of foamed whole milk, and an eight-ounce drink with steamed nonfat milk, one shot of decaf espresso, and chocolate (but no whipped cream).

Don't fret if you don't get it right from the start. As with anything, practice makes perfect (and for a good case of the jitters unless you're drinking decaf). And since there seems to be an espresso stand on every Northwest street corner, you'll have plenty of chances to hone your technique. And there's one more benefit from learning to do coffee right—if the high-tech industry stock boom ever fizzles, you can always get a job as a barista.

LIVING IN BEERVANA LIVING IN BEERVANA LIVING IN BEER

Maybe it's all the rain, but the Pacific Northwest does seem dominated by fluids. We've discussed coffee elsewhere, but when you don't want to set your brain on 220 volts, it's time for the Northwest's other liquid gift to mankind—good beer. Benjamin Franklin said, "Beer is proof that God loves us and wants us to be happy." No wonder so many consider the Northwest to be God's country. While the craft brewing or "microbrew" revolution started in California, and many parts of the country now boast fine regional beers, the Pacific Northwest is really where the movement reached critical mass.

Of course, the advent of microbrews has led to some changes. The days of simply hauling your rear end onto a barstool and ordering a schooner of Rainier, Olympia, or Blitz Weinhard have long since passed (except for a few dive bars, God bless 'em). The standard size of a beer is now the pint. Most bars offer a standard sixteen-ounce pint, the better brew pubs offer a twenty-ounce "Imperial Pint," and some less reputable bars have a thick-bottomed pint glass that looks like sixteen ounces but holds just fourteen or so.

Craft brewers religiously hold to German beer purity principles, meaning the only ingredients are malt, hops, yeast, and water. If your beer is made with anything else (such as the rice used by major brewers), it's not a craft beer. Different styles of beer come from the different proportions of the ingredients, when they are added, and the aging process. Fanatics also reserve the craft beer label for those beers made by independent small brewers, rather than those brewed under contract by big breweries with extra capacity (Sam Adams is a "contract" beer). Others focus on hewing to the German purity standards as the test. Before coming down on one side or the other of this quasireligious debate, we suggest you drink a lot of beer and compare for yourself. It may take many tastings before you reach a conclusion—darn.

Malt gives the beer its basic body and character. Hops are used for flavor and Northwest beers are known the world over for their aggressively "hoppy" recipes. (Hops are related to the cannabis family, which may explain why people order so much pizza and nachos when drinking beer). If you're used to a major national beer, such as Budweiser, be prepared to spit out your first gulp of a Northwest beer (but don't worry—you'll soon learn to love it.)

Once you're comfortably resting on a barstool in a fine Northwest brew pub, the tap handles you see are likely to include the following styles:

Pale Ale

The name may be pale but the flavor isn't. The pale refers to the color, which is often deep gold or red (but still "paler" than a porter). Northwest pale ales are generally loaded with hops.

IPA

An even hoppier version is the India Pale Ale (IPA). IPA is modeled on the British version that was designed to survive the voyage to India. Hops are a preservative so they were used generously. IPA also tends to be higher in alcohol content.

Brown Ale

This darker beer relies more on malt than on hops. This beer is often described as having an almost "chocolate" tone and is often served with heavy meat dishes.

Hefewiezen

This wheat ale is brewed so people who don't like microbrews can pretend they're drinking a microbrew. Served with a wedge of lemon.

Porter

The dark, malty porter was America's first favorite beer, dating back to Revolutionary War days. It's heavier than the ales, lighter than stout.

Stout

Dark and thick, the stout was a beer to sip all evening when Guinness pioneered the style. The Russian version—the Imperial Stout—has a much higher alcohol content.

Scottish Ale

The initial style of Northwest craft brewing pioneer Bert Grant, the Scottish Ale has a very distinctive and somewhat bitter taste. Not for beginners, a true Scottish Ale also packs one of the highest alcohol wallops of the bunch.

In the search for market share, brewers have tried other varieties—fruit beers and lemon beers among them—but you can't go wrong sticking to the main ones. So next time you've got a few spare moments, pop into your favorite pub and name your poison, knowing it will be the finest poison in the world.

MEDIA MEDIA MEDIA MEDIA MEDIA

Almost Live!

Almost Live! began in 1984, an example of the creative local programming that Seattle's KING-TV had originally been known for. Initially, the show was hosted by Ross Shafer, a local stand-up comic, who presided over an hour-long mix of guests, music, and sketch comedy. John Keister, who had previous stints as an editor at the *University of Washington Daily* student newspaper and host of the short-lived *REV* television series, was a contributor to the show. When Shafer left for Hollywood in 1988, KING conducted a search to replace him. They eventually settled on Keister—a bald, edgy type who was as far from a slick television star as he could be. It showed, as he couldn't fit into the established *Almost Live!* format. Ratings plunged and KING almost pulled the plug. Then, KING got permission to move the show to just before *Saturday Night Live*. Keister and producer Bill Stainton cut the program to one-half hour, focusing exclusively on sketch comedy. The revamp worked and over the next decade, *Almost Live!* became a Seattle institution. While some skits could take place anywhere, *Almost Live!* was best known for spoofing Seattle foibles, with a particularly sharp take on neighborhoods such as Ballard (bad Scandinavian drivers) and suburbs such as Kent (big trucks and big hair). The relentlessly local flavor may explain why the show didn't catch on nationally during a tryout on Comedy Central. Some *Almost Live!* cast members have used the show as a springboard to bigger things, including Bill Nye, who took his Bill Nye the Science Guy character national. The core troupe of Keister, Tracy Conway, Pat Cashman, Steve Wilson, Nancy Guppy, Bill Stainton, and Bob Nelson remained intact until the show was abruptly canceled by KING's parent company in 1999.

Anderson, Pamela

Platinum blond bombshell Pamela Anderson is the only real reason to tune into *Baywatch* reruns (and the preferred computer screensaver for teenage boys in North America). Anderson was born on July 1, 1967, in Ladysmith, a small town about one hour north of Victoria on Vancouver Island. Since she was the first baby born on the one-hundredth anniversary of the Canadian Confederation she was dubbed "The Centennial Baby." When she was age twenty-one, Anderson moved to Vancouver and worked as a fitness instructor. In 1989, she was spotted at a B.C. Lions football game (wearing a Labatt's T-shirt), and her picture was flashed on the big screen at B.C. Place Stadium. She went on to become the Labatt's "Blue Zone" girl, which eventually led to her *Playboy* centerfold spread and beach bunny television stint. She also starred in the motion picture *Barb Wire*, which was inspired by a character originally created by Portland's Dark Horse Comics.

Argus

Before *Seattle Magazine* and the *Seattle Weekly* there was the *Argus*. First published in 1894, the paper was a biting conservative journal until the 1950s when it was purchased by Philip Bailey, who brought the paper into the mainstream with first-rate political and arts coverage. Later, *Argus* was acquired by John Murray, longtime general manager of the paper and a Washington state senator. Murray tried to mesh the *Argus* with an ever-expanding empire of local shopping papers and specialty publications. The mix didn't work and *Argus* expired in 1984. The paper's distinguished alumni include historian Murray Morgan, *Seattle Post-Intelligencer* columnists Emmett Watson and Mike Layton, and David Brewster and Roger Downey of *Seattle Weekly* fame.

Blackburn, Bob

The original play-by-play voice of the Seattle Supersonics, Bob Blackburn began his sports broadcasting career in the Beaver State as the voice of Oregon State University football. In 1967, the fledgling Seattle Supersonics tapped him to be their first announcer and a twenty-five-year association was born. Perhaps the highlight of Blackburn's career was calling the final seconds of game five of the 1979 National Basketball Association (NBA) championship series between the Supersonics and the Washington Bullets which clinched Seattle's first (and still only) professional sports championship. Seeking a younger and more marketable voice for the franchise, Blackburn was unceremoniously partnered and then finally dumped in 1992 to make way for current Sonics play-by-play broadcaster Kevin Calabro (a fine announcer in his own right). Public backlash against the way Blackburn was let go forced the Sonics to honor him with a special night when his "microphone" was officially retired by the team.

Boreson, Stan

Beloved Northwest entertainer Stan Boreson is the "King of Scandinavian Humor." A native of Everett, Washington, Boreson appeared in his first local television show *Campus Capers* while attending the University of Washington in the late forties and early fifties. His success with the show led to a second television program

called *Two B's at the Keys* with local musician Art Barduhn. Along with his trusty accordion and "songs his Uncle Torvald taught him," Boreson specialized in transforming popular American songs into humorous Norwegian and Swedish dialect renditions. The songs were successful enough for Boreson to release several albums (some with the late Doug Setterberg) including a popular Christmas collection. His most famous Seattle television show was *King's Clubhouse*, which ran for fourteen years on KING-TV and made him a hero to a generation of Seattle-area baby boomers from the late fifties through the sixties. The secret password on *King's Clubhouse* was "Zero Dachus, Mucho Cracus, Hullaballooza Bub," and longtime locals are fond of uttering the phrase in front of newcomers to prove their Northwest roots. The program won a number of children's programming awards before bowing out after a fourteen-year run. Boreson still performs at festivals and celebrations throughout the United States and Canada and has appeared several times on Garrison Keillor's radio programs.

Brakeman Bill

Popular afternoon children's show on Tacoma's independent KTNT Channel 11 TV station in the fifties, sixties, and early seventies hosted by former cameraman Bill McLain who played railroad engineer Brakeman Bill. Along with his irreverent puppet sidekick Crazy Donkey, the *Brakeman Bill* show used a model train setup as an identifying gimmick. The format of the show consisted of cartoons and comedy shenanigans with Bill and Crazy Donkey (voiced by Channel 11's Warren Reed who also hosted the station's late movie show). Before giving way to syndicated situation

Brakeman Bill kept the trains running on time for Puget Sound kids.

(Photo courtesy of the Tacoma Public Library, Richards Collection, photo D94438-1)

comedies and talk shows, *Brakeman Bill* was one of the longest-running local kids' programs in the country.

Brougham, Royal

Royal Brougham, the one-time dean of American sportswriters, was known affectionately to his readers for almost seventy years as "Your Old Neighbor." Born in St. Louis in 1894, Brougham attended Seattle's Franklin High School before applying for a job as a copy boy at the *Seattle Post-Intelligencer* (*P-I*) in 1910. A decade later, Brougham was named sports editor, a post he would hold until 1968. In addition to local and regional sports stars, Brougham was an acquaintance and friend to such twentieth-century sports legends as Babe Ruth, Jack Dempsey, Jesse Owens, and Babe Zaharias. He was also a tireless fund-raiser for local charities and a crusader for athletic programs and facilities for young people. In 1936, he founded the *P-I* Man of the Year banquet (today the Sports Star of the Year banquet) to honor the region's top athlete—one of the oldest awards banquets of its kind in the nation. While Brougham was

never considered a great writer, his longtime colleague at the *P-I* Emmett Watson claimed he had the surest instinct for a story and what quickened the reader's interest. Brougham suffered a heart attack in October 1978 during a Seattle Seahawks football game and died early the next morning at the age of eighty-four. The main thoroughfare by the Kingdome was subsequently named Royal Brougham Way in his honor.

Bullitt, Dorothy

A pioneer in American broadcasting and the founder of the Northwest KING broadcasting empire, Dorothy Bullitt was born in 1892, the daughter of a wealthy sawmill owner and real estate mogul. She married a southern lawyer named Alexander Scott Bullitt who was a prominent figure in the Roosevelt administration. When he died unexpectedly of cancer, Dorothy was forced to learn his business quickly and soon proved to be no slouch in what had traditionally been a man's world. Not content to simply master the real estate market, Bullitt purchased some

Dorothy Bullitt was the founder of the KING Broadcasting empire. KING Mike was an early logo for the flagship TV station.

(Photo courtesy of PEMCO Webster and Stevens Collection, Museum of History and Industry)

local radio stations and in 1949 established the first television station in the Northwest—today's KING-TV in Seattle. She later added to the KING broadcasting empire by acquiring other Northwest stations including KREM-TV in Spokane and KGW-TV in Portland. Perhaps her best-loved project was KING-FM—a classical music station that began broadcasting in 1948. Dorothy Bullitt died in 1989. Her broadcasting empire was sold three years later, and proceeds from the sale helped fund the Bullitt Foundation, a leading environmental grant maker. Her beloved KING-FM stayed with the Bullitt family under the corporate name Classic Radio, Inc. In 1994, Classic Radio, Inc. was donated to a consortia of Seattle arts organizations known as "Beethoven."

⚡ Cecil & Dipstik

During the late seventies, the editorial pages of the *Seattle Post-Intelligencer* (*P-I*) featured a sociopolitical comic strip called *Cecil & Dipstik*. Drawn by longtime *P-I* artist Ray Collins, the character of Cecil

The gentle humor and philosophy of Ray Collins' ***Cecil & Dipstik*** **were Seattle favorites.**
(Cartoon courtesy of Ray Collins)

C. Addle was indigenous to Puget Sound, a little naive but with an air of innocence about him. Dipstik Duck was the minority opinion in Collins's world and had a lot of concern for the dim but lovable Cecil. Together they would sit on their friend Log, waxing philosophic about everything from nuclear power to punk rock. After Collins retired from the paper in 1979, he tried to make a go of the strip through syndication. Unfortunately, *Cecil & Dipstik* didn't translate well outside the Northwest and Collins retired the duo in 1981. Many of the best cartoons were collected in three books and the strip has recently made a comeback on Collins's Joy of Cartooning Web site.

⚡ Chong, Tommy

Far out, man! Tommy Chong, the drugged-out hippie-half of the classic seventies comedy duo Cheech and Chong, met his future partner in Vancouver. Born in Edmonton to a Chinese father and Scotch-Irish mother, Tommy Chong was a budding guitarist when he headed for the music scene in Vancouver shortly after finishing school. He became a member of

Bobby Taylor and the Vancouvers and cowrote their one hit song, "Does Your Mama Know About Me?" While touring with the band, Chong was influenced by improvisational comedy troupes like Chicago's Second City and the Committee in San Francisco. He eventually left the band to form his own improvisational comedy group called City Works in a Vancouver strip club owned by his family. It was in City Works that Chong met Cheech Marin and the duo found a chemistry that would propel them to a string of successful comedy albums and movies. Since their breakup in the mid-eighties, Chong has continued to make movies and tour as a stand-up comic, most recently with his wife as his partner.

Cinerama Theater

For years, Seattle's Cinerama Theater was the epitome of the ultimate movie-going experience. Opened in 1963, the theater features a spectacularly wide screen designed to accommodate special three-projector "Cinerama" process movies. Unfortunately, "Cinerama" never caught on, and while the theater was retrofitted to show normal films, competition from suburban multiplexes ultimately led to its decline. Cut to 1998 when pop culture savior Paul Allen—who had attended movies there in the 1960s—bought the Cinerama and embarked on a painstaking and expensive restoration. The theater reopened to rave reviews in 1999 and is designed to be a showcase for new movie technology.

Cody, Wayne

Before "jock talk" radio stations started spawning cookie-cutter announcers who are better at insulting callers than reporting the scores, the Seattle sports scene featured a rotund and jocular television and radio broadcaster affectionately known as "The Mound of Sound." From 1978 to 1992, Wayne Cody was (literally) the biggest personality on the local Seattle sports scene. The Midwest son of vaudeville performers, Cody worked for local CBS affiliate KIRO, usually as their main sports anchor on radio and TV, and as host of the Seattle Seahawks' pregame radio show. Never known for being a sports expert, the three-hundred-pound-plus Cody was more of an entertainer—a throwback "personality" in the style of former NBC *Today* show weatherman Willard Scott. Cody once brought a live horse into the TV studio to help report his beloved Longacres racing results. He did a sportscast from a hot tub and

in one memorable promotion called "Watch Wayne Disappear," tried (and failed) to lose weight over the course of several months on the air. Such antics earned him the enmity of the local sports media elite, but made him extremely popular with the public. He was so popular, in fact, that a chain of Cody's restaurants was opened in the Puget Sound offering meat, spuds, and stiff drinks—real "Wayner cuisine." Cody was "retired" by KIRO in 1992, but has surfaced occasionally to cover sports on a Northwest cable news channel.

Cram, Bob

Seattle-area cartoonist and illustrator Bob Cram is best remembered for his stint on KING-TV as one of their "cartooning weathermen." For nine years, Cram made watching the weather uniquely Northwest by doodling his way through low-pressure systems and partly cloudy days. Cram also illustrated Seattle impresario Bill Speidel's books on local cuisine called *You Can't Eat Mount Rainier* and *You Still Can't Eat Mount Rainier* and served as the longtime television spokesman for the local QFC supermarket chain. Most recently, Cram provided the illustrations to Dave Winfield's *The Complete Baseball Player* and the humorous *Gringolandia*, a wry look at American culture written with James Gallant and Lorenzo Milam (an original founder of Seattle's KRAB-FM community radio station).

Enerson, Jean

Seattle broadcaster Jean Enerson was one of the first television news anchorwomen in the country. A native of the Northwest, Enerson is no mere talking head, having graduated from Stanford University with a bachelor of arts in political science and a master of arts in broadcasting and film. Enerson was hired by KING-TV in 1968 and was promoted to the anchor desk in

1972. Consistently rated the city's most trusted and popular news personality, Enerson was part of journalism history in 1988 when she became the first American journalist to appear live on Soviet television. She has also hosted numerous special news programs on subjects ranging from Asia to AIDS. A 1994 inductee to the National Academy of Television Arts and Sciences (Seattle chapter), Enerson is still coanchoring KING's Channel 5 evening newscasts.

Farmer, Frances

Frances Farmer was an idealistic student at West Seattle High School when she first made a national name for herself by writing an essay in 1931 about the death of God, earning the hostility of local Christians who sought to portray her as a pawn of atheistic Communists. Unbowed, Farmer went on to attend the University of Washington Drama and her talents eventually took her to Hollywood where she became a popular film star. Her strong will and combative nature, however, put her at odds with studio moguls, and she often drank too much and took too many pills. As her career began to spin downward, Farmer's mother "rescued" her daughter by arranging a series of confinements in increasingly harsh mental institutions culminating with a stay at Western State Hospital in Steilacoom, Washington. Farmer was eventually lobotomized and lived out her days hosting a daytime television show in Indianapolis, a hollow shell of her former "free-spirited" self. Farmer's story is told in the 1982 motion picture *Frances*.

Fish, Byron

Longtime Seattle writer and columnist, Byron Fish signed his work with a small hand-drawn fish and the words "His Mark." Fish provided the words and Bob and Ira Spring provided the pictures for a series of popular outdoor books about the Northwest, but he is best known for his sketch "Free At Last." A favorite retirement gift, the sketch shows a buck-naked man running gleefully down the road.

Flying Karamazov Brothers

The greatest juggling and cheap theatrics act to ever come out of Port Townsend, Washington, the Flying Karamazov Brothers (Dmitri, Ivan, Smerdyakov, and Rakitin) have been juggling their way to fame and fortune for over a quarter century. Beginning as street performers in San Francisco in 1973, the Flying Karamazov Brothers (who are not related) have gained worldwide acclaim with their highly entertaining and hilarious vaudevillian shows as well as their own adaptations of famous plays such as *The Three Moscowteers* and Shakespeare's *The Comedy of Errors*. The brothers also have numerous television appearances to their credit and starred with Michael Douglas, Kathleen Turner, and Danny DeVito in the hit movie *The Jewel of the Nile*.

Fox, Michael J.

The puckish star of the blockbuster *Back to the Future* movies and the television shows *Spin City* and *Family Ties*, Michael J. Fox was born in 1961 in Edmonton, Alberta, but was raised in the Vancouver area. He attended Burnaby Central High School but dropped out in his senior year. After a short stint as costar of the CBC television show *Leo and Me*, Fox was off to Los Angeles where he eventually landed the role of Alex Keaton, earning three Emmy Awards and worldwide popularity.

French, Jim

Once upon a time, radio stations offered a potpourri of music, talk, news, and light entertainment presided over by a cadre of radio "personalities." One of the most memorable radio personalities in the Seattle market was Jim French. He grew up in Southern California and got his start on a Pasadena station. After a stint in the military, French landed a job at KING-AM 1090 in Seattle in the early fifties. He later migrated to KVI-AM 570 and finished his career at KIRO-AM 710. A versatile radio host, French specialized in author and celebrity interviews and for many years was the most recognizable commercial voice in the industry. French also began writing and producing radio dramas, first locally on Seattle radio stations as the *Mystery Playhouse* and now syndicated nationally as *Imagination Theater*. Although retired from day-to-day radio, French continues to write and produce radio plays and does occasional commercial voiceover work.

Gay, Henry

Henry Gay, the Northwest's version of legendary newspaper satirist H. L. Mencken, was the editor and publisher of the *Shelton-Mason County Journal*. For more than thirty years, Gay was a feisty and cantankerous columnist who never failed to drive home a point with deadly satirical precision. Born into a newspaper family in Monterey, California, Gay bought the *Journal* in 1966 and quickly became one of the most entertaining columnists in the region. As writer Roger Downey noted, Gay specialized in railing against "stupidity, illogic and malice in public life," and fellow columnist Emmett Watson wrote that Gay "used language as a weapon—against cant, sophistry, conceit, hypocrisy [and] crookedness." In the late sixties when schools were suspending students with long hair, it was Gay who reminded his readers about another longhaired troublemaker who the authorities eventually had to crucify. When Washington voters elected the

colorful Dixy Lee Ray, Gay had a field day criticizing her controversial "foot in mouth" statements. The winner of numerous journalism awards and a mentor to other small publishers, Gay died of cancer in January 1999.

George, Chief Dan

The most famous First Nations actor from Vancouver began his film career when he was far past mid-life. Dan George, or "Teswahno," was born in 1899 on the Burrard Indian Reserve. Until he was sixty years old, he worked as a longshoreman, logger, and musician and was chief of the Squamish Band of Burrard Inlet from 1951 to 1963. In 1959, George was "discovered" and had a number of roles as a Native American elder on Canadian television and stage. In 1967, he delivered a stunning recitation of the "Lament for Confederation" at Vancouver's Centennial celebrations at Empire Stadium. The speech was a poignant reminder of what Canada had been and what his people had lost. George's first major Hollywood role was as Old Lodge Skins in the 1970 film *Little Big Man*—a performance that earned him a Best Supporting Actor nomination. He also made appearances in *Harry and Tonto* (1974) and *The Outlaw Josey Wales* (1975). Chief Dan George authored the books *My Heart Soars* (1974) and *My Spirit Soars* (1982), the latter being released following his death in 1981.

Georgia Straight, The

Vancouver's *Georgia Straight* is the sole-surviving, independently owned North American "underground" newspaper from the 1960s. Born during the "Summer of Love" in 1967, the *Straight* was instantly controversial. The paper printed instructions for growing marijuana, talked frankly about sex, and criticized the police force. Local officials tried to ban its sale on the streets of their cities and Vancouver Mayor Tom Campbell tried to pull its business license. Unlike a number of former radical weeklies that started to focus more on entertainment than current affairs during the 1980s, the *Straight* has succeeded in staying true to its journalistic roots, and its writers continue to win numerous reporting awards. A 1997 book, *The Georgia Straight: What the Hell Happened?* celebrated the paper's thirtieth anniversary by compiling three decades of its best columns, stories, and features.

Groening, Matt

The creative genius behind the most successful animated television show of all time is Portland native Matt Groening. The son of an advertising executive, Groening was a student at the Evergreen State College in Olympia where he honed his comic talents with the help of fellow Greener and comic artist Lynda Barry. After moving to Los Angeles in 1977 with the intention of becoming a writer, Groening began to record his observations about life in L.A. in a comic strip called *Life in Hell*. The strip appeared for the first time in the weekly *Los Angeles Reader* in 1980 and now appears in more than 250 newspapers worldwide. In 1987, Groening was asked to contribute some animated segments that would appear between skits on the *Tracey Ullman Show*. For these skits, Groening created the *Simpsons*, a cartoon family that became so popular the FOX network gave them their own show, debuting in 1990. Since then, Groening has won numerous Emmys for the *Simpsons* and has succeeded in single-handedly bringing animation back to prime time. Some of the show's characters are named after his family, including Homer (his father), Marge (his mother), and Lisa and Maggie (his sisters).

Gross, Pete

The original "Voice of the Seahawks," Pete Gross was the radio broadcaster for the team from its inaugural season in 1976, until cancer prematurely claimed his life in 1992. Known for his enthusiastic play calling and high-pitched signature call "Touchdown Seahawks," Gross kept Hawk fans loyal through the best and worst of seasons. Only two days before he passed away, Gross was honored in a special Kingdome ceremony during a Monday Night Football game by having his name placed in the Seahawks' "Ring of Honor." Since his death, a Pete Gross House has been established at Seattle's Fred Hutchinson Cancer Research Center to house the families of cancer patients undergoing treatment at the Center.

Hairbreadth Husky

For twenty-one years (1960 to 1981), followers of University of Washington football were sure to check the front page of the *Seattle Post-Intelligencer* (P-I) sports section each game day to enjoy the adventures of *Hairbreadth Husky*. The creation of P-I cartoonist Bob McCausland, *Hairbreadth Husky* hilariously told the ups and downs of the Dawgs' football season through the eyes of this lovable mutt. Each week, Hairbreadth would run into his old pals Tommy Trojan (the West Coast bully with the death's-head sword); Eugene, the dyspeptic Oregon Duck; U. C. Alley, the big, bad bear from Los Angeles; and Hairbreadth's country cousin, Clem Cougar. Also featuring cartoon drawings of head coaches Jim Owens, Don James, and many of their assistants, *Hairbreadth Husky* was the most popular sports cartoon in Western Washington for two decades. A book of McCausland's best cartoons was published by Madrona Press in 1982.

⅏ Hardwick, Bob

At one time, Robert E. Lee Hardwick was Seattle's highest-paid radio personality and a winner of *Billboard Magazine*'s "Personality of the Year" award. When he committed suicide in 1992, he had been fired from his last job and was largely forgotten by the Seattle radio audience that had once made him number one. In some ways, Hardwick's demise mirrored the demise of "personality radio" in the Northwest. He began his career in 1959 at KVI, one of the top personality stations in the country. His show was a mix of music, patter, skits, and stunts. One Hardwick highlight came when he supervised the voyage of Namu the killer whale to the Seattle aquarium. While popular, Hardwick also could be impetuous (much like Jack Paar on the national level). In 1980, he walked out of KVI and started working at a rival station, only to return in a few months amid a flurry of litigation. He left KVI for good in 1984, appearing occasionally in commercials, until he returned to KING radio in 1990. By then the radio business had left the Hardwick style behind, and his KING tenure (as well as his life) ended just two years later.

⅏ Hart, Roger

One of Portland's premier Top 40 disc jockeys, Roger Hart is best remembered for bringing Paul Revere and the Raiders from the dance halls to the big time. In 1963, the Raiders had moved from Boise to Portland, holding down day jobs while trying to get a break. In addition to his disc jockey duties at KISN radio, Hart was beginning to promote dance concerts, featuring groups such as the Wailers. In his search for another band, Hart was introduced to Paul Revere and the Raiders and soon booked the group at the Lake Oswego Armory. Hart also released a Raiders' album on his own Sande label (now very collectable).

Hart became the group's manager, and negotiated a recording contract with Columbia Records, launching the Raiders' decade of national fame.

⅏ Helix

From 1967 to 1970, the *Helix* reigned as Seattle's entry in the underground press movement. While many underground publications lasted just a few issues, the *Helix* is distinguished by its longevity and its alumni, which include founder Paul Dorpat, now Seattle's leading historian, and Walt Crowley, liberal author and commentator. On the paper's second anniversary, Crowley would note that "*Helix* is not a newspaper, it is a psycho-drama. What you see every week is merely a by-product of a larger process. *Helix* is a highly charged gestalt, an integrated force field generated by a constellation of powerful and hungry egos." He also described the layout process as "sexual more in an anal sense than an erotic." You have to remember, it was the sixties. People really talked like that. Other *Helix* contributors included novelist Tom Robbins, future *Seattle Weekly* contributor Roger Downey, and mainstream local television newsmen Mike James and Don McGaffin, who wrote under the collective pseudonym Gabby Hayes.

⅏ Hill, Sandy

Former Miss Washington and Seattle KIRO-TV personality Sandy Hill turned her bubbly energy into national fame as cohost of ABC's *Good Morning America*. A native of Centralia, Washington, Hill had no broadcasting background and only one year of college when she was hired by KIRO in the late sixties to be an on-air "personality." Although the critics howled, Hill quickly became a viewer favorite, seemingly on the station twenty-four hours a day. At one time she anchored the noon news, hosted KIRO's afternoon *Big Money Movie*, handled the weather during the 6:30 P.M. and 11:00 P.M. newscasts, and served as the station's goodwill ambassador at supermarket openings and community celebrations. Her good looks and screen presence landed her in Los Angeles where she was a coanchor for KNXT and later a reporter for KABC before her three-year stint on *Good Morning America*. Most recently, Hill has been working in the film industry as a location manager and had a small role in the 1994 TV movie *Without Warning*.

Horsey, David

Longtime political cartoonist for the *Seattle Post-Intelligencer* (*P-I*), David Horsey won the Pulitzer Prize in 1999 for twenty cartoons published in 1998, many of which parodied the Clinton-Lewinsky affair. It was the first Pulitzer in the paper's 130-plus-year history. Horsey joined the *P-I* in 1979 (replacing Ray Collins of *Cecil & Dipstik* fame) after a stint with the *Bellevue Journal-American*. He also attended the University of Washington where he served as editor and cartoonist for the *Daily*, the school's student newspaper.

Hume, Ed

The Northwest's most popular television gardening expert is Seattle's venerable Ed Hume. For three decades, Hume has been advising Northwest green thumbs about the best way to fertilize rhododendrons and prune juniper tams. Hume first made a regional name for himself with a local gardening program on KOMO-TV in Seattle. His current weekly television program, *Gardening in America*, can be seen in approximately fifty million households across the United States and Japan. Hume also writes gardening articles for newspapers and magazines, makes numerous personal appearances, and markets Ed Hume brand seeds.

Jackson, Keith

Whoa, Nellie! Did you know that Keith Jackson, the "Voice of College Football," got his start in the Pacific Northwest? After graduating from Washington State University in Pullman (where he broadcast college games for the campus radio station), Georgian farm boy Jackson was hired as a reporter for KOMO-TV, Seattle's ABC network affiliate. At first he coanchored the 6:30 P.M. and 10:30 P.M. newscasts, teaming with Herb Robinson to become the West Coast's first two-person news team. For eight of his ten years in Seattle, Jackson was the voice of Husky football, calling back-to-back Rose Bowl victories during the Jim Owens "Purple Gang" glory years in the early sixties. Jackson also broadcast Seattle Rainiers baseball games (replacing legendary broadcaster Leo Lassen), Seattle University basketball, and the Gold Cup hydroplane races. Jackson's talent eventually got him noticed by ABC sports where he has been broadcasting college football for more than three decades.

Joint Operating Agreement

For many years, Seattle's two major newspapers, the *Seattle Post-Intelligencer* (*P-I*) and the *Seattle Times*, engaged in a fierce battle for readership in the Northwest's biggest city. The *P-I* was the scrappy, liberal morning paper, owned since 1921 by the Hearst Corporation. The *Times* was the stodgy, conservative afternoon paper owned for generations by Seattle's Blethen family. The *P-I* was Avis and the *Times* was Hertz and the competition was intense. If the *P-I* carried a story as a headline in the morning, you could expect the *Times* to bury that same story deep in the classifieds and vice versa. In 1983, the competition ended

Critics say that the Joint Operating Agreement between the *Seattle Times* and the *Seattle Post-Intelligencer* saved the *P-I* but cost the paper its spark.

(Photo from *Seattle Post-Intelligencer* Collection, Museum of History and Industry)

KJR Seattle – Channel 95

For fans of Top 40 radio around the world, the jingle "KJR Seattle . . . Channel 95" brings instant recognition. Under the leadership of Pat O'Day, the station became known as the one that could break a band nationally. Whereas other cities had their local favorites—Portland listeners tuned into KISN, where DJs such as Roger Hart and Roger W. Morgan spun the hits, and in Vancouver, Red Robinson and Fred Latremouille held forth—it was KJR that moved the needle on the Billboard charts. The station began broadcasting in 1921, but it was under the ownership of Danny Kaye and Lester Smith that KJR gained national prominence. In the late fifties, Smith discovered the commercial power of rock music and switched KJR's format. In the early sixties with the arrival of Pat O'Day, the station became a Top 40 powerhouse. Rivals, such as KOL, would define themselves in terms of KJR—when KJR had its "millionaire" give out money around town, KOL launched the "cheapskate" who would beg for spare change. Among the DJs who kept the KJR listeners loyal over the years were Gary Lockwood, Charlie Brown, Emperor Lee Smith, Lan Roberts, Tom Murphy, and Norm Gregory. While many of those DJs continued on in Seattle radio, KJR's glory days ended in the eighties, with Kaye and Smith selling out to Metromedia. Eventually, KJR was purchased by local billboard magnate and Supersonics owner Barry Ackerley and turned into a twenty-four-hour sports radio station.

Lassen, Leo

Perhaps the most famous Seattle radio sportscaster in history was a man known to his listeners as the "Great Gabbo"—the voice of Seattle Pacific Coast League baseball for almost three decades. Leo Lassen was born just before the

when both papers entered into a Joint Operating Agreement (JOA) permitted under the federal Newspaper Preservation Act. Under the agreement, the *Times* is responsible for the advertising, circulation, promotion, and production of both papers while the news and editorial functions remain separate. Although this move kept both papers afloat (the *P-I* had been struggling financially for years), the old rivalry was gone and the editorial boards of both papers have since moved to the middle of the political spectrum. In 1999, the JOA was amended to permit the *Times* to switch from an afternoon to a morning paper, going head-to-head each day with its old rival.

turn of the twentieth century and raised in North Seattle. Although he couldn't play baseball himself due to a childhood accident, he became closely associated with the sport, first as a reporter for the *Seattle Star* and then, beginning in 1931, as the voice of Seattle minor league baseball teams (Indians and Rainiers). For the next twenty-nine years, baseball fans throughout the Northwest heard Lassen's trademark metallic voice and rapid-fire delivery on their home radios. He was a master at painting an audio portrait of the game and his knowledge of baseball was unsurpassed. Lassen was also adept at timing and suspense—necessary skills in the early days when he had to re-create away games by reading sketchy details from a telegraph machine. Lassen's audience began to decline in the 1950s as television marched into Puget Sound homes, and he left the booth forever in 1960. Lassen retired to his home in Seattle's Wallingford neighborhood to tend his roses, never to attend another game. He died in 1975 and while he had no known relatives and few close friends, hundreds turned out in the rain to pay their respects to Seattle's "Mr. Baseball."

Lee, Bruce

Although he was born in San Francisco, raised in Hong Kong, and became famous in California, Bruce Lee's connection to Seattle is a key part of his legend and lore. When Lee was nineteen years old, he moved to Seattle to work for local restaurateur Ruby Chow—a power in the Asian community and a former member of the King County Council. He studied philosophy at the University of Washington, married local girl Linda Emery (it is claimed their first date was in the Space Needle's revolving restaurant), and left Ruby Chow's restaurant to establish his Jun Fan Kung-Fu Institute. After five years in Seattle, Lee returned to California where his role as Kato on *The Green Hor-*

net would make him a star. Lee died in Hong Kong in 1973 of a cerebral edema (swelling of the brain) and was brought back to Seattle for burial at Lake View Cemetery overlooking Lake Washington. A month after his death, his film *Enter the Dragon* premiered in Los Angeles, making him a posthumous international film star.

McCune, Don

Don McCune was a longtime radio and television personality who specialized in covering the history of the Pacific Northwest. McCune began his broadcasting career as a disc jockey on KRSC in Seattle in 1943. After the war, he moved to Alaska to manage a radio and television station and became known as the "Voice of Alaska" as an NBC correspondent. In 1957, McCune returned to Seattle to star in a local kids' show on KOMO called *Captain Puget*. As skipper of the *Windward Four*, McCune took Western Washington children on TV voyages around Puget Sound and sang sea chanteys

Don McCune, the host of *Exploration Northwest*, was also the children's favorite Captain Puget.

(Photo courtesy of Linda McCune)

(often with legendary Seattle restaurateur Ivar Haglund) for ten years. In 1960, McCune created an outdoor adventure show called *Exploration Northwest*, which took viewers to every corner of the Northwest, exploring topics from the Great Seattle Fire to the Klondike Gold Rush. *Exploration Northwest* ran for twenty-one seasons and earned McCune most of his twenty-six Emmy Awards for regional programming. His signature sign-off "Smooth sailing and goodbye for now" is remembered fondly by longtime Northwesterners, and an era in local broadcasting ended when McCune died of cancer in 1993 at the age of seventy-three. A special library of his works has been established at Washington State University and his widow Linda McCune continues to re-release his *Exploration Northwest* programs on videocassette.

Mulligan, Terry David

Terry David Mulligan has been one of Vancouver's most recognizable broadcasting personalities and a fixture on the city's music scene for decades. After an abortive career as a Mountie in Red Deer, Alberta, Mulligan discovered rock music and spent the next twenty years as a disc jockey at such Terminal City radio stations as CFUN and CHUM. Mulligan also helped program Canada's first "underground" FM radio station CKLG-FM 99 (now CFOX) where he worked with the legendary "Captain Midnight," J. B. Shayne. Mulligan hosted CBC Radio's rock magazine *Great Canadian Goldrush* and the CBC video program *Good Rockin' Tonight*. Often referred to as "the Dick Clark of Canada," Mulligan has had roles in a number of movies and TV programs and was a longtime commercial spokesman for Molson. Since 1985, Mulligan has worked for Much Music—a Canadian twenty-four-hour video music channel.

Murrow, Edward R.

The twentieth century's most celebrated and influential news reporter grew up in Washington State. Edward R. Murrow was born Egbert Murrow in 1908 in North Carolina and grew up on the Samish flats just south of Bellingham, Washington. In 1926, he went off to attend Washington State College (WSC) in Pullman. At the time, WSC had the country's first college courses in broadcasting and one of the first college radio stations. Murrow was active in drama and student politics while working at the campus radio station. Five years after he graduated in 1930, Murrow landed at CBS and soon became their European director, leading to his legendary "This . . . is London" broadcasts from Great Britain during the early days of World War II. Murrow was a fixture at CBS for twenty-five years before becoming director of the U.S. Information Agency during the Kennedy administration. He died of cancer in 1965. The communications school at Washington State University is named for Murrow and an award for outstanding achievement in broadcasting is presented each year in his honor.

Nelson, Larry

In the golden age of "full-service" AM stations that emphasized news, banter, and middle-of-the-road music, the main man in Seattle morning radio was KOMO's Larry Nelson. A native Northwesterner, Nelson started his morning stint in 1968 and quickly became one of the most popular disc jockeys in town. He was as casual as the Northwest, relaxed and always ready with a humorous quip. Nelson once claimed that he tried to create a kitchen atmosphere on his morning show, just like your next-door neighbor who might stop in for a cup of coffee and a cruller. He loved to salute listener-nominated "good sons," "super dads," and "wonder moms."

He read goopy poetry and for many years hosted the Saturday morning "Husky Tailgate Party" on KOMO before every University of Washington football game. Nelson's low-profile, laid-back attitude was often scoffed at by radio business insiders, but the format was enormously popular with listeners, making him one of the town's highest-paid disc jockeys and its most familiar morning voice. When KOMO finally switched to a news-talk format in 1996, Nelson stepped aside rather than contribute to a format he wasn't comfortable with. His last broadcast was from Seattle's 13 Coins Restaurant. It was a fitting finale since Nelson had been there to cover its grand opening in 1967.

Niehaus, Dave

Although the current popularity of the Seattle Mariners would lead one to believe that every game was worth listening to no matter what, this wasn't always the case. For most of the team's first two decades, the season was over before the all-star break, and the only thing that kept Northwesterners tuned into the action was the voice of radio and television play-by-play radio announcer Dave Niehaus. He has been with the Mariners since opening day in 1977, and his emotion-laden play calling keeps fans tuned in, whatever the team's fortunes. Dave's signature calls of "My Oh My" (a great play), "Fly Away" (home-run call), and "Get out the rye bread and mustard Grandma, it's grand salami time" (grand slam home-run call) have become part of Northwest baseball vocabulary. When heart trouble forced Niehaus off the mike for several weeks at the end of the 1996 season, thousands of baseball fans throughout the Northwest and the nation sent well wishes. Since then, a healthier Niehaus is back at the mike calling the action as "Junior steps to

the plate, and here's the pitch . . . swung on and belted, DEEP to right field. . . ."

Nye, Bill

Mr. Wizard with a comic edge, Bill Nye is a former cast member of KING-TV's *Almost Live!* show where he debuted his Bill Nye the Science Guy character. Nye would use outrageous contraptions to demonstrate scientific principles and he soon became an audience favorite. Nye's schtick was right in line with the new national emphasis on science education, and he soon became the star of a nationally distributed kids' science show, author of a number of popular books, and proprietor of the Nye Labs Web site.

O'Day, Pat

As Paul Berg, he might have never made it out of the small radio stations of Astoria, Oregon, and Longview, Washington. As Pat O'Day, he became Seattle's most influential disc jockey, leading KJR-AM 950 radio during its Top 40 heyday in the sixties and seventies. During his

Paul Berg, under personality moniker Pat O'Day, led KJR Seattle to Top 40 glory.

(Photo from *Seattle Post-Intelligencer Collection*, Museum of History and Industry)

tenure, KJR was a key national station that could make or break a record. According to a representative for Columbia Records, "We're home with the bacon when KJR charts a record." O'Day believed in personality radio and had an uncanny ability to pick and develop disc jockey talent. Radio consultant Bill Gavin once said of O'Day: "He's creative and imaginative, and he believes in communicating with his listeners. Unlike most Top 40 stations, KJR is not just a jukebox grinding out one hit after another with a minimum of personality." O'Day's drive made him successful but also controversial, especially as he parlayed his radio influence into a virtual lock on the teen dance circuit and concert promotion business. When Buffalo Springfield played an O'Day–promoted show, Steven Stills told *Seattle Magazine*, "We haven't heard a good word from any musicians about O'Day. The really good groups all consider him only a commercial huckster." KJR began a slow decline (along with the rest of Top 40 radio) in the seventies. Later, O'Day would be influential in establishing the city's first "new wave" station (KYYX), but he never again regained the influence and sway he possessed during KJR's prime. O'Day has been inducted into the Rock and Roll Hall of Fame, and for many years he was the primary announcer for the Seattle Seafair hydroplane races.

J. P. Patches, the mayor of the city dump, and his girlfriend, Gertrude, are still going strong.
(Photo courtesy of Chris Wedes)

Patches, J. P.

When Seattle's KIRO television went on the air in 1958, its first live program was a children's show called *J. P. Patches*. A retired clown from the "Ding-a-Ling Brothers Circus," J. P. (played by Chris Wedes) took up residency at the City Dump and soon became the favorite of children throughout the Northwest. The weekday morning show featured cartoons, zany characters (like his "dressed-in-drag" sidekick Gertrude played by Bob Nelson), and skits. J. P. also hosted numerous guests, many of them children who came to see the "Mayor" of the City Dump. After ratings for the show began to decline in the mid-seventies, KIRO-TV pulled *J. P. Patches* from their weekday lineup in 1978 and relegated the show to Saturday mornings. Not long after, the show disappeared from the airwaves entirely. Several years later, however, a *J. P. Patches* video retrospective was released and Seattle baby boomers anxious to relive their childhood memories welcomed J. P. and Gertrude back into the spotlight. The duo continues to make personal appearances around the Puget Sound area making new friends and reminiscing with their now middle-aged "Patches Pals."

Pitchmen

Every region has its great television pitchmen—sales guys who will scream, cajole, yodel—whatever it takes to get you to buy this car, refrigerator, or television set TODAY! In the Northwest you couldn't have watched more than five minutes of television in the seventies without seeing Seattle's Dick Balch—a longhaired car dealer who would finish almost every commercial by bashing a car with his ever-present sledge-hammer. Or how about Glen Grant, wearing a bad toupee and offering to "stand on his head to sell you a car"? Appliance buyers could see Tom Peterson in Portland, described by the *Oregonian* as "the buzz saw with the buzz cut," while Puget Sounders had Jack Roberts, a man who proclaimed he "won't be undersold" while his buxom wife smashed him with a cream pie. It remains to be seen whether modernists like Western Washington mattress empress Sunny Kobe Cook and Portland car dealer Scott Thomason, whose disembodied head floats from signs throughout Portland, can compete with the classics.

Ramblin' Rod

Rod Anders was the undisputed master of Portland kids' television for three decades, entertaining generations of moppets as Ramblin' Rod. Anders landed at Portland's KPTV in 1964 to host the *Popeye* cartoon block. He adapted the Ramblin' Rod name from a prior stint as a disc jockey. Like most local kids' shows, *Ramblin Rod* was a low-budget and endearing mix of cartoons and slapstick, with an enthusiastic peanut gallery of kids cheering every move. By the 1990s, the format was an anachronism—probably more popular with hungover college students than overly sophisticated children raised on Nickelodeon. KPTV cut out daily broadcasts of *Ramblin' Rod* in 1996, relegating the show to a weekend slot.

Rivers, Bob

The morning man at KISW radio in Seattle for the past decade, Bob Rivers has become nationally known for his "Twisted Tunes"—perfect soundalikes of rock classics with a lyrical twist. In Rivers's world, the Guess Who's "American Woman" becomes a lonely guy's "Inflatable Woman." "Walking in a Winter Wonderland" becomes a tribute to

men who like "Walkin' Round in Women's Underwear." Rivers came to Seattle from Baltimore after winning national attention for staying on the air continuously during the Orioles' famous twenty-one-game losing streak at the start of the 1988 season. Several collections of Rivers's parodies have been released on CD.

Robertson, Bob

The voice of Washington State University (WSU) Cougar football network for more than three decades is Bob Robertson, the current dean of Northwest sports broadcasters. His trademark line, "Always be a good sport, be a good sport all ways," may be corny, but it's characteristic of this "old-school" broadcaster who prefers to emphasize the positive and doesn't

Bob Robertson is the dean of Northwest sportscasters and the voice of WSU Cougar football.
(Photo courtesy of Washington State University Athletics)

apologize for being a true "homer." Robertson attended Western Washington University in Bellingham in the 1940s and worked at the campus radio station. In addition to Cougar football, Robertson has worked pro wrestling, Tacoma Stars indoor soccer, Husky football from 1969 to 1971, and Tacoma Rainiers (formerly Tigers) Triple-A baseball. It's WSU football, however, that has been Robertson's life off and on since the 1964 season, and he is as much a fixture in the Palouse as Cougar Gold cheese and keggers.

Robinson, Red

Vancouver's Red Robinson is Canada's best-known rock and roll disc jockey. Born in 1937 in Comox, B.C., Robinson was the first Canadian DJ to program rock and roll on a regular basis and the first to play Elvis Presley records. When the King appeared at Vancouver's Empire Stadium in 1957, Robinson was on hand to introduce him. He was also the master of ceremonies when the Beatles played there in 1964 and temporarily earned the enmity of John Lennon when he walked out on stage during the group's performance to quiet the crowd. After four years on Vancouver radio, Dorothy Bullitt and the KING broadcasting empire lured Robinson away to KGW in Portland in 1958. Red helped turn the Rose City station into a Top 40 powerhouse and hosted a program called *Portland Bandstand* before returning to Vancouver. In addition to gigs on various Vancouver radio stations, Robinson also hosted CBC television shows such as *Let's Go* (1963–65) and *Trivia* (1977–79). Winner of numerous broadcasting awards, he was elected in 1995 as a pioneer disc jockey to the Rock and Roll Hall of Fame in Cleveland—one of only three from Canada. In 1997, Robinson was inducted into the Canadian Association of Broadcasters Hall of Fame. He is currently the morning host on CISL-

Red Robinson, Vancouver's pioneer rock-and-roll disc jockey, is still spinning the hits.
(Photo courtesy of KVOS-TV)

AM 650 in Richmond, B.C., and is in his eleventh season as host of *Red's Classic Theater*, shown Sunday evenings on KVOS Channel 12 in Bellingham.

Rodeo Grandmas

Four senior horsewomen from Ellensburg became television stars in 1993 when Washington Mutual Bank tapped them to star in its commercials. The Rodeo Grandmas were portrayed as saving Washington Mutual customers from the evil predations of the big, out-of-state (i.e., California) banking chains. They were an instant hit, becoming staples of parades and festivals throughout the state. The Grandmas' future was thrown in doubt in late 1998 when Judy Golladay, a founding Grandma, died of cancer, but the remaining members plan to carry on.

Schonely, Bill

The original radio play-by-play voice of the Portland Trail Blazers, Bill Schonely began his career in Seattle, calling games for the University of Washington Husky football team, the Seattle Totems hockey team, the Seattle Pilots baseball team, and the occasional professional wrestling match. In 1971, he was named play-by-play announcer for the new Portland Trail Blazers basketball franchise, a position he held until the end of the 1997–98 season. Early in his Trail Blazers career, Schonely coined the phrase "Rip City" as a signature call when a key shot was made. The term soon became a nickname for the city of Portland itself, a mark of the affection held for Schonely.

◰ Seattle International Film Festival

What began in 1976 as an eighteen-film schedule at one art-house theater in Seattle has now grown into the largest film festival in the country and one of the top film festivals in the world. The Seattle International Film Festival is held annually for twenty-five days from the middle of May to the middle of June and attracts more than 135,000 movie lovers. More than two hundred filmmakers and film professionals attend the festival each year which is oriented primarily to filmgoers rather than industry personnel. The success of the festival is no surprise considering Seattle has the highest per capita movie-going frequency of any U.S. city.

◰ Seattle Weekly, The

Originally founded in 1976 as the *Weekly* by former *Seattle Magazine* staffer and *Argus* editor David Brewster, the *Seattle Weekly* carved out its niche from the beginning. Speaking with the *Seattle Post-Intelligencer* (*PI*), Brewster said the paper was looking for readers who were in " . . . the rising educated class—people in their thirties and forties who by their youth and education have more ideas." Initial investors reportedly included Starbucks founder Gordon Bowker, Democratic Party bigwig Gerald

Grinstein, and arts patron Bagley Wright. After a shaky start, the paper went on to become the bible of Seattle's elite readers. While some considered the paper little more than pretentious yuppie snobbery and others found it a thoughtful and unique voice, no one denied its influence—or the influence of Brewster on the paper. The *Seattle Weekly* crusaded for a city of discourse and ideas, from fighting the Joint Operating Agreement between the *Seattle Times* and *P-I*, to Brewster's failed attempt to establish a "Mark Tobey Pub" where ideas and beer would mix freely. By 1997, Brewster and his initial group of investors were ready to sell, finding a willing buyer in Leonard Stern, pet-food magnate and publisher of the *Village Voice*. Brewster retreated to the editorial page of the *Seattle Times*, while the new ownership made the paper edgier and tougher—in short, more urban than urbane (they even added a sex columnist).

◰ Shayne, J. B. (Captain Midnight)

J. B. Shayne, one of Vancouver's most colorful radio personalities during the past three decades, was greatly influenced by Seattle disc jockeys Pat O'Day and Lan Roberts, listening to them on his transistor radio while growing up in Vancouver's Kerrisdale neighborhood. Beginning on CKLG-FM 99 in the sixties, Shayne developed the persona of Captain Midnight during his graveyard shift. He also created the character of sportscaster Chuck Stake on the station's morning program. When Shayne and others attempted to unionize the CKLG workforce, they were unceremoniously fired. He rebounded in the 1970s and 1980s with Canada's first music video program (*Nite Dreems*) hosted by a new character called Raouel Casablanca. The success of *Nite Dreems* led to a Saturday night radio program on CBC called *Neon Nites*, earning his largest audience. In the nineties, Shayne was part of the Morning Dream Team at Coast 800 that featured the famous Hollywood North Report. Today, Shayne does voice work, hoping for another crack at the radio or TV limelight.

◤ Smith, Dr. Lendon

Portland's Dr. Lendon Smith was one of the most visible and popular doctors in the country from the sixties to the eighties. A graduate of Reed College and the University of Oregon medical school, Smith became a practicing pediatrician in the early fifties. His early work using nutritional approaches to treat hyperactive children brought him worldwide attention. His books like *Feed Your Kids Right* were best-sellers, and his colorful personality and sense of humor made him a frequent guest on the *Tonight Show*, the *Phil Donahue Show*, and others. Smith also had a series on ABC called *The Children's Doctor*, and his ABC Afterschool Special "My Mom's Having a Baby" is still one of the most widely distributed sex education presentations. Smith's career and theories that nutrition affects behavior have not been without controversy. The Oregon Board of Medical Examiners placed him on probation in 1973 for prescribing unnecessary medication to six adult patients, and in 1987, he permanently surrendered his medical license rather than face Board action on a charge of insurance fraud.

◤ Stranger, The

Seattle's alternative weekly, the *Stranger*, began in the early nineties as a small University District paper. Founder Tim Keck had earlier success starting the Madison, Wisconsin, satirical *Onion* before moving to Seattle. Keck sensed that the *Seattle Weekly* was stale and had little relevance to younger readers. He used irreverent writing, frank columns about sex, and a frisky personals section to quickly grow to parity with the older paper. Keck's greatest find was sex advice columnist Dan Savage, whose *Savage Love* column is now syndicated nationally. A gay activist, Savage used to require every letter to begin "Hey Faggot"—a shock to Seattle's politically correct sensibilities.

◤ Stratten, Dorothy

Vancouver's Dorothy Stratten became doubly famous for being named 1980 *Playboy* Playmate of the Year and for being tragically murdered later that year by her estranged husband, Paul Snider. Born Dorothy Ruth Hoogstraten in 1960, she posed for *Playboy* in 1979 and soon became one of Hugh Hefner's favorites. Shortly after finishing work on the Peter Bogdanovich film *They All Laughed*, Stratten was murdered by her jealous ex-husband. Her death inspired two films, *Star 80*, directed by Bob Fosse, and the TV movie *Death of a Centerfold*, starring Jamie Lee Curtis. Bogdanovich, who had fallen in love with Stratten, wrote *The Killing of the Unicorn—Dorothy Stratten 1960–1980*, which was less than kind in its treatment of Hefner and the *Playboy* star-making machine. Even Vancouver's Bryan Adams climbed aboard the Stratten bandwagon with the song "The Best Was Yet to Come."

◤ Strong, Anna Louise

Anna Louise Strong was a well-known American journalist who covered the early days of the labor movement and later became a Chinese communist sympathizer. Born in 1885 in Nebraska, Strong covered the 1918 Everett massacre trial involving the Industrial Workers of the World or "Wobblies" for the *New York*

Evening Post. An editorial published the following year in the *Seattle Union Record* helped shape the city's General Strike and is considered a landmark document in the history of the American Labor Movement. In the 1930s, Strong conducted a famous interview with Chairman Mao during which he coined his famous phrase "Paper Tiger." Strong spent the last years of her life living in China and is buried in the Revolutionary Martyrs Cemetery south of Beijing. Strong, portrayed by Diane Keaton, was a central character in the 1981 film *Reds* about Jack Reed.

Suzuki, David

David Suzuki is an award-winning scientist, environmentalist, and author best known for hosting the long-running CBC television show *The Nature of Things.* He was born in Vancouver in 1936 and grew up in Ontario before attending college in the United States. Repelled by racial tensions, Suzuki returned to Canada to teach at the University of Alberta and later at the University of British Columbia where he gained an international reputation as an expert geneticist. In 1980, Suzuki was tapped as host of the CBC television show *The Nature of Things.* Currently in its thirty-ninth season, the show explores hidden territories in the world of science, technology, and medicine. Suzuki's naturally engaging and inquisitive personality and ability to explain the complexities of science in a compelling and easily understood manner was an immediate hit, and the show became internationally famous. Suzuki is also the author of twenty-eight books (including ten books for children) and the founder of the David Suzuki Foundation, dedicated to environmental issues. He makes his home in Vancouver.

Van Sant, Gus

Portland's alternative director Gus Van Sant has been bringing his edgy vision to the screen since the 1980s. He reached mainstream fame with the 1997 film *Good Will Hunting,* gathering an Oscar nomination for best director in the process. Van Sant's first film to connect with a mainstream audience was *Drugstore Cowboy,* which was released in 1989 and starred Matt Dillon. In 1991, he released the finest film ever made about narcoleptic gay street hustlers, *My Own Private Idaho* (okay, it's a small category). His 1994 adaptation of Tom Robbins' sprawling *Even Cowgirls Get the Blues* was a flop, but Van Sant connected with the sharp satire *To Die For* in 1995, setting the stage for *Good Will Hunting.* In 1998, Van Sant released a near shot-for-shot remake of Alfred Hitchcock's *Psycho* to mixed reviews. In addition to films, Van Sant is a novelist (*Pink*) and a recording artist ("18 Songs about Golf").

David Suzuki, popular host of the *Nature of Things,* also heads an environmental foundation.

(Photo courtesy of David Suzuki)

Vinton, Will

If you loved or hated the California Raisins, you have Portland's Will Vinton to thank or blame. Vinton is the world's leading practitioner of clay animation, though recently he has branched out into other media. Hailing from McMinnville, Oregon, Vinton attended school in Berkeley, then returned home to Oregon to launch his animation empire. His first break came in 1974 when his short subject *Closed Mondays* won an Academy Award. Over the next decade, Vinton made a number of highly successful commercials and animated films. His commercials featuring the California Raisins made Vinton's "claymation" a staple. Despite his success, Vinton has remained firmly rooted in Portland, with an expansive studio in the city's Northwest section. The lobby of the studio contains awards and properties from various Vinton productions and is a must for any serious film or pop culture aficionado.

Visco, Tony

For a brief moment in the seventies, Tony Visco was the Puget Sound's answer to Tom Jones. When Tacoma's pathetic Channel 13 was purchased by new management, they decided to distinguish themselves by mounting a daily ninety-minute variety show taped live at Seattle's Trojan Horse restaurant. Enter Tony Visco, a twenty-seven-year old veteran of the Reno–Tahoe lounge circuit. Tony would belt out a tune, backed by a rock band, and then settle down to interview local celebrities, such as Merillee Rush, or notable visitors. Over the next couple of years, Channel 13's fortunes waned (it eventually collapsed in a hail of lawsuits), but Visco gamely soldiered on, even when he had to broadcast from the station's paltry studios. Visco eventually retreated back to the lounges.

Watson, Emmett

Emmett Watson has been the most popular and widely read newspaper columnist in Seattle for more than half a century. Since the early forties, Watson has worked for all the major Seattle papers, including the *Seattle Star*, the *Seattle Post-Intelligencer*, and currently the *Seattle Times*. His columns have profiled the famous and the obscure. He has taken readers along on his vacations as well as shared his personal hopes, dreams, and fears. He has chronicled the

The long-running columnist Emmett Watson is the champion of "Lesser Seattle."
(Photo from *Seattle Post-Intelligencer* Collection, Museum of History and Industry)

city's most important lore, such as the origin of the Space Needle as a crude drawing on Eddie Carlson's napkin in a restaurant in Germany. Many of Watson's most popular columns have dealt with his Lesser Seattle campaign—the antithesis of the local chamber of commerce's attempt to make Seattle a big-time metropolis. His Lesser Seattle movement has tried to fight off mindless growth and the Californication of Seattle in order to preserve what's left of the city's unique culture. The author of two books of essays about the people of Seattle as well as a collection of his best newspaper work, Watson's column currently appears twice a week in the *Seattle Times*.

⦿ Webster, Jack

Glasgow-born ex-newspaperman Jack Webster was Vancouver's most abrasive and hard-hitting radio and television talk show host for nearly half a century. Webster was working for the *Vancouver Sun* in 1953 when he was hired by CJOR to do two shows called *Spotlight at Noon* and *City Mike*. His irascible style won him a loyal listening audience as he ferreted out the scandals of the day. In 1963, Webster began a talk radio show on CKNW, and the public loved the way he brought the high and mighty to their knees with his gruff personality and cunning questions. He became one of Canada's best-known and highest-paid broadcasters and was a frequent guest panelist on CBC's popular TV show

Front Page Challenge. His radio success led to the creation of a television interview program on BCTV simply called *Webster*, which made him a household name throughout western Canada. Webster retired in 1987, a year later received the Order of Canada, and in 1989 was elected to the Canadian Association of Broadcasters Hall of Fame. Webster died in 1999 at the age of eighty.

⦿ Wee Willie Nelson

Wee Willie Nelson was a radio moniker used by country superstar Willie Nelson during his stint as a disc jockey in Vancouver, Washington, during the late fifties. Having a hard time making a living in Fort Worth, Texas, Nelson's mother in Portland sent money to have Nelson and his family come to the Northwest. He landed a job at KVAN radio in Vancouver holding down the midday slot. His second daughter was born there in 1957, and later the same year, he cut his first record using equipment borrowed from the radio station. After an agent heard his song and urged him to head back east to pursue a country music career, he demanded a big pay increase from the station manager, was rebuffed, and left the radio business for a "slightly" more lucrative music career.

⦿ Weiden and Kennedy

When Dan Weiden and David Kennedy started their advertising agency in 1982, there probably were doubters. But something inside of them said, "Just do it." Good advice, because that phrase landed Weiden and Kennedy (W&K) in the front ranks of national advertising firms. W&K is known for edgy and quirky ad campaigns for Nike,

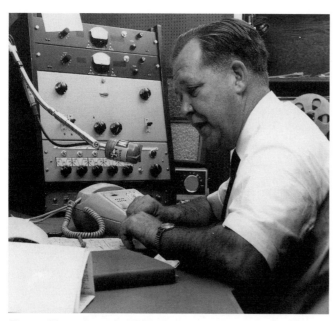

The gruff interviewer Jack Webster was a Vancouver radio and television mainstay for three decades.
(Photo courtesy of the Vancouver Public Library, photo 79296)

Microsoft, ESPN, and Miller Brewing, among others. Two W&K campaigns—for Nike and ESPN SportsCenter—were named by *Adweek* magazine as among the top twenty ad campaigns of the past twenty years. W&K caused a bit of a stir in Portland when its Miller campaign ("It's time for a good old macrobrew") appeared to take dead aim at the craft brewing industry—a serious offense in Beervana.

ⓦ Willamette Week

Founded in 1974 by Ron Buel and a group of local investors, *Willamette Week* (*WW*) has survived the vagaries of alternative press economics to become one of the oldest and strongest publications of its type in the nation. For the first few years, the paper charged for copies, but that changed after it was purchased by Mark Zusman and Richard Meeker in 1983. The small loss of sales revenues was more than made up by an explosion in advertiser interest. Now, *WW* circulates more than eighty thousand copies a week, claiming a readership of nearly two hundred thousand. Like most alternative weeklies, *WW* is a mix of local news, commentary, a generous and respected entertainment section, and a frisky set of personal ads. The paper takes special glee in poking the *Oregonian* for slow and stodgy coverage. Today's *WW* is successful enough that it draws criticism itself—from lefties, who want more political coverage, and from corporations, who dislike the paper's sometimes edgy tone. Meeker and Zusman say they have no interest in selling the paper to a national chain—in fact, they branched out in 1997, purchasing the *Santa Fe New Mexico Reporter*.

ⓦ Wunda Wunda

One of the most beloved local television shows for very young Seattle-area children was a storytelling program called *Wunda Wunda*. Named for the lead character played by Ruth Prins, *Wunda Wunda* was a harlequin-like clown who told stories for younger children from the Wunda House, accompanied by organist Elliott Brown and a variety of video effects and backgrounds (sometimes including live animals). Kids would wait each week for the theme, which began, "Wunda Wunda is my name, boys and girls I'm glad you came, we'll have fun as I explain, how we play our Wunda games." *Wunda Wunda* ran on KING-TV from 1953 to 1972 and received numerous awards, including a Peabody Award for excellence in children's programming.

HOLLYWOOD NORTH—MOVIES IN THE NORTHWEST

Have you ever gone to a movie and said, "Hey—I've been to that place"? If you're a film fan in the Northwest, that experience has been more common in the past two decades as filmmakers drawn by spectacular locations (and the cheap Canadian dollar) have found our region a studio away from home. "Hollywood North" is the generic term used to describe filmmaking and the film industry in the Pacific Northwest. Currently, British Columbia is far ahead of its southern neighbors for possession of that title, given the rapid growth in the B.C. movie industry over the past decade. Film production companies are British Columbia's fourth-largest employer group, worth more than $400 million annually to the provincial economy and employing more than six thousand people—numbers that Washington and Oregon can only dream about.

Although Canada's cheaper currency has given B.C. a distinct advantage, Washington and Oregon film offices still regularly "troll" Southern California to market their distinctive film locations. The Washington film community has also pushed state tax breaks for the film industry as a means of leveling the uneven currency playing field.

So, how did all this get started? Hollywood filmmakers made early forays into the Pacific Northwest during the 1920s and 1930s, looking for realistic settings for their films. The gold rush melodrama *The Winds of Change* (1925) was filmed in Vancouver, and Clark Gable's *Call of the Wild* (1935) was shot near Mount Baker in northwest Washington State. The Marie Dressler and Wallace Beery comedy *Tugboat Annie* (1933) was filmed on location in Seattle, another in a long line of Seattle slights to Tacoma since the Tugboat Annie character was based on Thea Foss, a turn-of-the-century tugboat operator in the City of Destiny.

In Oregon, Buster Keaton came north to film the silent classic *The General* (1927) in the tiny town of Cottage Grove. While town fathers probably thought this was the beginning of a long Hollywood love affair, it would be another half century before Cottage Grove would again grace the silver screen in the comedy classic *Animal House* (1978). The climactic Faber College homecoming parade finale was filmed on the town's Main Street in November 1977. Cottage Grove officials are anxiously preparing for their next feature film appearance around the year 2027.

Despite this early activity, the forties and fifties would produce only a handful of "on location" pictures, and it seemed for a time that Hollywood's interest in the Northwest had waned. All of that changed in the early sixties when Washington State Governor Albert Rosellini convinced MGM Studios to feature the Seattle World's Fair as the backdrop to Elvis Presley's twelfth feature-length film. Thus, the modern era of Northwest moviemaking was born when the King met the Space Needle in *It Happened at the World's Fair* (1963). Rumor has it that Elvis liked the fries so much at Seattle's Dick's Drive-In that he still keeps a secret apartment in Wallingford.

By the late sixties and early seventies, the pace of moviemaking in the Northwest picked up considerably. Robert Altman's *That Cold Day in the Park* (1969) was shot in Vancouver, and he returned the next year to shoot *McCabe and Mrs. Miller* (1970). Mike Nichols followed with his steamy *Carnal Knowledge* (1971), starring Jack Nicholson. Nicholson also starred in the classic *Five Easy Pieces* (1970), which was shot in Washington State's San Juan Islands. When Mount Hood's Timberline Lodge served as the spooky ski resort in *The Shining* (1980), Nicholson earned the distinction of being the only major actor to appear in films shot in all three Northwest locales.

In Seattle, movies like *Cinderella Liberty* (1973) and *The Parallax View* (1974) have become cult favorites, though most seventies films in the Northwest were standard production line potboilers. The Jet City also had its own run of those "tough cops who play by their own rules" films that were popular at the time. John Wayne (*McQ*, 1974) and Connie Stevens (*Scorchy*, 1976) each portrayed a Dirty Harry- and Harriet-type character during the decade. The Willamette Valley town of Eugene made movie history in the late seventies as the setting for the fictitious Faber College. After more than fifty other colleges and universities had turned him down, director John Landis persuaded the University of Oregon to let him film the comedy classic *Animal House* (1978) on their campus. Bet they didn't read the script.

With the formation of state and provincial

In town to film *It Happened at the World's Fair,* Elvis Presley hams it up with Governor Albert Rosellini.
(Photo from *Seattle Post-Intelligencer* Collection, Museum of History and Industry)

film offices in the seventies, the Northwest became better known and the number of films shot here grew significantly. Fort Worden State Park in Port Townsend, Washington, served as a backdrop for the Richard Gere breakout flick *An Officer and a Gentleman* (1981). Jessica Lange was nominated for a Best Actress Oscar for her portrayal of doomed Seattle-born actress Frances Farmer in the biopic *Frances* (1982), and teenagers flocked to see Matthew Broderick and bratpacker Ally Sheedy in the nuclear thriller *Wargames* (1983), which was partially filmed in and around Seattle. Sylvester Stallone's *First Blood* (1982) was shot on location in Hope, British Columbia, and is considered the best of the Rambo movies (although that's not saying a lot).

After a bit of a dry spell, Oregon moviemaking was reinvigorated in the late eighties with Portland director Gus Van Sant's *Drugstore Cowboy* (1989) and quirky Scottish director Bill Forsyth's *Breaking In* (1989), both of which were shot in the Rose City. Madonna came to both Portland and Olympia to shoot the steamy *Body of Evidence* (1992), causing a minor stir as large crowds flocked to catch a glimpse of pop music's sexiest diva (our necks are still sore from all the craning).

The early nineties saw a number of film studios spring up in the Vancouver area. North Shore Studios was built by Hollywood writer-producer Stephen J. Cannell (of *Rockford Files* fame), and Burnaby's Bridge Studios (which is a converted steel company) has been used for such pictures as *Bird on a Wire* (1990), *Look Who's Talking* (1989), and *Jumanji* (1995).

Although Washington has yet to build enough studio space to compete with Vancouver, the state wasn't completely ignored in the early nineties. Filmmaker Cameron Crowe (who is married to Heart's Nancy Wilson), made two youth-oriented pictures in Seattle, *Say Anything* (1989) and *Singles* (1992), the latter his ode to the city's now passe grunge music scene. The popular *Free Willy* pictures were shot on location in the San Juan Islands, rekindling local memories of the rescue of Namu during the sixties. Perhaps the high point for Emerald City filmmaking was the release of the Tom Hanks and Meg Ryan blockbuster *Sleepless in Seattle* (1993). A strong contender for the top-ten all-time "date movies" list, the flick helped usher another wave of immigration to "the most liveable city in America!" (provided you live in a gorgeous houseboat, make a huge salary as a funky architect, have cool friends like Rob Reiner, etc.). Still, Vancouver currently reigns as the North-

west film capital. The truest sign of Vancouver's prominence can be seen in movies like *Stakeout* (1987), *Stay Tuned* (1992), *Another Stakeout* (1992), and *Man of the House* (1996). Each of these films was purported to be set in Seattle, but all were actually filmed in Vancouver, proving you can fool most of the flatworms most of the time. "Look Ma, aren't those mountains purdy. That sure is colorful money they use thar in the Northwest." Oh well. We're just jealous because it seems that "Hollywood North" has finally turned into "Hollywood Great White North" (with apologies to the McKenzie Brothers).

Throughout the history of network television, there have been a handful of shows that define a city or a region in the minds of the nation's viewers. What TV fans think of Boston without *Cheers*, Minneapolis without *The Mary Tyler Moore Show*, or Boulder without *Mork and Mindy*? All right, maybe not the last one.

The popular and critical success of *The X-Files*, *Frasier*, and *Northern Exposure* has probably accomplished the same thing for the Pacific Northwest, for better or worse. And although Northwesterners like to think they're too cool to care when a hit series spotlights the region, they still love to focus on picky mistakes. "Can you believe Frasier said U Double U! I mean, everybody knows it's U-Dub! Who's writing this show? Turn back to *Animal Planet*."

We know the real truth. Despite their outward indifference, Northwesterners are starstruck just like everybody else. The streets of Seattle were packed when the cast and crew of *Frasier* showed up in September 1997 to film the one-hundredth episode of the show on location in the Emerald City. And when *The X-Files* producers decided to move the series back to Los Angeles in 1998, you could hear the moaning all the way from Kamloops to Klamath Falls.

Despite the success of shows like *Frasier*, other Northwest-based or filmed series weren't on the prime-time schedule long enough for the ink to dry in the program guide—but that doesn't mean they weren't good! Here are ten of the most significant and interesting Northwest TV shows.

The Adventures of Tugboat Annie

Based in part on the life of Thea Foss, a turn-of-the-century tugboat operator from Tacoma, *The Adventures of Tugboat Annie* debuted in syndication in 1958. This Canadian-produced show was set in the fictional town of Seacoma (a cross between Seattle and Tacoma) and found Annie and her nemesis, Captain Horatio Bullwinkle, involved in endless schemes to outwit each other. Although thirty-nine episodes were produced over two years, the show never really caught on and was rarely seen after its initial run.

Here Come the Brides

The first bona fide network television show set in the Northwest, *Here Come the Brides* ran for two full seasons in prime time on **ABC** between 1968 and 1970. It was loosely based on the life of Seattle businessman **Asa Mercer** who had twice brought unmarried women ("Mercer Girls") from **New England** because he was having trouble retaining a labor force due to the lack of marriageable women. While *Here Come the Brides* had more historical inaccuracies than a Russian textbook, it did focus popular attention on Seattle with its cast of young stars, novel story line, and catchy theme song. Come on now, everybody sing: "The bluest skies you've ever seen are in Seattle." A *Here Come the Brides* fan club formed several years ago and a thirtieth-anniversary reunion held in 1998 in Los Angeles was attended by fan club members as well as former cast members.

The Beachcombers

A long-running (but unexciting) **CBC**-produced drama series that was set along the Pacific Coast of British Columbia, *The Beachcombers* debuted in 1972. The show followed the exploits of Nick Adonidas (played by the late **Bruno Gerussi**), a middle-aged beachcomber who motored up and down the coastline looking for salvage and adventure. Nick lived above a coffee shop owned by Molly Carmody who resided there with her two grandchildren. The show also featured Jesse Jim, Nick's First Nations partner. Initially shown on Sundays immediately following *Walt Disney*, *The Beachcombers* was widely popular in Canada and was sold in syndication around the world. The show ended its run in 1990.

Hello Larry

Hello Larry was **McLean Stevenson's** third and final shot at a network show of his own following his much-publicized departure from *M.A.S.H.* In this sitcom outing, Stevenson played Larry Alder, a radio talk show host who had just moved to Portland with his two daughters following his divorce. His call-in show on the fictional radio station **KLOW** was produced by Morgan Winslow (played by **Joanna Gleason**). Other costars included Harlem Globetrotters great Meadowlark Lemon as the owner of a local sporting goods store, and legendary blues singer Ruth Brown as Larry's schoolteacher neighbor. While **Kelsey Grammer** would find success behind a Northwest radio mike fifteen years later, *Hello Larry* lasted only fifteen months.

A Year in the Life

Joshua Brand and John Falsey produced this **NBC** drama that starred the late actor Richard Kiley as Joe Gardner, the patriarch of a large, upper-middle-class Seattle-area family. Joe was a widower (it's a little-known TV rule that all patriarchs must be widowers) with four adult children who had been brought back together after the untimely death of their mother. *A Year in the Life* was filled with every politically correct stereotype that typified Northwest living in the mid- to late eighties. Joe's kids were either yuppies or ex-hippies struggling with career angst, parenting angst, or relationship angst. While Kiley managed to win an Emmy Award for his efforts, it didn't keep *A Year in the Life* from expiring after the first season.

Danger Bay

This eighties half-hour television show was set in the Vancouver Aquarium in Stanley Park. *Danger Bay's* environmentally themed stories revolved around aquarium research director Dr. Grant "Doc" Roberts (Donnelly Rhodes) and his two children Jonah (Christopher Crabb) and Nicole (Ocean Hellman), who were always helping Dad with some Greenpeace-style mission such as rescuing an injured harbor seal or tracking down careless polluters. The show ran from 1984 to 1989 and can still be seen in reruns on the Disney Channel.

Twin Peaks

The most overhyped Northwest television show of all time was David Lynch's bizarre soap opera *Twin Peaks*. Set in the fictional town of Twin Peaks (located in Washington State somewhere near the Canadian border), the show starred University of Washington drama school graduate Kyle MacLachlan as FBI Agent Dale Cooper. Cooper spent his days investigating the brutal murder of a local high school student named Laura Palmer and visiting the MAR-T Cafe for damn good coffee and cherry pie. While this sounds like standard television fare, the other characters and story lines in *Twin Peaks* made *South Park* look like *Mr. Rogers' Neighborhood*.

Northern Exposure

Okay, so it was set in Alaska—it was filmed in the Northwest. Sue us. While *Northern Exposure* was as quirky as *Twin Peaks*, it wasn't downright weird, and what began as a summer replacement series in 1990 went on to become a mainstay of the CBS prime-time lineup for five seasons. The show chronicled the plight of Dr. Joel Fleishman (Rob Morrow), a recent New York medical intern forced to repay his scholarship by serving four years as the town doctor in Cicely, Alaska. The series was filmed on location in Roslyn, Washington, a small town on the eastern side of the Cascade mountain range. Story lines revolved around Fleishman's reactions to the eccentric characters who lived in the town.

Frasier

The most successful television show ever set in the Northwest is *Frasier*, a spin-off of a character originally created on the Boston-based TV hit *Cheers*. Kelsey Grammer plays the title role of Dr. Frasier Crane, the psychiatrist host of a local Seattle radio call-in show. When Frasier isn't dispensing pop psychology advice to the Emerald City masses, there are the predictable run-ins with his irascible father, Martin; his father's goofy English caretaker, Daphne; and fellow psychiatrist brother, Niles, played to the anal-retentive hilt by actor David Hyde Pierce. To celebrate the series' one-hundredth episode, cast and crew filmed a special show on location in Seattle in September 1997. Afterward, they promptly departed for a soundstage in Los Angeles.

The X-Files

The X-Files is Vancouver's heaviest export since Bachman-Turner Overdrive as well as the only Northwest television show to inspire a major theatrical motion picture. The series follows the adventures of FBI Agents Fox Mulder (David Duchovny) and Dana Scully (Gillian Anderson) who investigate cases with unexplainable elements. For the first five seasons, the show was shot on location in and around Vancouver and the lower mainland. Although the setting of the show rotates from episode to episode, Canadian fans grew accustomed to the sudden appearance of familiar landmarks such as the Grouse Mountain cable car tram ride and Tim Horton's donut shops (aliens like donuts, eh?). Sorry to say that in 1998 the aliens abducted *The X-Files* and moved it to Los Angeles.

MUSIC MUSIC MUSIC MUSIC

54-40

Perhaps Vancouver's premier "political rock" act (though DOA might also make that claim), 54-40 debuted at the Smilin' Buddah Cabaret in 1980. The name was derived from U.S. President James Polk's campaign slogan "54-40 or fight," which encouraged Americans to push the border with Canada to the fifty-fourth parallel. Their sharp melodies and political edge made it a campus favorite up and down the West Coast. Despite continued popularity in Canada, the 54-40 were unable to break through to a mass American audience. In the early nineties, they regrooved their sound to be softer (one of their songs was even covered by L.L. Bean poster band Hootie and the Blowfish), and 54-40 has continued to "soldier" on.

Adams, Bryan

The king of Canadian pop music, Bryan Adams was born in Kingston, Ontario, but raised in Vancouver following his parents' divorce. After graduating from high school, he formed a songwriting partnership with Jim Vallance of the Vancouver band Prism. Adams's commercial breakthrough came in 1983 with the album "Cuts Like a Knife," which featured a killer video of the title track, and the song "Straight from the Heart," which reached the Top Ten before the album was even released. Adams's 1984 release "Reckless" put him on the worldwide pop music map—six singles were released including "Run to You," "Heaven," and "Summer of '69," and the album sold more than five million copies. Bryan Adams helped organize the Canadian musicians' benefit for the famine in Ethiopia and headlined the Prince's Trust Fund charity concert in 1987 at Wembley Stadium. He also wrote the song "Everything I Do (I Do It for You)" for the 1991 film *Robin Hood: Prince of Thieves*, which spent fifteen weeks on the charts and was followed by the triple-platinum album "Waking Up the Neighbors." While his sales have recently slowed, Adams continues to perform and record.

Allen, Bruce

Born in 1945, Bruce Allen is a world-famous Vancouver-based talent manager who has hit it big three times: first with Bachman-Turner Overdrive in the seventies, then with Loverboy, and again with Bryan Adams in the eighties. Allen still manages a wide range of musicians (including Adams and country star Martina McBride) from offices in the historic Gastown District and hosts a popular radio show on CFOX radio Sunday evenings. *Vancouver* magazine recently named Allen one of the ten most influential arts and entertainment figures in the city.

Anderson, Ernestine

The first lady of Seattle jazz, Ernestine Anderson was born in Houston, Texas, in 1928. Her father moved the family to Seattle when she was fifteen, in part to keep Ernestine away from the temptations of the Houston nightclubs where she was beginning to sing. The Seattle jazz community, however, soon recognized her singing ability, and she began performing professionally in local clubs. In the early fifties, Anderson left town to sing with Lionel Hampton, among others. Her first album "Hot Cargo" was released in 1958, and she was featured on the cover of *Time* magazine as the "best new voice in the business." Despite this success, Anderson became disillusioned with the music industry during the sixties and withdrew from public life. In 1974, she was coaxed out of retirement to perform at Red Kelly's club in Tumwater, Washington, and her singing career was back on track. Anderson also was the namesake of a successful Pioneer Square jazz club. A series of successful albums on the Concord label followed, and she remains a strong force on the Northwest jazz scene today.

Bachman-Turner Overdrive

The "heavyweights" of the rock music scene in the seventies, Vancouver's Bachman-Turner Overdrive (later just "BTO") began in 1970 when guitarist Randy Bachman (formerly of the Guess Who), his brother Rob, Chad Allen, and C. F. "Fred" Turner formed a band called Brave Belt. After two albums on the Reprise label (and only modest success in Canada), Allen was replaced by Randy's brother Tim, and the group changed their named to Bachman-Turner Overdrive (the word "Overdrive" was borrowed from a trade magazine for truck drivers). BTO ruled in the Northwest, touring incessantly and playing anywhere they could be headliners. With chords as chunky as the band members and a new Mercury recording contract, BTO released their self-titled debut album in 1973, the first of four enormously successful recordings. Between 1973 and 1977, it was almost impossible to tune into any FM rock station in North America without hearing "Takin' Care of Business," "Roll On Down the Highway," "You Ain't Seen Nothin' Yet," and the BTO classic "Let It Ride." Randy Bachman left the band in the late seventies, though he would return for periodic reunions until the early nineties. BTO (version 6.0) continues to per-

form, releasing a CD anthology in 1993 and a new European album in 1997. Randy Bachman continues to record and tour as a solo artist. To make original BTO fans feel really old, Randy Bachman's son Tal has emerged as a successful artist on his own.

Blackwell, Bumps

Born in 1918, Seattle music promoter Robert "Bumps" Blackwell was part of the city's Jackson Street jazz scene, promoting a "junior band" that included the likes of Quincy Jones and jazz bassist Buddy Catlett. Blackwell was known for his promotional skills as well as his ability to take jazz music across racial lines. When the jazz scene in Seattle cooled in the late forties, Blackwell moved to Los Angeles, eventually becoming the producer for many of Little Richard's early hits. Blackwell continued to produce records until his death in 1985.

Bobby Taylor and the Vancouvers

Vancouver-based pop-soul band Bobby Taylor and the Vancouvers are probably more noteworthy for the individual members and discovery of Michael Jackson and the Jackson 5 than their musical abilities. Formed in Vancouver in the early sixties, the group at one time featured a young Seattle guitarist named Jimi Hendrix in its lineup. Bobby Taylor and the Vancouvers' biggest hit was "Does Your Mama Know About Me?" which was cowritten by the band's guitarist Tommy Chong, who went on to team with Cheech Marin as one-half of the 1970s comedy duo Cheech and Chong. After a couple other marginal singles, the group disbanded. Vocalist Taylor went on pursue a solo career.

Bobrow, Norm

Jazz performer and promoter, radio personality, newspaper columnist, restaurateur, and raconteur, Norm Bobrow is one of a handful of "renaissance men" who helped shape Seattle popular culture over four decades. *Seattle Times* columnist Don Duncan once wrote, "Trying to distill Bobrow in a newspaper-column size is like trying to dry up Lake Washington with a blotter. He is a bundle of paradoxes: Athlete and esthete, hard competitor and gentle philosopher, freedom-loving male and advocate of hearth and home." After moving from New York with his family in the thirties, Bobrow attended Roosevelt High School and then the University of Washington (UW). At the UW, he acted in and produced student shows, sparking the impresario in him. Soon, Bobrow was promoting shows around Seattle's famed Jackson Street jazz and blues scene—his first in 1941 featuring Fats Waller was later credited by *Downbeat Magazine* as being the first American theatrical jazz concert. Bobrow later founded the Colony nightclub, hosting the best music in the city and bringing Pat Suzuki to stardom in his cabaret productions. When Suzuki went to New York to seek Broadway fame, Bobrow went along as her manager, but he ultimately returned to Seattle. In other incarnations, Bobrow managed KXA radio, handled publicity for the Seattle Sounders soccer team, and wrote a column with his wife for the *Seattle Times* (*He Says, She Says*), continuing to promote fine jazz along the way.

Brothers Four, The

The Brothers Four were a popular folk quartet, formed in 1958 by University of Washington fraternity brothers Bob Flick, Mike Kirkland, John Paine, and Dick Foley. The group was discovered at the famous Hungry I in San Francisco by Dave Brubeck's manager and

Norm Bobrow is a jazz impresario and Seattle's man about town.
(Photo from *Seattle Post-Intelligencer* Collection, Museum of History and Industry)

soon signed a recording contract with Columbia Records. Their first two albums reached the U.S. Top 20 and their biggest hit "Greenfields" rose to number two, selling more than one million copies. The group continues to occasionally perform. Dick Foley went on to become a television personality on Seattle's KOMO-TV.

Charles, Ray

Ray Charles came to Seattle in the late forties as a teenager, staying for two years and honing the style that would bring him fame. Born in the South, Charles listened to advice to take his talent on the road. He picked Seattle and settled into the Jackson Street jazz scene. While in the city, Charles made his first radio and television appearances and cut his first single, "Confession Blues." He also met Quincy Jones and forged a lasting friendship. When asked by noted Seattle jazz historian Paul deBarros why he came to Seattle, Charles replied, "What do they call this—bar mitzvah?—where you come out as a man? I think Seattle was kind of like that for me."

Cherry Poppin' Daddies

Though best known nationally as a key instigator of the swing revival, the Cherry Poppin' Daddies have been playing an energetic mix of rock, swing, ska, and punk since forming in Eugene, Oregon, in 1989. Led by band founder and singer Steve Perry, the Daddies independently released a number of CDs before hitting it big in 1998 with "Zoot Suit Riot." The band is also noted for having one of the most politically incorrect names to ever make the national charts, with newspapers often listing the band as CPDs or simply the Daddies.

Chilliwack

The Vancouver band Chilliwack formed in the late sixties as the Classics and later changed to the Collectors. At that time, the group consisted of Bill Henderson, Claire Lawrence, Ross Turney, Howie Vickers, and Glenn Miller. The Collectors released two albums before changing their name again in 1971 to Chilliwack. The band then had a run of Canadian hits, beginning with "Lonesome Mary" and "What You Gonna Do?" Vickers and Miller eventually left and were replaced by Brian McLeod and Howard Froese. Chilliwack disbanded in the mid-eighties after a couple of reunion concerts. McLeod, who penned many of the group's later hits, died of cancer in 1992. Recently, Henderson has re-formed a new version of Chilliwack, playing occasional "classic rock" festival shows.

Commodore Ballroom

From the 1930s until its closing in 1996, the Commodore was downtown Vancouver's premier concert venue, featuring a "bouncing" dance floor. The Commodore operated as a speakeasy in its early years, becoming a rock palace in the 1960s. During its run, the Commodore hosted everything from big bands to rockers such as U2, the Clash, and Courtney Love. In early 1999,

Patrons at Vancouver's classic Commodore Ballroom felt very "swellegant."
(Photo courtesy of the Vancouver Public Library, photo 70488)

hospitality executive Roger Gibson and Bryan Adams's manager Bruce Allen announced plans to lease, renovate, and reopen the Commodore as a concert hall.

Cowboys, The

During the eighties, the Cowboys (along with their rivals the Heats) were kings of the Seattle bar scene. Led by wildman Ian Fisher, the Cowboys played a rock/reggae mix and were famed for volcanic live shows. They were unable to turn their local popularity into a national record deal and faded away by the end of the decade. The Cowboys' records have now been re-released on compact disc.

Cray, Robert

During the seventies Robert "Young Bob" Cray gigged furiously up and down the I-5 corridor from Eugene to Bellingham, establishing a reputation as a premier young blues star. From 1976 to 1982, the Cray band also featured a fiery harp player and singer named Curtis Salgado who inspired John Belushi to create the Blues Brothers during the filming of *Animal House* in Eugene in 1977. (Cray himself can be seen briefly in *Animal House* as a member of the Otis Day and the Knights band.) After Salgado left, Cray stepped to the microphone and achieved a national breakout in 1983 with the album "Strong Persuader." Over the next several years, Cray jettisoned his early band and moved to a sound that mixed soul and blues music. Cray continues to record and tour, though his base of operations is now the San Francisco Bay area.

⚡ Crazy 8s

The much-loved late eighties Portland band Crazy 8s helped pave the way for the swing and ska revival, though it never reaped national rewards for itself. The band is legendary for its "day of the eights" shows on August 8, 1988, when it played eight shows throughout the day at different locations, including one on the back of a flatbed truck cruising through downtown. The 8s broke up in 1995, but the band occasionally reunites for shows.

⚡ Crosby, Bing

Though he acted in Hollywood, touted Florida orange juice, and crooned the world over, Harry Lillis "Bing" Crosby was a Northwest boy. Born in Tacoma in 1903, Crosby inherited his famous nickname from the comic strip *The Bingville Bugle*. In 1906, his family moved to Spokane, where Crosby attended Gonzaga College. "Der Bingle" became a major benefactor for Gonzaga, which honors its favorite son with a statue in front of the student center and a "Crosbyana" room full of memorabilia. Crosby, always an avid golfer, died on October 14, 1977, only minutes after carding an 85 on the La Moraleja golf course near Madrid, Spain.

⚡ Crystal Ballroom

Opened in 1914, the Crystal Ballroom was Portland's grand concert venue until it closed in 1968. Some of the acts to appear at the Crystal were James Brown, Ike and Tina Turner, Big Brother and the Holding Company, and the Grateful Dead. While the music was first-line, the Crystal's claim to fame was its "floating" dance floor. A system of rockers and ball bearings was installed under the floor so it had a fluid motion, which could be adjusted for different dance styles. The always-tasteful McMenamin brothers made the Crystal a part of their crusade to revive cool Northwest places, renovating and reopening the ballroom in 1997. As part of the complex, the McMenamins opened Ringler's Annex, a tribute to Crystal founder Montrose Ringler.

Bing "Der Bingle" Crosby pulls into Union Station in his hometown of Tacoma.
(Photo courtesy of the Tacoma Public Library, Richards Collection, photo D13217-3)

deLay, Paul

A formidable man, Paul deLay is one of the Northwest's premier blues harp players, singers, and songwriters. A Portland native, deLay first hit the scene in 1970, finally forming his own band in 1979. Over the next decade the Paul deLay Band became a local favorite. The band's career was interrupted when deLay was sentenced to federal prison in 1990 for cocaine trafficking. In a remarkable gesture, the core of his razor-sharp band stayed together, teaming up with singer Linda Hornbuckle and renaming itself No deLay while awaiting the leader's return. When a clean and sober deLay emerged from prison in the mid-nineties the band picked up steam, signing a national record deal and beginning to tour nationally and in Europe. Guitarist Peter Damman also serves as talent coordinator for the long-running Portland Waterfront Blues Festival.

After a stint in "Club Fed," Paul deLay gained national blues prominence.

(Photo by Ross Hamilton)

Dennon, Jerry

Record producer and honcho of the Seattle-based Jerden label, Jerry Dennon first released the Kingsmen's classic recording of "Louie Louie." Jerden recorded many Northwest groups including the Dynamics, Don and the Goodtimes, Ian Whitcomb, and the Sonics. He also launched the short-lived Northwest music magazine *Disc a Go Go* in the sixties. In the nineties, Dennon, now living on Bainbridge Island near Seattle, has reactivated the Jerden label, releasing mostly archival material.

DOA

Vancouver's Joe Keithley, better known as "Joey Shithead," has led the longest-running punk act in Canada since forming DOA in 1978. The original DOA lineup, featuring Randy Rampage on bass and Chuck Biscuits on drums, produced uncompromising political punk, characterized by their 1984 anthology "Bloodied but Unbowed." Despite numerous personnel changes, including the tragic house-fire death of later drummer Ken "Dimwit" Jensen, Keithley soldiered on, gaining a new generation of fans that admired his persistence and integrity as well as the music.

Don and the Goodtimes

Keyboardist Don Gallucci had been an original member of the Kingsmen but was forced to quit when the group started to tour because he was still in high school. Undeterred, Gallucci and his friend Bob Holden formed the Goodtimes in Portland in 1964. Jim Valley, who went on to join Paul Revere and the Raiders, was also an early member. With Gallucci's driving organ, the group recorded a number of regional classics such as "Little Sally Tease" and "Sweets for My Sweet." Toward the end of 1966, Dick Clark asked the Goodtimes to become regulars on his teen show *Where the Action Is*, where the Raiders had gained national fame. The group soon signed with Epic Records and had a minor national hit with "I Could Be So Good to You." Unfortunately, ABC canceled *Where the Action Is* and the "Goodtimes" were over.

𝖂 Doug and the Slugs

Formed in 1977, Doug and the Slugs were Vancouver's entry in the power pop sweepstakes of tight bands with sharp lyrics and impossibly catchy melodies. Their sound caught on enough to get an American record deal, but the Slugs didn't expand their appeal to a wide audience. Returning to their base, band leader Doug Bennett and his mates remained active into the mid-1990s.

𝖂 duMaurier Jazz Festival

Every summer, top-name jazz musicians flock to Vancouver for this citywide event. Over a ten-day period, major concerts and intimate nightclub gigs abound, along with a smattering of free shows. The festival began in 1985 when Vancouver's Coastal Jazz and Blues Society launched a small event, hoping to attract a corporate sponsor in time for Expo '86. The duMaurier tobacco company signed on, and the festival has grown ever since. Canadian antismoking legislation prohibiting cigarette companies from being "name sponsors" will force the festival to change its name by 2001.

𝖂 Dynamics, The

A regionally popular group formed by the Afdem brothers (Terry and Jeff), Seattle's Dynamics were staples of the Northwest dance-hall circuit with a blend of blues and rock. In the early sixties, the group added vocal sensation Jimmy Hanna, recording an influential live album at Parker's Ballroom. Hanna left to form his own band, and by the mid-sixties, with a national hit proving elusive, the band renamed itself the Springfield Rifle. The Rifle scored one minor national hit in 1968, "That's All I Really Need," but couldn't follow up. The group disbanded in the late sixties, and Jeff Afdem went on to form a short-lived jazz group called the Springfield Flute.

𝖂 Eagles Auditorium

Also known as the Eagles Hippodrome, the Eagles Auditorium was the premier place during the sixties for hard rock concerts in Seattle (not to mention rampant drug use). Everyone who was anyone played the Eagles, from blues players such as Albert Collins to rockers such as Alice Cooper. The venue also hosted Seattle's first "Trips Festival," a wild music and light show attended by six thousand. After falling dark in the early seventies, the Eagles briefly reopened as a punk rock venue in 1983. The revival didn't last and the funky old hall (located next to the downtown convention center) has been turned into more tasteful digs for Seattle's A Contemporary Theater (ACT).

𝖂 Englehart, Little Bill

Reputed to have formed the first rock band in Tacoma, Little Bill Englehart had a national chart hit in 1959 with "I Love an Angel." Little Bill's original Bluenotes included bassist Buck Ormsby, who later would join the Wailers. Little Bill and Ormsby also discovered legendary Northwest rock front-man Rockin' Robin Roberts singing on a bench at the Puyallup Fair. Little Bill has reemerged on the scene in recent years, playing the tavern and festival circuit, releasing a number of blues-tinged recordings, and penning a column for local blues newspapers.

🎵 Experience Music Project

Microsoft cofounder Paul Allen buys what most guys would love to buy—except he shops on a scale befitting one of the world's richest men. If you liked Jimi Hendrix, you might buy a boxed set and a video. Allen bought a bunch of Hendrix's guitars and planned an entire museum to honor the guitarist. That Hendrix project has now morphed into the Experience Music Project (EMP). The EMP, which is building a state-of-the-art facility at the Seattle Center, will spotlight Northwest music and Hendrix in the context of a broader look at rock and roll. The original sheet music to "Louie Louie," Nirvana's original contract, the mixing board from Hendrix's Electric Lady Studio, and rare Northwest recordings are among the seventy thousand artifacts collected by the museum (so far). The unusual design of the museum (some describe it as looking like clumps of crumpled, colored foil) has drawn both interest and criticism.

🎵 Fleetwoods, The

The Fleetwoods—Gary Troxell, Gretchen Christopher, and Barbara Ellis—were one of the nation's most popular doo-wop groups in the late fifties and early sixties. Taking their name from the local Olympia telephone prefix, the Fleetwoods formed while attending high school in the capitol city and began performing a song called "Come Softly to Me" at various events around town. Seattle-based Dolphin (later Dolton) Records released the song in early 1959, and it became an instant hit, climbing to number one on the pop charts and number five on the R&B charts. Their next single "Mr. Blue" was also a number-one hit the same year. When Troxell left the group at the end of 1959 after being drafted

by the Navy, singer Vic Dana replaced him. The Fleetwoods continued to have a string of Top 40 hits, but disbanded in 1963 as doo-wop music gave way to the British Invasion. While not widely remembered today, the *All Music Guide* notes that the Fleetwoods were "one of the few white vocal groups of the late fifties and early sixties to enjoy success not only on the pop charts, but also the R&B charts."

🎵 G, Kenny

Though jazz critics and purists hack up a hairball at the mention of his name, Kenny "G" Gorelick has built a huge following for his smooth, airy instrumentals. Born in Seattle in 1959, Kenny G began playing professional sax at the tender age of seventeen in Barry White's Love Unlimited Orchestra. After that stint, he enrolled at the University of Washington, keeping his hand in music by playing in a local funk band. After college, he returned to music full time, starting with the Jeff Lorber Fusion, and then launching a solo career in the early eighties. Since then, he has become an automatic million-selling artist. The "G man" is also known for his unusual ability to use a special breathing technique to sustain a single note for up to forty-five minutes.

🎵 Garage Rock

Garage Rock is shorthand for the raw and raucous music that emerged from the Northwest in the late fifties and early sixties. While garage bands could be found throughout the region, Tacoma is usually recognized as "ground zero" of this influential scene. Some Tacoma bands, such as the Wailers, played a New Orleans-flavored rhythm and blues. Others, such as the Sonics, made a volcanic thrash that later influenced grunge bands like Nirvana. Everyone played "Louie Louie." Because the Northwest was out of the mainstream of the rock industry, local bands had to adopt a "do-it-your-self" (DIY) ethic, promoting their own shows, releasing their own records, and publishing their own music. While the Northwest scene didn't make a huge national commercial splash, it had an influence out of proportion to its sales. Some musicians, such as Jerry Miller and Don Stevenson of Seattle's Frantics, were recruited to form other important bands (in this case Moby Grape). British acts, including the Beatles and the Kinks, have acknowledged that the Northwest-sound musicians—particularly the model of writing, performing, and producing music as a self-contained unit—influenced their approach. Later, punk bands, which embraced the DIY approach, looked to the early Northwest rockers for inspiration. Recently, a new generation has begun to discover the roots of Northwest music as early records by the Wailers and the Sonics have been rereleased on CD.

Grunge Rock

Grunge Rock is the nickname for the dirge-like, slow, angst-filled rock that emanated from Seattle in the late eighties and early nineties. Grunge bands were known for their flannel shirts, unkempt manner, and grinding music. As loud as punk but slowed way down, grunge seemed a fine match for Seattle's prodigious gray and rainy weather—in a word, foreboding. Other attributes of the grunge scene were a fierce independence, rejection of rock star trappings, and "do-it-yourself" ethic that influenced a rise in self-released CDs and self-promoted shows. The Seattle music scene—with grunge at its center—is reasonably captured by Cameron Crowe's 1992 movie *Singles*, which featured cameos by members of

Pearl Jam and Soundgarden, along with Sub Pop label founder Bruce Pavitt. During this period, record company executives camped in Seattle, signing virtually every band that had an aggressive name and could string together three chords. A backlash ensued, leading to songs such as the Smithereens' "Sick of Seattle." Prototypical grunge bands include the Melvins, Nirvana, Soundgarden, early Pearl Jam, and Mudhoney. By the mid-nineties the term had died out, killed partly by local musicians who saw it as limiting and stereotypical.

Guitar, Bonnie

Born Bonnie Buckingham in Seattle in 1923, Bonnie Guitar was an accomplished session guitarist in Los Angeles in the 1950s when she made her debut on the country charts in 1958 with her composition "Dark Moon." That same year, she formed the locally famous Dolton record label in Seattle and began to record local acts, including a doo-wop trio from Olympia called the Fleetwoods, which had two million-selling records for Dolton. Wishing to concentrate on her own career, Bonnie sold Dolton and in the 1960s scored Top 10 country hits with "I'm Living in Two Worlds," "(You've Got Yourself) A Woman in Love," and "I Believe in Love." Bonnie Guitar continued to tour and record into the 1980s.

Guthrie, Woody

His Northwest stay may have been brief, but Woody Guthrie left a legacy of music to the region during the early forties. As part of the effort to bring electricity to rural areas, the Bonneville Power Administration had been building dams, running transmission lines, and encouraging local areas to form public power districts. BPA was running into serious friction from private power interests and needed to find a strategy to captivate the public. They hired Guthrie to write a series of folk songs, telling the story of bringing electricity to the public. One of the songs—"Roll on Columbia"—has been recognized as Washington State's official folk song.

◼ Heart

The queens of FM radio throughout the 1970s and 1980s, Seattle's Heart formed in the mid-1970s, playing "Zeppelin-style" rock to adoring audiences throughout the Northwest. Fronted by Ann Wilson—one of the premier female rock singers of all time—and her guitar-slinging sister Nancy, Heart churned out a steady stream of hits. Heart's debut album, "Dreamboat Annie," which was recorded in Vancouver and released on the local Mushroom label, went on to become one of the biggest regional hits ever. A legal row ensued with Mushroom claiming to be owed a second album and the band wanting to jump to a major label. As a result, fans soon found themselves presented with two new Heart albums—the major label "Little Queen" and the cobbled-together Mushroom product "Magazine." Despite the contractual troubles, the band soon established itself as the premier woman-fronted band of its day, with hits including "Barracuda" and "Even It Up." By the early 1980s, Heart's fortunes began to slide, in-band romances crumbled, and sales began to decline. Early members, including guitarist Roger Fisher, bassist Steve Fossen, and drummer Michael DeRosier, were replaced. It looked like a "Heart attack," but in the mid-1980s Heart changed labels and became wildly popular practitioners of the romantic power ballad. In recent years, Heart has been largely inactive. The Wilson sisters have begun a new, acoustic band called the Lovemongers and have toured as a duo. Nancy Wilson has released a solo album, and Ann Wilson has dabbled in cabaret singing.

◼ Heats, The

Fronted by songwriters Steve Pearson and Don Short, the Heats (originally the Heaters) were Seattle's entry in the power-pop sweepstakes of the early 1980s. They packed local clubs, and though their songs were radio-friendly three-minute gems, they were unable to break out nationally. A local label has released a Heats retrospective, including their local single hit "I Don't Like Your Face." The Heats recently reunited for a series of gigs around the Puget Sound area.

◼ Hendrix, Jimi

Born Johnny Allen Hendrix in 1942 (later renamed James Marshall Hendrix by his father), the boy who would become the world's most famous rock guitarist grew up in Seattle's Central Area. During the period that Hendrix attended Meany Junior High School and Garfield High School, he learned to play the electric guitar. He formed his first band, the Velvetones, in 1958 and later teamed up with a local group called the Rocking Kings. Hendrix also frequented the Seattle club Birdland, where local music giant Dave Lewis held court. Lewis would let the young Hendrix sit in with his band on occasion, though his experimental style would leave the audience perplexed. Hendrix left Seattle in 1961 to join the U.S. Army, ultimately landing in New York. During this period, Hendrix served as a session player and sideman for bands, including Bobby Taylor and the Vancouvers. After his death in 1970, Hendrix was buried in Renton's Greenwood Memorial Park. His grave is a frequent stop for rock fans. In the early 1990s,

Microsoft cofounder Paul Allen, a Hendrix fan and all-around incredibly rich guy, announced plans to build a Hendrix museum in Seattle, which eventually evolved into the Experience Music Project.

Hovhaness, Alan

Recognized as one of the most distinctive and prolific American classical composers, Alan Hovhaness was born in Somerville, Massachusetts, and roamed the world before settling in the Seattle area in 1972. His most highly regarded symphonies, including "Mount Saint Helens," have drawn on Northwest themes and have been recorded by the Seattle Symphony Orchestra under the direction of Gerard Schwarz.

Johnny and the Distractions

Led by a dramatic and passionate singer named Jon Koonce, Johnny and the Distractions ruled the Portland bar scene in the early 1980s. Distractions concerts were high-energy affairs. According to a former band member, "We would start shows with the band playing this driving, building rhythm. And he'd (Koonce) start at the back of the stage, running, and dive off the front of the stage, land on his knees, and slide across the dance floor. He used to do that all the time. It just ruined his knees, but he didn't care. Whatever it took—that was his whole attitude about rock 'n' roll." The Distractions made it to A&M records, but their national career stalled and they retreated to the Northwest. Koonce later formed a well-received roots rock trio called the Gas Hogs and continues to perform in Portland. A Distractions compilation CD is available on Portland's Burnside Records label.

Jones, Quincy

Quincy Jones spent his childhood in Bremerton, Washington, and moved to Seattle in 1947. He played in the Garfield High School concert band and was eventually recruited into the Bumps Blackwell Junior Band, the creation of an influential local music promoter. During this period, Jones forged enduring relationships with the cream of Seattle musicians, including Ray Charles. Jones's first real break came with Lionel Hampton's Orchestra in the early 1950s, and he has become a music business legend.

Jr. Cadillac

Throughout the 1970s and early 1980s, Seattle's Jr. Cadillac was the Northwest's premier bar band. Formed in 1970 by Ned Neltner, formerly with the Gas Company, and Buck Ormsby, previously with the Wailers, the band plays danceable, rhythm-and-blues-influenced rock and roll. A big national break never came, but Jr. Cadillac continues on, touring relentlessly and releasing strong albums on its own Great Northwest Record Company label. Though the band works a reduced schedule today, it continues to produce fine original music and cover an eclectic mix of older songs. Cadillac was featured on *Northern Exposure* in the popular episode "Mud and Blood."

K Records

A much-admired label from Olympia, K Records is a prototype of the DIY (do-it-yourself) spirit of Northwest music. Label instigator Calvin Johnson returned to Olympia to attend college and was involved in 1977 with a Northwest fanzine *Sub Pop* (which would later give rise to that famous record label). Johnson also worked at KAOS radio, the Olympia community station located at the Evergreen State College and distinguished by a fierce commitment to independent music. The combination led Johnson in the early 1980s to form K Records, which has become—along with the later arriving Kill

Rock Stars—a label with influence out of proportion to its sales. Johnson also is a recording artist with two bands—Beat Happening and Dub Narcotic Sound System.

▥ Katims, Milton

As conductor of the Seattle Symphony from the 1950s to the early 1970s, Milton Katims became a star in his own right, even appearing on the cover of the 1966 Seattle phone book. Although not ranked among the great conductors of our time, Katims was flamboyant and not afraid to take symphony music to the people. He organized neighborhood concerts, family concerts, and a "music in the schools" program, showing that symphony music wasn't just the province of the cultural elite. As the 1970s dawned, however, Katims's star began to wane and he was unceremoniously shown the door in 1973. In an act of gracelessness, the Symphony didn't invite Katims back as a guest conductor until 1992.

Seattle Symphony Conductor Milton Katims became a cultural superstar in the 1960s.
(Photo from *Seattle Post-Intelligencer* Collection, Museum of History and Industry)

▥ Kaye Smith Studios

The Northwest's first entry into the world of big-time recording studios, Seattle's Kaye Smith was named for its founders, entertainer Danny Kaye and radioman Lester Smith. During the seventies, the studio played host to the biggest acts of the day, including BTO and Steve Miller. In the early nineties, Heart's Ann and Nancy Wilson bought the studio with Seattle producer Steve Lawson, renaming it Bad Animals and opening a state-of-the-art recording room that attracted R.E.M. and Soundgarden. The Wilson sisters have since sold their interest but the studio lives on, now concentrating on media post-production and commercial work.

▥ Kelly, Red

Longtime Northwest jazzman and club owner Red Kelly is also famous as the instigator of the biggest spoof on Washington State politics in history. Born Thomas Kelly in 1927, he is a first-rate bassist, having played with the likes of Harry James, Stan Kenton, and Woody Herman. In 1974, Kelly opened the Tumwater Conservatory. While there, besides helping to relaunch Ernestine Anderson's career, he formed the OWL party, which stood for Out With Logic, On With Lunacy, running several very tongue-in-cheek candidates for state office. Kelly later opened Kelly's Nightclub in Tacoma.

▥ Kingsmen, The

In 1963, a modestly successful Portland band named the Kingsmen gathered at producer Ken Chase's Northwest Recording Studio to create three minutes of rock history. Because the studio was designed for voice recordings, not music, the microphones were placed in awkward locations. Lead singer Jack Ely had to stand on his tiptoes and shout the

Wet & Wired

lyrics to the ceiling. The resulting garble became the glorious noise of "Louie Louie." Whether it was because of the drunken party feel of the song or the controversy over the "dirty" lyrics buried in the muddy vocal, "Louie Louie" was a world-wide smash. There was just one problem. Jack Ely had left the band to form his own "Kings-men" group. The remaining members carried on, but none sounded like Ely, so they lip-synched their hit to his vocal. Litigation ensued, with the result that Ely could no longer use the band's name, and the band could no longer use his vocal track. The Kingsmen persevered, touring throughout the sixties and releasing a number of successful albums, though never again reaching the heights of "Louie Louie." A re-formed version of the Kingsmen (not including Ely) remains popular on the Northwest club and fair circuit. In 1998, the Kingsmen won a long-standing lawsuit over unpaid royalties for "Louie Louie."

The Kingsmen: "Louie Louie, we gotta load the truck now."
(Photo from *Seattle Post-Intelligencer* Collection, Museum of History and Industry)

Lake Hills Roller Rink

During the 1960s, Lake Hills Roller Rink (located in the Seattle suburb of Bellevue) was a premier stop for disc jockey Pat O'Day's dance circuit, hosting all the major regional bands. During the eighties Lake Hills got a second life, becoming what one critic called the "epicenter of Eastside heavy metal." Local metal legends such as Culprit and Overlord were Lake Hills regulars, paving the way for the grunge scene to come. One Bellevue band, Rail and Company (later just Rail), gained fame in 1983 by winning MTV's Basement Tapes competition. Rail became a frequent opening act for groups such as Van Halen and Blue Oyster Cult, but was unable to break through to national fame.

Lewis, Dave

When he died of cancer in 1998, Dave Lewis was unknown to most Northwest music fans. In the 1960s, however, keyboardist Lewis was one of the most popular Seattle musicians, breaking through to a national audience with songs such as "Little Green Thing" and "David's Mood." Local music scholars credit Lewis as the originator of the Seattle "jungle beat"—a heavily syncopated sound best heard on the Kingsmen's hit version of "Louie Louie" (which Lewis claimed to be his arrangement). Lewis often played local clubs such as the Birdland where in the late fifties a young boy named Jimi Hendrix would beg to sit in. Lewis would agree and the boy would unleash the first of the guitar solos that would propel Hendrix to fame a decade later.

Little Mountain Sound

The famous recording studio Little Mountain Sound in Vancouver is best known as home to some of the great "air-punching" rock anthems of the 1980s. Drawn by the talents of in-house producer Bruce Fairbairn, groups like Bon Jovi, Motley Crue, Whitesnake, the Cult, AC/DC, David Lee Roth, and the granddaddy of them all, Aerosmith, recorded some of their most commercially successful albums at Little Mountain Sound. Bon Jovi's breakthrough "Slippery When Wet" album was a tribute to the legendary Vancouver strip clubs favored by many bands recording at Little Mountain. The studio also inadvertently became known as the "Betty Ford Center" of recording studios as many of these bands had long-standing drug and alcohol abuse problems and came to Vancouver to dry out and reclaim their musical success. One of the more notorious stunts at Little Mountain Sound was pulled by singer David Lee Roth, who commissioned a painting of one of his favorite strippers on the outside studio wall. Local authorities were not amused.

⚡ Love, Courtney

Courtney Love is the leader of Hole, one of the most critically and commercially successful alternative bands of the nineties. For many, however, Love's music has been overshadowed by her marriage to Nirvana's leader Kurt Cobain. She married Cobain in 1992, giving birth to their daughter, Frances (named after tragic Seattle movie star Frances Farmer), and fighting allegations of heroin abuse. After Cobain committed suicide in April 1994, Love stunned a memorial gathering at the Seattle Center by reading a raw, profane, and cathartic missive to her dead husband. Two months later Hole bassist Kristen Pfaff was found dead of a heroin overdose in Seattle, but Love slogged on, finding a replacement and continuing to tour. Branching out, Love won an Academy Award nomination for her portrayal of Larry Flynt's wife Althea in *The*

People vs. Larry Flynt. She also has continued to record and tour with Hole.

⚡ Loverboy

Quintessential 1980s arena rock band Loverboy hailed from Vancouver. Front man Mike Reno wailed, Paul Dean played chunky lead guitar, bassist Scott Smith and drummer Matt Frenette set down a fat bottom, and Doug Johnston washed it all with keyboards. (A pop culture side note: Frenette is reported to have suggested a nose job to a pre-rock star Courtney Love when he saw her performing at one of Vancouver's notorious strip clubs.) Hit after hit followed, including "Turn Me Loose" and "The Kid is Hot Tonight." After a short run at the top, album sales dried up, and by the end of the 1980s the band was no more. In the late 1990s Loverboy re-formed (sans spandex pants), playing nightclubs and releasing new material, though not with their early results.

⚡ McLachlan, Sarah

Born in Halifax, female rock diva Sarah McLachlan was persuaded to move west by Mark Jowett (one of the founders of Nettwerk Productions) when her band opened for his group, Moev. McLachlan moved to Vancouver in 1987 and soon began a solo career. Her fame built slowly but steadily, breaking through in the United States with "Fumbling Toward Ecstacy" (1993). McLachlan's next album, "Surfacing" (1997), established her at the top ranks of rock stars. Whatever McLachlan's career holds, however, she is destined to be remembered as the founder, inspiration, guru, star, and motivator of the Lillith Fair, an all-female-package rock tour that captured the imagination of concertgoers and record buyers during the late 1990s.

⚡ Melvins, The

Hailing from Montesano, Washington, the Melvins are credited with inventing grunge, taking hardcore punk music, slowing it down, and making it sonically dense. The Melvins were featured on Sub Pop's Deep Six compilation, often considered the "ground zero" of grunge music. Melvins guitarist Buzz Osborne (also known as King Buzzo) and drummer Dale Crover were in early bands with a resident of nearby Aberdeen named Kurt Cobain. Osborne and Crover eventually moved to California, where the Melvins live on, having survived a major label deal to return to their grunge indy roots.

⚡ Mother Love Bone

Considered a forerunner of the grunge "Seattle Sound" of the early 1990s, Mother Love Bone featured the powerful vocals of Andrew Wood fronting the bass of Jeff Ament and the guitar of Stone Gossard. Wood died of a heroin overdose just before the release of the band's debut recording, "Apple." Ament and Gossard went on to form the highly successful Pearl Jam.

⚡ Munsel, Patrice

Spokane songbird Patrice Munsel gained fame in 1943 as the youngest (seventeen years old) performer ever signed by New York's Metropolitan Opera. She remained with the Met until 1958, starring in numerous productions, including *Die Fledermaus*. After leaving the Met, Munsel broadened her repertoire, starring in musical comedies and nightclub shows, and lecturing across the country. In 1974, Munsel

made a triumphant return to Spokane to appear at Expo '74. The official Expo commemorative book noted, "She sang their favorites, from *Madame Butterfly* to the Beatles, with a fillip of hard rock. The capacity audience loved every minute of it—even to the display of her pet, a boa constrictor."

⚡ Music Millennium

Owner Terry Currier has kept Portland's Music Millennium a fiercely independent outpost for three decades, featuring a wide selection of local music. Currier is legendary for taking on the big record distributors who wanted to crack down on used record sales. He held a Garth Brooks CD barbecue, attracting media attention and backing off the big boys. Currier also founded Burnside Records, releasing albums by local favorites Johnny and the Distractions and Terry Robb, among others.

Music Millennium owner Terry Currier protested record company policies by holding a Garth Brooks CD barbecue.
(Photo courtesy of Music Millennium)

⚡ Muzak

Seattle-based provider of "background and foreground audio environments" (yes, that's the new name for elevator music), Muzak has been around since the 1920s, but it was in the mid-1980s that the company entered into a private-label agreement with Yesco, the Seattle originators of "foreground" music. While Muzak re-recorded songs for background play, Yesco compiled reel-to-reel tapes of current original artist hits to be used as foreground music. Muzak's most lasting contribution to modern pop culture may have been as an employer for many members of Seattle's grunge musicians during the mid-1980s, as well as future Sub Pop honcho Bruce Pavitt.

⚡ Nettwerk Productions

The Vancouver-based label and management company Nettwerk Productions was formed originally in the late 1980s to pro-

Seattle's Muzak invades Vancouver's PNE (Pacific National Exhibition) in the early 1960s.
(Photo courtesy of the Pacific National Exhibition, City of Vancouver Archives, photo CVA180-2349)

mote the music of the band Moev. The label distinguished itself by its mission of bringing Vancouver alternative music to the world. Its biggest coup came when a label founder discovered the young Sarah McLachlan in Halifax and persuaded her to come west to start a solo career.

⚡ Nirvana

The suicide of Kurt Cobain in 1994 provoked a catharsis in Seattle. Thousands gathered at the Seattle Center to mourn the musician, news reports were filled with remembrance and speculation. All this for a musician whose band (at the time) had released just three studio albums (like Jimi Hendrix) and a collection of B-sides. Cobain and Nirvana came to symbolize Seattle grunge to the world—flannel shirts, dark lyrics, and hard

Nirvana's Kurt Cobain was the Seattle grunge sound to millions worldwide.
(Photo by Tom Reese, *Seattle Times*)

Wet & Wired

music. Nirvana formed in Aberdeen, Washington, a coastal mill town where Cobain hooked up with bassist Krist Novoselic. They perfected their sound in Olympia, often playing shows in the dorms at the Evergreen State College. Nirvana signed with the then-new Sub Pop label and recorded the album "Bleach" for a pittance. After "Bleach," the group replaced drummer Chad Channing with Dave Grohl and the lineup that would storm the world was complete. Nirvana signed to Geffen Records (the deal included a royalty for Sub Pop that helped keep that label afloat) and their now-classic album "Nevermind" was released in 1991. It sold more than thirteen million copies, contained the anthemic "Smells Like Teen Spirit," and gave birth to a highly successful Weird Al Yankovic parody. Controversy dogged the band, which struggled with Cobain's heroin addiction and the need to produce a follow-up record. Rumors surfaced that the next album "In Utero" had been rejected for being unlistenable but, while the album was harder edged, it became a sizable hit. During this period, Cobain married Courtney Love and fathered a child named Frances Bean Cobain (after tormented Seattle actress Frances Farmer). Ultimately, the pressure cracked Cobain. He attempted suicide in Italy with an overdose of pills. The next time, he took no chances. After leaving a rehab program he returned to Seattle, purchased a shotgun, and around April 8, 1994, shot himself to death in his Lake Washington home. Two posthumous live albums have been released, one of which (MTV Unplugged) won a Grammy Award. Since Nirvana, Krist Novoselic has gone on to form the band Sweet 75, meeting with limited commercial success. Novoselic also has become politically prominent, forming JAMPAC, which advocates on issues of interest to musicians. Dave Grohl formed the highly successful Foo Fighters. In 1999, Cobain was named artist of the decade by *Rolling Stone* magazine, and "Nevermind" was named the top Northwest album of all time by the *Rocket*, an influential Seattle-based music publication.

Nixon, Marni

The most famous behind-the-scenes vocalist in motion picture history, Marni Nixon was also the host of a popular kids' show in Seattle for many years. Nixon provided the singing voice for Audrey Hepburn in *My Fair Lady*, Deborah Kerr in *The King and I*, and Natalie Wood in *West Side Story*. She also played the role of Sister Sophia in the film *The Sound of Music*. Her Northwest connection came as host of a children's TV show called *Boomerang*, which aired on Seattle's ABC-affiliate KOMO during the 1970s.

Noah, Tim

Kids' performer without peer, Tim Noah has been entertaining Northwest children since the late seventies. An early member of the Seattle kid music band Tickle Tune Typhoon, Noah went off on his own, recording and releasing his albums. He struck paydirt in the mid-eighties with an album and video titled "In Search of the Wow Wow Wibble Wobble Wozzie Woodle Woo," leading to a national recording contract. An energetic performer, Noah blends rock and roll moves and songs with kid-friendly lyrics. Most recently, Noah has been hosting a Seattle-produced kids' television show called *How 'Bout That*, along with his frequent concert appearances in the Puget Sound area.

Northcott, Tom

A Canadian folksinger whose career has spanned four decades, Tom Northcott began singing in 1963 in Vancouver coffeehouses, notably the Inquisition. Northcott eventually signed with Warner Brothers and recorded several songs, including "Girl from the North Country," "The Rainmaker," and his most famous single, "I Think It's Gonna Rain Today." In 1969, Northcott built a recording studio in Vancouver, producing acts including the Irish Rovers. Although he stopped performing in 1973, he resurfaced in 1990 when his song "The Trouble with Love" hit the country charts.

Page, Jim

Seattle's premier protest singer Jim Page got his start working the streets around the Pike Place Public Market and the University of Washington campus. He soon earned a reputation for tuneful, witty, and pointed songs advocating the interests of the oppressed. As the folk music market struggled in the eighties, Page increasingly toured in Europe, releasing several albums. In recent years, Page has split his time between Europe and the Seattle area.

Parker's Ballroom

One of the last standing examples of the "roadhouse," Parker's Ballroom (located on Aurora Avenue just north of Seattle) was built in 1928 and hosted the best in jazz, big-band, and swing music in the 1930s and 1940s. During the 1950s rock and roll acts began to appear at Parker's—in 1956 the old roadhouse served as the location for a locally televised teen dance party. Music changed, and so did Parker's, which evolved into a hard rock concert hall during the 1960s and 1970s (changing its name to the Aquarius). The Aquarius was a beer- and marijuana-saturated regular stop for national acts, both up and coming and old and fading. Heart was a frequent starring act at the Aquarius, recording songs that were eventually released on the disputed "Magazine" album. By the early nineties, the music stopped and the Aquarius became a sports bar, but recently the original name Parker's was restored along with occasional live concerts.

Paul Revere and the Raiders

One of the most successful groups ever to hail from the Pacific Northwest, Paul Revere and the Raiders were formed in Boise in 1961 when keyboardist Paul Revere hooked up with vocalist/sax player Mark Lindsay. They relocated to Portland and eventually were discovered by popular KISN disc jockey Roger Hart, who became the group's manager. As with most Northwest bands, the Raiders recorded a version of "Louie Louie." Though it wasn't a national success, it did lead to a contract with Columbia Records. The band moved to Los Angeles and became regulars on the Dick Clark-produced show *Where the Action Is*, honing a reputation for wild, comedic performances with stage costumes direct from the Revolutionary War. A string of hits followed, including "Just Like Me," "Kicks," "Hungry," and the Raiders' stab at social consciousness, "Indian Reservation." Numerous personnel changes and changing tastes sapped the original band, which packed it in by the early 1970s. Today Lindsay performs as a solo act, and Paul Revere continues to lead a group of Raiders on the casino and fair circuit.

Pearl Jam

Formed after Mother Love Bone vocalist Andrew Wood died from a heroin overdose, Pearl Jam became the most successful band to emerge from Seattle during the 1990s. Mother Love Bone bassist Jeff Ament and guitarist Stone Gossard found singer Eddie Vedder, guitarist Mike McReady, and drummer Dave

Krusen and went on to make a powerful noise. The band's first album "Ten" sold more than nine million copies, but Pearl Jam was distinctly uncomfortable with rock star fame. When they released their second album in 1993 ("Vs"), the band refused to shoot any music videos. Pearl Jam embarked on a tour of smaller venues in 1994 to be closer to fans. And, in one of the most brilliantly futile gestures in rock history, Pearl Jam refused to let Ticketmaster handle ticket sales for their 1994 summer tour. All the while, Pearl Jam rotated drummers, first to Dave Abbruzzese, then to Jack Irons, and most recently to former Soundgarden member Matt Cameron. In an unusual side project, Pearl Jam recorded an album with Neil Young in 1995 ("Mirror Ball"), though the band is not credited as a unit. Many observers believed that Pearl Jam had seen its fifteen minutes at the top, but the band rebounded strongly in 1998, kissing and making up with Ticketmaster, mounting a critically and commercially successful tour, and releasing a live album. Most recently, Pearl Jam released a popular version of the 1960s' chestnut "Last Kiss," donating profits to Kosovo refugee relief.

Pied Pumkin

Vancouver's Pied Pumkin was formed in the early seventies by guitarist Joe Mock from Regina, Saskatchewan, dulcimer player Rick Scott, a native Texan who had fled to Canada to avoid the Vietnam War, and vocalist Shari Ulrich. Their swinging folk sound made them the toast of the hippie dance circuit for a number of years, before Ulrich left for a solo career. (Scott and Mock carried on as the "Pear of Pied Pumkin.") On their own Squash label, the band (with and without Ulrich) released the albums "Pied Pumkin String Ensemble," "Pied Pumkin Allah Mode," and "The Pear of Pied Pumkin." Another album fol-

lowed in 1980 with a larger group of musicians, and both Mock and Scott toured again in 1989 to promote "The Lost Squash Tapes." The group, including Ulrich, has recently re-formed to perform several reunion concerts in the Vancouver area.

Poppy Family

Vancouver-based purveyors of soft hippie pop, the Poppy Family were led by songwriter/producer Terry Jacks with his wife, Susan, on lead vocals. After a string of hits, including "Which Way You Goin' Billy" and "Where Evil Grows," Terry Jacks left the band, and he and Susan divorced. Terry Jacks reemerged in 1973 with a macabre song that consistently makes the lists of worst songs ever recorded—"Seasons in the Sun." The public disagreed, snapping up more than eleven million copies. He couldn't follow up the success, however, and retreated to a career in music production. Susan Jacks eventually moved to Nashville and attempted to come back as a country singer, with limited success.

Presidents of the United States of America

Formed in Seattle in 1993 by Chris Ballew, Dave Dederer, and Jason Finn, the Presidents had a short but brilliant run at the top. Characterized by goofy, catchy songs ("Lump"), the group was known for its odd instrumentation—Ballew played a two-string bass and Dederer a three-string guitar. It didn't matter—their first locally released album was picked up by Columbia and went straight to the Top 10. A second album, though strong, failed to sustain the momentum, and the Presidents disbanded in early 1998. Since then, the group has occasionally reunited, most recently to work with Seattle rapper Sir Mix-A-Lot.

Quarterflash

A popular "arena rock" act of the early 1980s, Quarterflash began as the Portland band Seafood Mama. Led by the husband and wife team of Marv and Rindy Ross, Seafood Mama featured a loose, swinging sound, Rindy's soulful vocals and sax, and the impossibly catchy song "Harden My Heart." As Seafood Mama, the band did sell-out business at top nightclubs throughout the Northwest. When Geffen Records signed the Rosses to a national deal, the name Seafood Mama and the other band members were jettisoned in favor of a harder rock sound. "Harden My Heart" reached number one on the rock charts, and over the next few years Quarterflash produced four albums and sold more than two million records. Toward the mid-1980s the hits dried up, and the Rosses folded Quarterflash in 1991, returning to Portland. After a three-year break, they formed a new Quarterflash, appearing locally, and also began occasionally appearing again under the name Seafood Mama. Today, the Rosses have once again hung up the Quarterflash name, instead appearing in musical productions based on Oregon history.

Rainbow Tavern

During the seventies, Seattle's Rainbow Tavern was the very definition of "funky dive." Located in the University District, the small club had metal folding chairs, grungy toilets, cheap Rainier beer, and big-time music. Local bar favorites such as Jr. Cadillac held court at the Rainbow, and soon-to-be-famous bluesman Robert Cray was a regular. A victim of changing tastes, the Rainbow closed in the mid-1980s, to be replaced by a strip club and, later, an Irish pub.

Reilly and Maloney

Along with Birkenstock sandals, a low REI co-op number, and an aging Volvo, a Reilly and Maloney album in the collection was essential equipment for "Northwest Mellow People." When they joined forces in San Francisco in 1969, David Maloney and Ginny Reilly could not have predicted the hold they would exert on the Northwest folk music scene. In the rest of the country their name drew nods of recognition; here they were major concert draws and their albums best-sellers. Playing locations like the Silver Spoon (a funky and fondly remembered restaurant and folk club in Duvall, Washington, near Seattle), Reilly and Maloney charmed audiences with gentle tunes and good humor. When they split up in 1989, their final concert was held at Seattle's elegant Fifth Avenue Theater. During the ensuing decade, Reilly performed infrequently, branching out into jazzier music, while Maloney continued to work the folk circuit, often appearing as a children's musician. In 1999, Reilly and Maloney reunited for a series of well-received concerts.

Roberts, Rockin' Robin

Legendary vocalist for the Wailers, Rockin' Robin Roberts was discovered by Little Bill Englehart and future Wailer Buck Ormsby singing on a bench at the Puyallup Fair. Roberts's intense R&B style helped the Wailers' version of "Louie Louie" become an enormous regional hit. Roberts left the Wailers in the mid-1960s and moved to California. A possible reunion was in the works when he tragically died in a 1967 car accident. Recently, fans in Tacoma raised donations to buy a proper headstone for Roberts's grave, and the reunited Wailers have played benefit concerts to fund a music scholarship in his name.

⚡ Rush, Merilee

With her backing band the Turnabouts, Seattle's Merilee Rush was the Northwest's musical sweetheart for two decades. Rush worked the Northwest teen dance circuit relentlessly—a local writer described her as ". . . pleasantly plump in all the right places. She would smile all the time and when she bounced up and down as she played her organ, her hair would swing from side to side. She was the PTA-approved 'girl next door'—live and in person." After landing some local hits, Rush signed with national label Bell Records. During a tour of the South, opening for Paul Revere and the Raiders, Rush was discovered by legendary Nashville producer Chips Moman who had her record "Angel of the Morning." The success of that single made Rush a top touring and television attraction, but eventually the hits and exposure dried up and she returned to the Seattle area. Rush performed regularly into the 1980s and now makes occasional appearances.

⚡ Salgado, Curtis

A top-notch blues vocalist and harp player, Portland's Curtis Salgado fronted early versions of the Robert Cray band and Roomful of Blues before launching a solo career. His records are excellent and performances dynamic, but Salgado was guaranteed at least a footnote in pop culture history in Eugene in 1977. It was during the filming of *Animal House* that John Belushi caught Salgado's performance at the Eugene Hotel with Robert Cray. Salgado and Belushi became friends and spent many evenings listening to the blues, with Salgado providing a tutorial on blues music and blues style. These after-hours sessions

became the creative fuel for the Blues Brothers. In fact, careful liner note readers will see that the first Blues Brothers album is dedicated to Salgado (though the royalties went to Belushi).

⚡ Schuur, Diane

Diane Schuur is a Seattle jazz vocalist who has sometimes favored pop standards to the dismay of jazz fans and critics. Blind since her birth in 1953, Schuur (also known by the nickname "Deedles") has a remarkable three and one-half octave range. Discovered at the Monterey Jazz Festival in 1979 by jazz legend Stan Getz, she soon signed a recording contract with GRP Records. She has continued to record and tour to the present day. Schuur has been awarded two Grammys and has performed at the White House. More recent recordings have returned to her jazz roots.

⚡ Shank, Bud

One of the charter members of the West Coast jazz movement, Bud Shank hails from Port Townsend, Washington. Shank first came to prominence as a member of both the Charlie Barnett and Stan Kenton big bands in the 1940s, followed by a long stint with the Lighthouse All-Stars. A respected saxophonist, composer, and arranger, Shank has an instantly recognizable "cool sound" that made him a highly sought-after studio musician for film and television work in the 1950s and 1960s. In 1974, he formed the LA Four (with Ray Brown, Laurindo Almeida, and Jeff Hamilton), popularizing Latin-flavored and chamber jazz. For fifteen years, Shank has sponsored the Bud Shank Jazz Workshop held in concurrence with the annual Port Townsend Jazz Festival in July. Although more than seventy years old, Shank maintains an ambitious performing, recording, and teaching schedule.

🎜 Sir Mix-A-Lot

The Northwest will never be known as a rap hotbed, but when Seattle's Sir Mix-A-Lot is in the house a good time will be had by all. Mix-A-Lot began recording in the late 1980s, but it was 1992's "Mack Daddy" that put him on the national map, thanks largely to the single "Baby Got Back," a raucous tribute to the glories of oversized female posteriors. Locally, Mix-A-Lot is beloved for his song "Posse on Broadway," which takes its audience on a cruise through his favorite Seattle spots, including "Dick's where the cool hang out." Mix-A-Lot's commercial star waned during the mid-1990s, though he recently has been plotting a comeback with members of the Presidents of the United States of America.

🎜 Sky River Rock Festival

One of the first outdoor rock festivals in the world was held between August 31 and September 2, 1968, on a muddy pasture near the Skykomish River and the town of Sultan, Washington. Billed as the "Sky River Rock Festival and Lighter than Air Fair," the event featured musical acts such as the Grateful Dead, Country Joe and the Fish, and Santana, as well as comedian Richard Pryor and the San Francisco Mime Troupe. Employees of Seattle's underground newspaper the *Helix* had much to do with the festival's organization and promotion, which drew twenty thousand people during the three-day celebration.

🎜 Sonics, The

The original "bad boys" of Northwest rock and roll, the Sonics formed in 1963 in Tacoma in the wake of the success of other Northwest "garage rock" bands such as the Kingsmen and the Wailers. Featuring the screeching, feedback-laden guitar playing of Larry Parypa and the harrowing vocals of Gerry Roslie, the Sonics quickly earned a reputation as a raunchy and gritty band that sounded like punk rock long before anyone knew what to call it. Noted rock critic Dave Marsh has called the Sonics "the rhythmic and attitudinal grandfathers of Nirvana, Soundgarden, and Pearl Jam." Their most famous song "The Witch" became the all-time best-selling local rock single in Northwest history, and other songs like "Psycho," "Strychnine," and "He's Waitin" were admired by everyone from Bruce Springsteen to the Sex Pistols. Despite their regional popularity, the Sonics were never able to build a national audience and disbanded by the end of the 1960s. Roslie tried to re-form the band in 1979 with a new lineup but met with limited success. A compilation CD titled "The Ultimate Sonics" was released in 1994, rejuvenating local and national interest in the band.

🎜 Soundgarden

For more than a decade, Soundgarden helped define the dark and dense grunge sound. Vocalist Chris Cornell and guitarist Kim Thayil labored for years in the clubs of Seattle, releasing numerous singles, EPs, and albums on small labels before getting a major label deal in 1990. The real commercial breakthrough occurred in 1994 with "Superunknown," launching the band into the front ranks of American rock groups. Never comfortable with stardom, the band continued on until 1997. Seattle residents also enjoyed Thayil—a hirsute giant—in a recurring skit on KING-TV's *Almost Live!* show in which he and other members of the Seattle heavy-metal music community proclaimed various people, products, and places to be "LAME!" with much tossing of their abundant locks.

Spanish Castle

The most famous dance hall in the Pacific Northwest, the Spanish Castle near Midway on Pacific Highway South in Seattle had been a popular ballroom in the 1920s and 1930s. In 1959, the Castle reopened as a rock and roll club, playing host to national acts such as Jerry Lee Lewis, Roy Orbison, and Jan and Dean, as well as Northwest bands such as the Frantics, the Dynamics, Little Bill and the Bluenotes, and the Ventures. A local teenager named Jimi Hendrix attended many of the Castle shows and later recorded a tribute song called "Spanish Castle Magic" for his second album, "Axis: Bold as Love."

Sub Pop Records

Sub Pop Records is a Northwest label that stood at the epicenter of the Seattle sound. Bruce Pavitt was a student at the Evergreen State College in 1979 when he launched a small 'zine called *Subterranean Pop*. Thrown at the face of disco and corporate rock, Sub Pop trumpeted alternative music, eventually resulting in a number of compilation cassettes. Pavitt folded the 'zine and started a column in the *Rocket*, a Seattle-based regional music magazine. In 1988, Pavitt hooked up with Jonathan Poneman and they pooled their resources to create Sub Pop Records. Early releases included singles by Green River, Soundgarden, and Nirvana. Pavitt and Poneman may have had impeccable taste in music, but their lack of business savvy almost took the label down. Then Geffen Records signed Sub Pop act Nirvana, resulting in royalty payments that served as financial "CPR" for the label. Sub Pop continued to be the bellwether of the Seattle sound, but the glory days were over as bigger Sub Pop acts, such as Soundgarden, left for major labels. In 1994, Warner Music bought a 49 percent stake in the company. By 1997, Pavitt and Poneman were feuding, but they eventually reached an accommodation. Today the label remains active, though dogged by periodic rumors of financial turmoil.

Ventures, The

The most popular rock instrumental group of all time, the Ventures were formed in Tacoma in 1960 by Bob Bogle and Don Wilson, both construction workers who played guitar in their off hours. Adding Nokie Edwards on guitar and bass and Howie Johnson on drums, the Ventures first hit the national charts with the infectious

The Ventures, the greatest-selling instrumental rock band in the world, are from Tacoma.
(Photo courtesy of the Tacoma Public Library, Richards Collection, photo A126221-35)

"Walk, Don't Run." Mel Taylor replaced Johnson in the drummer's chair in 1963, a slot he held until his death in 1997. Edwards drifted in and out of the band, replaced by Nashville session ace Gerry McGee, but the Ventures' original sound—surf-informed rock instrumentals—has never strayed. Fittingly, the group's best-known song may be the "Theme from Hawaii Five-O." During dry spells in the United States, the Ventures took their act abroad, finding their greatest success in Japan. Today's Ventures include Bogle, Wilson, McGee, and Mel Taylor's son Leon.

Wailers, The

Often considered the most influential early Northwest rock band, the Wailers formed in Tacoma in 1958. Playing raucous rhythm-and-blues-influenced songs, the Wailers went on to dominate the regional dance scene for more than a decade, formed their own self-contained recording and publishing empire, and caught the notice of key British rockers, including the Beatles and the Kinks. Early group members included John Greek and Rich Dangel on guitar, Mark Marush on sax, Mike Burk on drums, Kent Morrill on keyboards and vocals, and Buck Ormsby on bass. While early Wailers songs, including the hit "Tall Cool One," were instrumentals, by the early sixties they began to add vocals. At one point, the Wailers added songbird Gail Harris and wildman Rockin' Robin Roberts to the mix, turning their show into a full-out rock and roll revue. Despite their enormous popularity in the Northwest, the group was unable to fully break out nationally. Members came and went—some of the later members like saxman Ron Gardner became Northwest stars in their own right—and a long decline

began. By 1970 it was over, but twenty-five years later it was starting up again. As a new generation of Seattle musicians emerged, the Wailers were rediscovered. Reunion concerts followed, attended by the Seattle rock music elite, and by 1998, a core group of Wailers (Ormsby, Dangel, and Morrill) was playing well-received shows, re-releasing old material and recording new songs.

Zulu Records

A longtime Vancouver independent record company previously known as Quintessence Records, Zulu Records is home to numerous local indies. Zulu also has released important compilations of Vancouver's late 1970s and early 1980s music, featuring Terminal City favorites the Modernettes, Young Canadians, and Pointed Sticks.

Tacoma's hard-working Wailers were regional garage rock favorites in the 1950s and 1960s.
(Photo courtesy of the Tacoma Public Library, Richards Collection, photo A120694-4)

Despite the increasing fragmentation of radio formats and the fickle tastes of the record-buying public, there is still something special about scoring a number-one hit. For a musician, it's the ultimate sign of mass acceptance (except for being on the cover of Rolling Stone, but that was Dr. Hook's song and they're not from the Northwest, so it doesn't count). Over the years, Northwest artists have had a decent share of number-one hits, particularly for a region whose claim to fame has been low-budget, "do-it-yourself" garage and grunge music. Who are our number-one hitmakers and what songs took them to the top?

Portland's **Raiders** (formerly Paul Revere and the Raiders) rode social consciousness to the top in August 1971 with their version of "Indian Reservation." (Remember the droning beat and the lyric "Cherokee people, Cherokee tribe, so proud you lived, so proud you died"?) After hearing a version of the song by Don Fardon that was a hit in Britain, Raiders lead singer Mark Lindsay pegged the song for a solo record. Instead, he chose to record and release the song under the Raiders banner, giving the group its last chart hit. Ironically, the Raiders' only number-one single was a departure from the driving party music that was their original claim to fame. The single sold more than three million copies and, at the time, was the biggest-selling single ever for Columbia Records.

In 1974, the beefy boys of Vancouver's **Bachman-Turner Overdrive** were close to the top of the rock world. The band's second album, featuring "Takin' Care of Business" and "Let it Ride," had broken the band to a national audience. Now it was time to record a follow-up. During the sessions for what would become the "Not Fragile" release, Randy Bachman penned a little ditty and deliberately stuttered the vocals as an inside joke for his brother. It seems that Gary Bachman, the band's first manager, had a speech impediment, and the song was intended to be a private brotherly tribute. While the song wasn't intended for release, everyone who heard it thought "potential big hit." A re-recording with straight vocals didn't have the same effect, so finally Bachman relented and let "You Ain't Seen Nothin' Yet" out as a single. Whereas critics slammed the song as derivative of the Who's "My Generation," the fans ate it up. By November of

1974, the song climbed to number one on the singles chart, propelling sales of the album as well. The song and album would be BTO's commercial peak.

Seattle is not known as a rap town (some folks here consider Kenny G funky), but during the summer of 1992 **Sir Mix-A-Lot** got us some respect. During a video shoot for an early single, Mix-A-Lot heard women on the set complaining that they couldn't get work because their bottoms were—uh—too bottomy. Sensing injustice (not to mention a potential hit), Mix began concocting his paean to posterior pulchritude. His tribute to tush, "Baby Got Back," spent five weeks at number one beginning in August 1992. The single's success propelled the album "Mack Daddy" to be the biggest of Mix's career. In a cheeky promotional move, Mix-A-Lot's record label hauled a giant inflatable buttocks from record store to record store. A later tribute to a different part of the female anatomy ("Put 'em on the Glass") reached a commercial dead end.

The first Northwest band to score two number-one hits was the **Fleetwoods,** who took "Come Softly to Me" to the top in April 1959. The Olympia-based vocal trio had been performing the song in high school and caught the ear of record producer Bob Reisdorff. The original version was called "Come Softly" but the producer thought the title a bit raunchy and added the additional words (hard to imagine that happening today). The Fleetwoods scored their second number-one hit in November with the follow-up "Mr. Blue," a tune that had been originally intended for the legendary R&B group the Platters. The Fleetwoods continued to record until the mid-1960s but the British invasion soon spelled doom for their style of gentle balladeering.

Given **Heart's** enormous mainstream success and radio-friendly songs, it's a little surprising that they have only two number-one hits,

both coming during their mid-1980s comeback. The Seattle-based band earned its fame on the Northwest bar band circuit, blending powerful rock with cosmic ballads reminiscent of Led Zeppelin. The formula ran dry by the early 1980s, and it looked like Heart was a spent force. New producer Ron Nevison encouraged Heart to augment their own songs with outside material in an effort to restore chart success. Heart first reached number one with the power ballad "These Dreams" in March 1986, featuring a rare lead vocal by Nancy Wilson (the video also featured a generous sampling of her sizable charms). A similar dramatic approach took "Alone" up the charts in August 1987, this time sung by usual lead vocalist Ann Wilson.

That leaves us with the King of Northwest Number One—Vancouver's **Bryan Adams.** Adams won legions of fans throughout the Northwest for his rockers, but it once again took power ballads to reach the top of the chart. The first Adams song to land at the top was "Heaven," drawn from the multiplatinum "Reckless" release. The song had originally been recorded for the laughable movie *A Night in Heaven,* starring Christopher Atkins as a male stripper. After declining sales the next few years, Adams became the Kenny Loggins of the nineties—the master of the movie love song. The new approach yielded three more number-one songs. "Everything I Do (I Do It For You)" from *Robin Hood: Prince of Thieves* topped the charts in July 1991. "All For Love" (with Rod Stewart and Sting) from the *Three Musketeers* went to number one in January 1994. Finally, "Have You Ever Loved a Woman" from *Don Juan De Marco* hit the top in June 1995. Adams's sappy ballad approach hasn't won universal acclaim—the 1999 movie version of *South Park* features a fictitious apology from the Canadian government for his music.

And how did the two songs that defined different eras of Northwest music fare on the charts? While Northwest music fans love them, they couldn't scale the peak of the Billboard charts. The Kingsmen's version of the garage rock anthem "Louie Louie" topped out at number two for six weeks in 1963. Almost thirty years later, Nirvana's sonic blast "Smells Like Teen Spirit" edged up to number six in January 1992.

If the Northwest ever does secede from the rest of the United States, the choice for a national anthem will be easy—it's "Louie Louie" time. It may have been written by a Californian (the late Richard Berry), but "Louie Louie" has become the unofficial rock song of the Pacific Northwest. In 1985, the Washington State Legislature actually gave serious consideration to changing the state song from the lugubrious "Washington, My Home" to "Louie Louie," but soon thought better. For years, "Louie Louie" has been played at all Seattle Mariners home games during the seventh-inning stretch.

But which version of "Louie Louie" should we choose? While most people are familiar with the Kingsmen's garbled classic—particularly as drunkenly rendered by John Belushi and company in the film *Animal House*—that only scratches the surface of the available versions.

Feeling a little stressed? Then kick back with New Orleans clarinetist Pete Fountain's easy-listening version from the late 1960s. Need some more edge in your life? Look no farther than the metal band Motorhead, which cut a version in 1978. The 1960s British invasion weighed in with a version by the Kinks. Even Frank Zappa honored Louie, by including orchestral snippets of the tune on his 1968 masterpiece "Uncle Meat." If you're a purist, of course, you'll want the late composer Richard Berry's Caribbean-tinged lament. Not bad for a little ditty about a lonely sailor.

Although "Louie Louie" has been recorded by all manner of musicians, from all corners of the world, no place has a better feel for the song, or more recorded versions available, than the Pacific Northwest. Sorting through the versions takes time, but some stand out as being essential to a well-rounded Northwest record collection.

The Kingsmen

Though critics will argue over whether it's the best version, Portland's Kingsmen scored the biggest hit. The crude recording technique they used led to a wonderfully garbled vocal. Of course, this resulted in charges of obscene lyrics made by people who no doubt years later saw sexual images in every Disney film. Get a life, people—it's just a record. Insist on the original with Jack Ely on lead vocals or you'll be disappointed.

150

Paul Revere and the Raiders

Their version is distinguished by Mark Lindsay's big honking sax intro. The studio version, which was first released on Portland's Sande label in 1963, is the best. The Raiders, wearing what Paul Revere would later call their "Revolutionary War Fruit Suits," would ride this version of "Louie" to a national recording contract and fame on the ABC television show *Where the Action Is*.

The Wailers

A bit slower paced than the Kingsmen or Paul Revere, the Wailers' version also opens with a blast of saxophone, followed by Rockin' Robin Roberts chiming in on lead vocals. This 1961 version was a big regional hit for "the boys from Tacoma" and inspired the Raiders and Kingsmen to record their more successful takes. The Wailers were renowned for their live shows and never really captured their full energy on record.

The Sonics

Want to know where punk music came from? Listen to this. Northwest music writer Victor Moore says, "Gerry Roslie's vocal delivery is bereft of dynamics—he starts off like a hog caller on amphetamines (picture Sam Kinison with a band)." Produced in 1966 by Buck Ormsby of the Wailers for the Etiquette label, this version is worth seeking out, if only to amaze your children that people could play guitar like that back in the olden days.

Jr. Cadillac

Led by Ned Neltner, Seattle's Jr. Cadillac is the keeper of the flame of early Northwest music. Cadillac has cut "Louie" a number of times, but it's worth finding the Northwest version (complete with locally themed lyrics) they released in the mid-1980s when the Washington State Legislature actually considered making "Louie Louie" the state song. Like the Wailers' version, this "Louie" is slower paced and captures some of the Caribbean feel of the Richard Berry original.

Don and the Goodtimes

Don Gallucci was in the version of Portland's Kingsmen that recorded the hit version of "Louie Louie." Still in high school, Gallucci couldn't tour and had to leave the band. What to do? Form another band and cut your own version of "Louie Louie," of course. The Goodtimes' version is fun with lots of banter among the band members. In a bit of Northwest rock cross-pollination, Goodtimes lead guitarists Jim Valley and Charlie Coe both became members (at different times) of Paul Revere and the Raiders.

Little Bill and the Bluenotes

Little Bill's take on "Louie Louie" predates even the Wailers and is the most distinctive of the key Northwest versions. It's a slow, bluesy rendition that scored from airplay for the Tacoma band, but didn't reach hit status. Bluenotes bassist Buck Ormsby would go on to record "Louie" with the Wailers and Jr. Cadillac.

University of Washington Husky Marching Band

The Husky marching band is most famed for its lusty rendition of "Tequila," but it also tried its hand at "Louie Louie." It's perfect background music for lying in your hammock, imagining yourself sitting in Husky Stadium for a big game, eating a grapefruit that you had injected with vodka. Not that we are suggesting that people would actually do such a thing.

Tracking down the original albums that feature these "Louie" versions is a great way to start building a Northwest music collection. For those who want to cut to the chase, both Rhino Records and the Northwest-based Jerden label have released "Louie Louie" collections. The Rhino collection ranges far and wide for its "Louies," while the Jerden release features the key Northwest versions. If repeated listening triggers a "Louie" epiphany, you can also check out Eric Proedal's "Louie Report" (www.louielouie.net) for more history about the Northwest's number-one song.

ATTRACTIONS, PLACES, AND EVENTS

24-Hour Church of Elvis

A little slice of guerilla art plopped smack-dab in the middle of downtown Portland, the 24-Hour Church of Elvis has been spreading the vision of Stephanie Pierce since the mid-1980s. Pierce is a former telephone company lawyer who had a broader vision of how to spend her days. She chucked the law, worked on a cruise ship for a spell, and eventually landed in Portland, starting a number of "participative" art projects before gravitating to the King. Pierce's "Church"—which also uses the slogan "Art for the Smart"—is known for its display of spinning Elvis liquor bottles.

Alaskan Way Viaduct

If there is a really big earthquake in Seattle, the Alaskan Way Viaduct is one place you really don't want to be. An old double-stack highway, the Viaduct travels along the Seattle waterfront carrying nearly one hundred thousand cars a day from the Pike Place Public Market to Safeco Field. The Viaduct was erected between 1949 and 1953, well before current earthquake construction standards were adopted. It is built on fill and tide-flat deposits used to reclaim and extend the waterfront in the early 1900s. These deposits are considered likely to "liquefy" in the event of a severe quake. Transportation planners are studying whether the Viaduct can be reinforced to meet current earthquake codes or whether the structure must be torn down.

Alligator Palace Theater

The Northwest has long had a strain of "new vaudeville" performers (including the world-famous Flying Karamazov Brothers), but none have been more beloved than Reverend Chumleigh, who held court at the Alligator Palace in La Conner, Washington. The good reverend would appear accompanied by his faithful companion Brodie, Dog of the Future (billed as the only dog in the world with a doctorate in economics). Chumleigh was a regular at street fairs and festivals, but in the seventies he established a home base in La Conner, opening the small Alligator Palace Theater and contributing to the

The spirit of the King lives on in the kitschy Portland 24-Hour Church of Elvis art gallery.
(Photo by John Farrand)

village's reputation as hippie artist haven. The Palace has since closed, but Chumleigh continues to make the rounds.

◢ Archie McPhee

The Northwest's best place to find rubber chickens, fake vomit, magic 8 balls, and other weird oddities is Archie McPhee, located in Seattle's Ballard District. Since 1986, pop culture artifacts of all kind can be found at Archie McPhee, along with in-store experiences like Motog, the Terrible Talking Tiki God; the world-famous Glow Chamber; and the infamous Row of Heads. An Archie McPhee catalog, strategically placed on the coffee table or commode, is a sure conversation starter.

◢ Architectural Novelties

Unlike Southern California, the Northwest is not overrun with weird roadside architecture, but the few examples that exist are cool enough to be considered worthy of Route 66

status. The Java Jive tavern, located in Tacoma's Nalley Valley, is shaped like an enormous coffeepot. Inside, the Jive has a tacky jungle motif (live monkeys used to be on display until animal-rights fans got squeamish). In Seattle's Georgetown neighborhood, the abandoned Hat and Boots gas station sits lonely behind a chain-link fence, begging for Paul Allen to open his pocketbook and finance a renovation. Built in 1953 as the "Premium Tex" gas station, the site features a large cowboy-hat-shaped building, where people paid for their gas, and an enormous pair of cowboy boots, which served as men's and women's restrooms. Closed since 1988, California car magnate Cal Worthington once tried to move the Hat and Boots to his Federal Way dealership, but even in disuse, Hat and Boots is jealously protected by its Georgetown neighbors. Finally, North Seattle's Greenlake neighborhood is home to the still operating Twin Tepees restaurant on Aurora Avenue (old Highway 99). Opened in 1937, the restaurant and bar are housed inside two connected concrete teepees. The menu is classic road food (with

particularly enormous breakfasts) and the drinks are plentiful and stiff.

◢ Asarco Smelter

Notorious for spewing arsenic for years throughout North Tacoma, the Asarco Smelter, with its huge smokestack, was a fixture of Tacoma industry (and environmental controversy) from the 1890s until its closure in 1985. Arsenic is a by-product of the copper smelting process, and emissions covered a wide circle around the plant, forcing area residents to stop growing vegetables and leading some to complain of a metallic taste in their mouths.

Tacoma's Java Jive tavern used to be home to two monkeys named, oddly enough, Java and Jive.
(Photo courtesy of the Tacoma Public Library)

156

Wet & Wired

As environmental awareness grew in the 1960s, the smelter came under increasing attack from people concerned about long-term health risks. The battle became a classic "environment vs. jobs" tussle, with Asarco finally closing the plant. A class-action lawsuit followed and was settled in 1995, with Asarco agreeing to pay nearby residents nearly $70 million and continue environmental cleanup at the former plant site.

B&I Circus Store

By roadside attraction standards, Tacoma's B&I Circus Store was world class. In the forties and early fifties, the store was a fairly standard clothing, hardware, and military surplus operation. Fortunately, owner Earl Irwin had a flair for promotion, luring customers with gimmicks such as dumping ice in the parking lot and offering cash to the person who correctly guessed when it would melt. Irwin also brought in the stars of the day, such as Duncan Reynaldo (the Cisco Kid), to wow the locals. However, Irwin's greatest triumph was yet to come. In the late 1950s, a circus ran into financial trouble and needed its llamas boarded. Sensing a great promotional opportunity, Irwin offered up his facility and the B&I was forever transformed. By the sixties, visitors to the B&I were greeted with a menagerie of bear cubs, a baby elephant, seals, lions, a baseball-playing chicken, and a cute gorilla named Ivan. In the more "natural" seventies, public attitudes toward animal displays began to change. Earl Irwin died in 1973 and his son Ron began to disperse the menagerie. Without the draw, B&I slowly declined and today the structure is an indoor "mini-mall" hosting an odd assortment of small vendors and an arcade.

Benson Hotel

Portland's classic downtown hotel was the brainchild of lumber baron Simon Benson, who wanted Portland to have a world-class hostelry. Using the finest European materials, the Benson opened its doors in 1912. The hotel was originally known as the "New Oregon" and was patterned on Chicago's luxurious Blackstone. After opening, the hotel almost folded, forcing Simon Benson to take over active management. Benson renamed the hotel after himself and restored its finances before selling out. During the 1950s and 1960s, the Benson's food service operation employed Max Birnbach, who later built Rose's restaurant into a local institution.

Bigfoot

Whether you call him Bigfoot, Yeti, or Sasquatch, sightings of the "wild man of the woods" abound in the Northwest (more than 250 sightings so far). The bigfoot is usually portrayed as a tall, hairy ape-man—think Chewbacca from *Star Wars* but worse-smelling and less articulate. Two Yakima-area residents, Roger Patterson and Bob Gimlin, were responsible for a famed 1967 filming of a bigfoot just south of the Oregon and California border. Over the years, the film has withstood numerous scientific studies, though many still believe it to be a brilliant hoax. Hollywood validated the Northwest's Bigfoot credentials in 1987 with the family hit *Harry and the Hendersons. Harry* was the story of what happens when a typical movie family adopts a typical movie Sasquatch and brings him home to live with them in Seattle's Wallingford neighborhood.

Boeing Bust

In 1970, overly optimistic projections about the demand for air travel and Congress's decision to shelve the Supersonic Transport (SST) project resulted in a major financial crisis for the Boeing Company. Between 1970 and 1972, Boeing laid off a total of sixty-five thousand employees—two-thirds of its total workforce. Since Boeing was (and still is) the largest private employer in the Puget Sound area, a major economic recession resulted with local unemployment running at 12 percent. Things got so bad that during the period, a famous billboard message appeared in the city that read, "Will the last person leaving Seattle please turn out the lights?" The Puget Sound economy has diversified greatly since the Boeing bust, but downturns at the "Lazy B" still send shivers down the spines of local economists.

⚡ Bubbleator

The spherical, glass-walled Bubbleator served as the centerpiece of the Washington State Pavilion at the 1962 Century 21 Exposition (Seattle World's Fair). Visitors to the exhibit would board the Bubbleator and rise into a "forest" of aluminum cubes on which were projected colored lights, films, and slides, all synchro-

To many longtime locals, the Seattle Center has not been the same since the Bubbleator was taken out of the Food Circus.

(Photo courtesy of the Special Collections Division, University of Washington Libraries, photo UW 13111)

nized to a space-age soundtrack. After the fair ended, the Bubbleator was purchased from the state for fifty-one hundred dollars and relocated to the Seattle Center Food Circus (later called the Center House), where it carried passengers between floors until the mid-seventies. Sold to private interests, the Bubbleator now resides in a backyard south of Seattle, but its memory lives on. The music played on the Bubbleator during the World's Fair has recently been re-released on compact disc ("Attilio Mineo Conducts Man in Space with Sounds").

⚡ Bumbershoot

Every Labor Day, the Seattle Center is crammed cheek to jowl with hundreds of thousands of arts fans, sampling national musical headliners, local favorites, and artists and craftspersons of all description. Bumbershoot has become one of the nation's top arts festivals, but its founding (as Festival 71) in 1971 was a bit more humble. Back then, the festival was free to attend and headlined by country novelty singer Sheb Wooley (remember "The Flying Purple People Eater"?). The name Bumbershoot didn't debut until 1973. For the next several years, Bumbershoot expanded in its number of days and ambitions, until financial losses triggered a door charge and a change in producer (to the folks behind the One Reel Vaudeville Show). The mix of acts was changed to include more crowd-drawing national headliners including Chuck Berry, Elvis Costello, the reunited Sex Pistols, Bonnie Raitt, and David Byrne. Fortunately, Bumbershoot still makes room for top blues and country acts, occasional comedy performers, and extensive art displays. With

Wet & Wired

nearly thirty years under its belt, Bumbershoot has matured into a reliable, predictable institution.

⚡ Butchart Gardens

What was once a bleak pit in a worked-out quarry has become one of the most famous attractions in the Pacific Northwest. The Butchart Gardens, located just outside Victoria, began in 1904 as the reclamation project of Jenny Butchart, wife of a prominent cement manufacturer. After exhausting a limestone quarry near the couple's home on Vancouver Island's Tod Inlet, Butchart began a refurbishment project that she called "Sunken Garden." Little by little, the gardens expanded and soon visitors began coming each year to see Butchart's creation. Still under family ownership, Butchart Gardens boasts more than one million bedding plants and seven hundred varieties ensuring uninterrupted blooming from March through October (just like it says on those ubiquitous giant billboards that pop up on interstate highways headed into the Northwest).

⚡ Century 21 Exposition (Seattle World's Fair)

More commonly known as the 1962 Seattle World's Fair, the Century 21 Exposition had originally been intended to occur in 1959, commemorating the fiftieth anniversary of Seattle's first big-time event, the Alaska-Yukon-Pacific Exposition. Better late than never, for the 1962 fair left a legacy that continues to shape Northwest popular culture. Running from April 21 to October 21, the fair drew nearly ten million visitors (and ended up in the black!). The science-heavy theme was settled on after the Soviet Union launched its Sputnik satellite in 1957, fueling American fears of a "science gap." The choice of a scientific theme helped attract funding and commitments

from major exhibitors. It also doomed the fair to looking a bit like a *Jetsons* rerun, but that's part of its charm. A significant architectural legacy from the fair stands today, guarded zealously by the Seattle electorate. Besides the Seattle Center grounds, the Space Needle, Monorail, and the Pacific Science Center all remain big tourist

Victoria's original "sunken gardens," Butchart Gardens beckons drivers from giant billboards on Interstate 5 and Interstate 90.
(Photo courtesy of the Vancouver Public Library, photo 38806)

draws. When the Seattle Supersonics demanded a new facility (Key Arena), the exterior shape of the old coliseum was preserved (even if the name wasn't). A less visible legacy was the network of business and political contacts that developed out of the fair-planning process. Led by Eddie Carlson (later chairman of Westin Hotels), the extended family of lawyers, bankers, business leaders, and public relations geniuses who built the fair would put their stamp on Seattle development for the next twenty years. Besides, Elvis filmed a movie there—what other world's fair can claim that?

Chinatown (Vancouver)

The Chinese are the largest ethnic group in Vancouver and the city's Chinatown is the second largest in North America, after San Francisco's. Chinese residency dates back to the 1850s when the Fraser Valley gold rush drew crowds of prospectors. Later, Chinese workers were exploited as a cheap source of labor to build the Canadian Pacific Railway. The Chinese in Canada were not allowed citizenship rights until 1947, so an elaborate social service network developed to meet the needs of Chinatown residents. Today's Chinatown is a mix of stores and restaurants and is home to a large cultural center. The area is located east of downtown and covers portions of ten city blocks.

Covered Bridges

An example of historic preservation at its best, Oregon's covered bridges were saved from extinction in the 1980s when citizens pressured the government to preserve and restore the remaining stock. Hundreds (estimates vary) of covered bridges were built to cross Oregon streams beginning in the mid-1800s. The abundance of timber provided a natural building material and the covers protected the bridges from premature rot in the moist climate. A 1947 index by the Oregon State Highway Department listed 286 bridges, and scholars believe many more existed on private land. By the 1980s, all but about fifty had been lost to modernization, lack of repair, and the elements. Lane County (on the western side of the state) is considered the covered bridge capital of Oregon, with a concentration near Eugene and Cottage Grove, including the Chambers Covered Railroad Bridge (the only remaining covered railroad bridge in the state). The bridges are a favorite of romantics—tradition requires stealing a kiss from your sweetheart when passing through a covered bridge.

Crater Lake

The deepest lake in the United States, Crater Lake rests in the crater of the Mount Mazama volcano, which exploded nearly eight thousand years ago. Crater Lake National Park is the fifth oldest, dating back to 1902. The lake, which is favored by photographers for its remarkable blue color, is 1,932 feet deep at its lowest point, with an average depth of 1,500 feet. It measures six miles wide.

D. B. Cooper Hijacking

On a rainy Thanksgiving eve in 1971, a man calling himself Dan Cooper boarded a 4:35 P.M. Northwest Orient Airlines flight bound for Seattle from Portland. Just moments after takeoff, the man handed a flight attendant a note that warned the crew that he had a bomb and would blow up the plane unless he was given two hundred thousand dollars in cash and four parachutes. About an hour later, the plane landed in Seattle where other passengers (except the crew) were permitted to disembark. The authorities met Cooper's demands and he ordered the plane to fly to Mexico via Reno at no more than ten thousand feet. He also insisted the wing flaps be kept partially down and the landing gear lowered, keeping the plane at a safe speed for jumping. About 8 P.M. Cooper lowered the rear stairway of the plane and thirteen minutes later as the plane crossed the Lewis River in Southwest Washington State, a slight bump in pressure was recorded. The FBI theorized that this is when Cooper jumped out of the plane because when it landed in Reno, Cooper, the money, and two of the parachutes were missing. Authorities leaked to the press that they were questioning a Daniel B. Cooper of Portland, but he was eventually cleared. Nevertheless, the press proceeded to use the infamous D. B. Cooper moniker in the headlines. While some of the ransom money was uncovered by accident in 1980, no trace of Cooper has ever been found and the case remains unsolved.

W Edgewater Inn

Built in the mid-fifties, this venerable Seattle waterfront hotel is most famous for the identities and antics of the rock stars who have stayed there over the years. The Beatles stayed at the Edgewater when they played Seattle in 1964—after their stay the management sold the rug in their room to a souvenir company to be cut up and sold to Beatle-crazy fans. Frank Zappa immortalized the now-banned practice of fishing from hotel windows in the 1971 song "Mud Shark." The Edgewater's rock and roll high point (or low point, depending on your view) came in 1970 when Led Zeppelin engaged in world-class debaucheries, which are chronicled in the book *Hammer of the Gods*. A recently remodeled Edgewater still welcomes guests at Pier 67.

W Empress Hotel

Built in 1908, the Empress Hotel is the most famous landmark in Victoria, British Columbia. The 481-room hotel was designed in the tradition of the stately hotels of Europe. The Empress has played host to kings and prime ministers, and its ivy-covered walls and imposing lobby are tourist favorites. The Empress is located in the center of Victoria's recreational and business district overlooking the picturesque inner harbor. Afternoon tea at the Empress has been a Northwest tradition for many years, drawing twice as many spectators as participants.

W Expo '74 (Spokane)

Largely forgotten today, Spokane's World's Fair was the pride of the Inland Empire in 1974, leaving the legacy of a redeveloped downtown Riverfront Park. Adopting an environmental theme, the fair ran from May 4 to November 3, drawing a respectable 5.2 million visitors. Expo '74 was built out of a dilapidated rail yard in the middle of the Spokane River. While the exhibition used the environment to sell the fair, critics were quick to note that the energy pavilion was sponsored by oil, electric, and nuclear power companies, and the agriculture pavilion was hosted by agribusiness and chemical firms. Expo entertainment was a stylistic smorgasbord, ranging from establishment favorites such as Bill Cosby and Lawrence Welk to then-current rock stars such as Grand Funk Railroad and the Northwest's own Bachman-Turner Overdrive. Lacking a true signature piece of architecture such as the Space Needle, Expo '74 quickly faded from memory after the gates closed, though Riverfront Park remains a popular tourist destination.

W Expo '86 (Vancouver)

In 1986, more than 170 acres of industrial desolation on Vancouver's False Creek was transformed into a sparkling and successful World's Fair. With the theme of "World in Motion—World in Touch," the fair celebrated transportation and communications. After previous expositions in New Orleans and Knoxville had been busts, Vancouver planners were wary. Their fears were unfounded as more than twenty-two million visitors attended, well above the projected fourteen million. Canada's national pavilion was located a mile away from the main fairground, in a stunning facility on Burrard Inlet that is now a mainstay of the downtown skyline.

Fairgoers could take a special train to the Canada exhibit, the first link in Vancouver's "Skytrain" light rail system. Part of Expo '86's appeal lay in its ability to surmount international tensions and convince both the United States and the Soviet Union to mount major exhibits. After the fair closed, a mixed-use development with housing, office space, parks, and entertainment venues took over the Expo site.

Floating and Sinking Bridges

Plopped right in the middle of the Seattle urban area, Lake Washington used to require ferries to carry folks from the east side to the city. In 1940, the Lacey V. Murrow floating bridge was put in service, linking Seattle and the east side via Mercer Island. Named for a former state highway director (and brother of legendary journalist Edward R. Murrow), the bridge was the world's first concrete floating bridge. The Evergreen Point Bridge (also known as the "520" bridge) followed in 1963. Although scenic, the bridges are choke points for the Seattle area's notorious traffic congestion. In the early nineties, during renovations to the Mercer Island floating bridge, portions sank, causing much local snickering and consternation. The state's other notable floating bridge spans Hood Canal on the Olympic Peninsula. Opened in 1961, the bridge links the north end of the Kitsap Peninsula with the Olympic Peninsula. The western half of the Hood Canal bridge met its demise during a windstorm in 1979. It was rebuilt and reopened in 1982.

Folklife Festival

Since 1972, the Northwest Folklife Festival has provided Northwesterners with a way to reconnect with the rootsy sixties. Every Memorial Day, the festival covers the Seattle Center with traditional arts, including music, dancing, arts, crafts, and foods. The Folklife Festival also features the largest collection of patchouli oil and old Birkenstocks in the world (all being worn by attendees and participants). In recent years the festival has run into financial problems—perhaps because it has always been free to the public.

Four Seasons Olympic Hotel

The Four Seasons Olympic Hotel sits on the site of the original University of Washington (UW) in downtown Seattle. After the UW moved to its current Montlake campus, a portion of the "Metropolitan Tract" was redeveloped into Seattle's premier hotel. The Olympic opened to the public in 1924, and its Renaissance styling gave Seattle a world-class showplace. By the late seventies, however, the grand hotel was on its heels—a victim of age and cramped quarters. A turnaround began in 1979 when the Olympic was given historic landmark status. Soon after the property was leased to the Four Seasons chain, which began a massive restoration. The grand reopening in 1982 signaled the Olympic's return to four-star status, which it maintains to the present.

Galloping Gertie

Built to span the Puget Sound Narrows between Tacoma and the Gig Harbor peninsula, the first Tacoma Narrows bridge opened July 1, 1940. An unusual suspension design was chosen, despite concerns raised by some engineers. Almost immediately drivers noticed that the bridge had a pronounced sway during breezes. The swaying action led to the bridge being dubbed "Galloping Gertie" by locals. Alas, on November 7, 1940—less than six months after opening—Gertie galloped straight to the bottom of the Narrows. A stiff wind of forty miles per hour caused the bridge to sway up to five feet. Police closed the structure at 10 A.M., and the roadbed began to break up one-half hour later. Shortly after 11 A.M. the remainder of the bridge broke free, with the center span plunging into the water below. The bridge was eventually rebuilt and voters recently approved a plan to construct a second Narrows bridge, next to the existing span. An environmental and engineering challenge that has surfaced is how to work around the wreckage of Gertie, still lodged on the bottom of the Narrows sixty years after it fell.

Gastown

The birthplace of Vancouver, Gastown was named for saloonkeeper Gassy Jack Deighton, who set up shop in 1867, providing booze to local millworkers. The area around his saloon became known as Gastown. It was incorporated in 1869 as the town of Granville, and in 1889 became the city of Vancouver. A fire that year destroyed the entire city, though it was soon rebuilt. After the

depression, the Gastown area became a skid row and remained so until the 1960s when historic preservation projects began the climb back. Like Pioneer Square in Seattle and Old Town in Portland, Gastown today is a mix of elegance and dereliction.

Goodwill Games

Ted Turner's monument to world peace, understanding, and his ego made their second appearance in Seattle in 1990. Drawing upon the fact that Seattle was a hotbed of the "citizen diplomacy" movement, Turner's faux Olympics provoked a collective yawn (and probably killed any chance of luring the real Olympics). Running from July 21 to August 5, the games did feature many top athletes, including track star Carl Lewis and swimmer Summer Sanders, as well as a first-rate arts festival. The United States wrestling team also defeated the Soviet Union (the first international meet loss for the Soviets in thirty years).

Green River Murders

The Green River murders are one of the great unsolved crimes of the century. Between 1982 and 1984, forty-nine women were murdered in the Seattle area, usually prostitutes picked up on the Sea-Tac airport strip. The case gets its name from the place where some of the first bodies were discovered, though later victims were found in wooded areas near Portland. At its height, the Green River task force had more than fifty investigators; now it has dwindled to one. Much suspicion focused on a man named William Stevens, who was cleared during the investigation, thanks to alibi testimony from his half-brother. The half-brother has since recanted and

Galloping Gertie: Bridge falls down, goes "boom"!
(Photo courtesy of the Tacoma Public Library)

many crime buffs believe that Stevens, who died in 1991, remains the most viable suspect. Others believe the killer is still active in another location, noting some similarities between the Green River murders and later killings in Spokane, San Diego, and most recently in Vancouver.

Greeners

Greeners is shorthand for students at the Evergreen State College. Located in Olympia, Evergreen is an alternative liberal arts school that shuns traditional classes and grades in favor of long interdisciplinary courses and detailed written evaluations. Founded in 1967, Evergreen's alternative ways got it in recurring trouble with conservative state legislators who took several runs at closing the school. Former Governor Dan Evans stepped in as college president in 1977, lending the school prestige and political clout. A number of national rankings placing Evergreen at the top tier of liberal arts schools didn't hurt either, and the immediate threat to the school appears to have passed. Famous Evergreen alumni include *Simpsons* creator Matt Groening, cartoonist Lynda Barry, and actor Michael Richards (Kramer on *Seinfeld*). Never content to shy from controversy, the school recently landed in the headlines when Mumia Abu Jamal (a death-row inmate convicted of killing a Philadelphia policeman) was selected to be one of the school's commencement speakers.

Hanford

Hanford is the definition of the gift that keeps on giving—even when you don't want it anymore. From the 1940s to the late 1980s, the U.S. Department of Energy's Hanford Site produced plutonium for nuclear weapons. The local area embraced the industry—for example, Richland High School's teams are called the Bombers, you can bowl at the Atomic Lanes, and the local hydroplane race was known for years as the Atomic Cup. Covering 560 square miles along the Columbia River, north of Richland, Hanford's name now has become synonymous with the environmental costs of nuclear research and production. Millions of gallons of spent nuclear materials and by-products of plutonium production were buried on site, in tanks that are now leaking. Some of the leaking waste has reached the groundwater and is making its way toward the river. Cleanup plans focus on "vitrifying" the waste by mixing it with glass and storing the resulting toxic bricks in dry underground storage.

Harrison Hot Springs

An old-line Northwest resort, popular among the "newlywed and nearly dead," Harrison Hot Springs is located on Harrison Lake, about ninety minutes east of Vancouver. The resort dates back to the mid-1800s and was named for Benjamin Harrison, a former deputy governor of the Hudson's Bay Company. Popular with local fur traders and natives for "healing powers," the hot springs were later discovered by European visitors. After the Canadian Pacific Railroad reached the area in 1885, the first hotel was built at the hot springs. The current Harrison resort was built in 1926.

Hershel at the Ballard Locks

A poster child for gluttony, Hershel was the collective name given to the sea lions that camped at Seattle's Ballard Locks beginning in the mid-1980s. It seems that the barrier of the locks helped boats but also slowed down salmon. Hershel discovered that this engineering quirk made the locks the equivalent of an all-you-can-eat seafood buffet. As Hershel was joined by numerous compadres, local fish advocates became concerned. Some proposed shooting the sea lions, but local sensitivities prevented such a violent denouement. As a result, humans spent the next few years looking very stupid while trying strategies such as putting up nets, setting off firecrackers, and blasting rock music underwater (hey—it worked on Noriega!). A local radio station even crafted a faux whale (dubbed Fake Willy) designed to scare the unwelcome diners. Ultimately, the sea lions were captured and sent away to aquariums.

Hippie Hollow

The center of "Lotus Land" in Canada during the mid- to late 1960s, Vancouver's so-called "Hippie Hollow" was located in the Kitsilano District on Fourth Avenue, between Maple and Vine. A true "Haight Ashbury of the North," Hippie Hollow attracted thousands of peace-loving Canadians as well as a bevy of young American men who were avoiding the Vietnam War draft. The area was also the physical as well as spiritual birthplace of Vancouver's underground newspaper the *Georgia Straight*. Today, the old Hippie Hollow area has been transformed into an upscale shopping district, featuring gourmet restaurants (like Bishop's) and trendy pubs. Like Hawthorne Street in Portland and the U-District in Seattle, the yuppie phenomenon swallowed the hippie movement, incense, love beads, and all.

Husky Stadium Collapse

By the mid-eighties, after Don James had restored the University of Washington (UW) Husky football team to national prominence, demand for tickets skyrocketed. Solution? Build a second grandstand for thousands of additional ticketholders. That's just what the UW set out to do, but during construction in February 1987, the new section creaked, groaned, and then gave way. The nearly $13 million addition took just twelve seconds to

collapse. Fortunately, no one was injured, and the addition was rebuilt. Like Tacoma's Galloping Gertie, this time it has stayed up—unlike the U-Dub's football fortunes.

Hutterite Colonies

Amish country in Washington State? Well, not quite. Hutterites are one of three Anabaptist groups in North America that can trace their origins to the Protestant Reformation in the sixteenth century. Like the Amish and the Mennonites, Hutterites are devout Christians and strict pacifists. Unlike those other groups, however, Hutterites live communally on large farms in the Canadian prairie provinces and in Montana, South Dakota, and Eastern Washington State. Distinguished by their German language and old-fashioned dress, there are four colonies of

Vancouver's "Hippie Hollow" in the Kitsilano neighborhood was the center of "Lotus Land" in the sixties.
(Photo courtesy of Pugstem Publications, City of Vancouver Archives, photo CVA134-41)

Attractions, Places, and Events

Hutterites in Washington: in Odessa in Lincoln County, near Warden in Grant County, another near Marlin in Grant County, and a Reardon colony fifteen miles west of Spokane.

Ivan the Gorilla

In 1964, the B&I Circus Store in Tacoma was looking for an animal to round out its eclectic collection. Owner Earl Irwin paid five thousand dollars for a pair of infant gorillas captured in West Africa. The female died, but the male—named Ivan—survived to become the centerpiece of the store and of a controversy. Ivan quickly became the star of B&I promotions, gaining some national fame with a guest spot on the *Daktari* television show. By 1967, Ivan had gained so much strength his keepers decided he needed to be permanently caged, and that's where he stayed for the next twenty-seven years. At first, Ivan was a major draw, but two forces were at work that would change his fate. First, zoos were beginning to place gorillas into natural habitats, allowing them to form groups rather than live in isolation. Second, animal-rights activism was beginning to grow and the notion of a robust gorilla living as a store display became unthinkable. In 1994, a deal was struck for Ivan to be transferred to the Atlanta Zoo, with the hope that eventually he would gain social skills and mate. In early 1998, after numerous false starts, Ivan finally figured out how all the parts work and mated with Kinyani, who Atlanta zookeepers described as "a very persistent, sexy little gorilla." At least Ivan didn't suffer the fate of the Northwest's other favorite gorilla—Bobo. Bobo ruled the Woodland Park Zoo during the 1950s and 1960s and was most notorious for failing to mate with Fifi, the female gorilla brought in to rouse his passions. Bobo died in 1968 and was stuffed to be displayed at Seattle's Museum of History and Industry.

The Tacoma B&I Store's most famous employee, the gorilla Ivan, is now retired and living in the Atlanta Zoo. (Photo courtesy of the Tacoma Public Library, Richards Collection, photo D163776-15L)

J. Z. Knight ("Ramtha")

When J. Z. Knight moved to Yelm, Washington, in 1981, most locals didn't know she was bringing someone with her. That someone was Ramtha, the spirit of a 35,000-year-old Atlantean Warrior for whom Knight asserts that she provides a channel. Knight established her Ramtha School of Enlightenment, and soon Yelm was New Age central. Followers—sometimes called "Ramsters"—descended on Yelm, buying houses and establishing businesses to be close to the school. Knight herself built an enormous mansion and horse farm in Yelm, hosting seminars in the barn that would attract hundreds. Famous Ramtha devotees, including Shirley Maclaine and Linda Evans, moved to the area, lending some celebrity glamour to the whole enterprise. Local preachers warned that Ramtha was surely a sign of the end times—or at least that Ramtha's followers were on the road to hell. Knight herself went through a very public and messy divorce in the mid-nineties, but lately things seem to have settled down as Knight and her students have blended into the local community. In 1998, Knight invited a number of religious scholars to investigate her work. While not validating Ramtha, they concluded that Knight's channeling sessions—in which she appears to undergo a personality shift into that of Ramtha—did not appear to be faked.

Jantzen Beach

Beginning in 1928, the Jantzen Beach amusement park was hallowed ground for Portland-area kids. Featuring a huge wooden roller coaster known as the Big Dipper, swimming pools, a variety of carnival rides and games, and a spectacular carousel, Jantzen Beach thrived until the mid-sixties. Changing public tastes and poor weather began to take their toll, but the final blow came when freeway expansion took out the Big Dipper (and with it the amusement park) in 1970. A shopping mall was constructed on the former park site, although the Jantzen Beach carousel was preserved as a part of the new complex.

John Wayne Marina

John Wayne had a special affinity for the Northwest. He shot one of his last movies in Seattle (a competent *Dirty Harry* clone called *McQ*), and he spent many summers cruising Puget Sound in his boat, the *Wild Goose*. Wayne's favorite harbor for the *Wild Goose* was in the banana belt of Sequim, Washington. He envisioned building a marina in Sequim Bay and, after his death, Wayne's family donated the land to make his dream a reality.

Kalakala

With much of the population separated by water, the Northwest is unusually reliant on passenger and auto ferries for transportation. Both Washington State and British Columbia boast large government-run ferry fleets that, despite the occasional controversy, provide affordable and reliable service. Before public ferries, there was a "mosquito fleet" of private ferries plying the water. A key remaining link to that era came home to Seattle in 1998 when the *Kalakala* was rescued from a rusting demise in Kodiak, Alaska. When it was commissioned in 1935, the *Kalakala* was an art-deco wonder, carrying up to one hundred autos and two thousand passengers on a sleek, rounded, space-age hull. Known

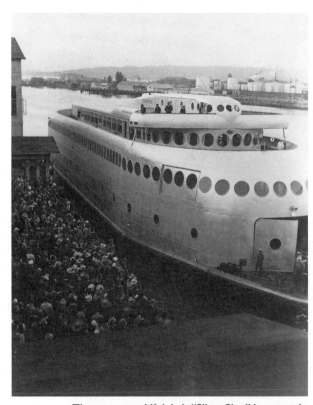

The once proud *Kalakala* "Silver Slug" is currently undergoing renovation on Seattle's Lake Union.
(Photo courtesy of the Tacoma Public Library, Richards Collection, photo D9978-4)

as the "silver slug," the *Kalakala* became part of the state ferry fleet when the private system was taken over in 1951. The boat remained in service until it was supplanted by the new state "super-ferries" in 1967. At that time, the *Kalakala* was moved to Alaska and converted to a crab and shrimp-processing factory. In 1995, the Seattle-based *Kalakala* Foundation began preparations to return the boat to Seattle and restore it to its former glory. Phase one of the mission was completed on November 6, 1998, when the boat redocked on the Seattle waterfront for the first time in thirty years.

Keiko

The star of the 1992 film *Free Willy* illustrated that sometimes life imitates movies. Keiko was captured in 1979 and by 1985 was performing at the Reino Aventura amusement park in Mexico City. It was there Keiko was featured in *Free Willy*, leading to an international campaign to improve his living conditions and ultimately return him to Icelandic waters. In 1996, Keiko was moved to a rehabilitation facility at the Oregon Coast Aquarium in Newport, becoming an instant tourist sensation. The Free Willy Foundation continued to make plans to return Keiko to Iceland, leading to tensions with aquarium supporters who were concerned about Keiko's health (and also about losing their star attraction). Nonetheless, in late 1998, Keiko was bundled up and flown to a specially constructed holding pen off the Icelandic coast. Early reports indicate that Keiko is adjusting well and plans are moving ahead to remove the pen and fully return the famed whale to the wild.

La Conner

Unofficial capital of the "Magic Skagit," La Conner, Washington, in the seventies and eighties was the epitome of laid-back, organic living. Home to artists such as painter Guy Anderson, writer Tom Robbins, and vaudevillian Reverend Chumleigh, La Conner is a funky little village nestled on the banks of the Swinomish Channel, about one hour north of Seattle. For a number of years, one of the police cars was a small Renault Le Car—perfect for a town surrounded by tulip fields and good vibes. Today, La Conner is a bit overrun by tourists, though the Skagit Valley continues to attract those interested in a slower, greener way of life.

Monorail

Seattle's beloved monorail train was built for the Seattle World's Fair in 1962. The 1.2-mile route connected downtown Seattle to the fair site with a futuristic-looking (at the time) "bullet train" gliding on a single concrete rail above the city. After the fair, the monorail remained one of Seattle's signature tourist attractions. What is less well known is that the Alweg Company, which built the monorail, had offered to build a loop around Lake Washington if the city would secure and donate the right of way. The city fathers declined the offer. Over the years the monorail has had to survive official indifference and outright hostility. To downtown leaders and the political establishment, the monorail is a hopeless anachronism. To Seattleites, the monorail is a pop culture treasure, and the citizenry got their revenge at the ballot box in 1997. As Puget Sound succumbed to gridlock, transportation planners struggled to get local voters to approve funding for an expensive light-rail system. Monorail boosters proposed and passed a ballot initiative directing that the system be extended throughout Seattle, and withholding the pay of any city council member who stood in the way. While it is unlikely that funding will be secured for a complete expansion, it appears that a longer monorail is in Seattle's future.

Mount Rainier

In 1792, Captain George Vancouver sailed into Puget Sound and saw a spectacular mountain looming above the landscape. He named the mountain for a colleague, Peter Rainier, and duly recorded the name on his charts. As the area became settled, however, the native name for the mountain surfaced—alternately reported as "Tahoma" or "Tacoma." Despite numerous attempts by boosters in the City of Destiny, Vancouver's name stuck and was forever memorialized when President McKinley signed legislation in 1899 making Mount Rainier National Park a reality. Hazard Stevens, son of Washington's territorial governor, made the first recorded ascent of the summit in 1870. Stevens believed that the inside of the mountain was inhabited by subterranean aliens, none of whom apparently greeted him when he reached the top. Today, Mount Rainier National Park is a favorite tourist destination, to the point of being overrun on beautiful summer days. The peak is also a favorite with climbers, with thousands making the trek each summer. Go while you can—Mount Rainier also has the distinction of being the largest volcano in the United States. Given Tacoma's luck over the years, after it blows up, we'll probably change the name.

Mount Saint Helens Eruption

In 1980, Mount Saint Helens (located between Seattle and Portland) provided Northwesterners with a rude reminder that the Cascade Range is filled with volcanoes. In the late seventies, Saint Helens had begun to show signs of life, with steam venting and minor earthquakes. Concerns about an eruption

Hazard Stevens, the first white man to ascend Mount Rainier in the 1870s, thought a race of subterranean beings lived inside. Really.
(Photo courtesy of the Tacoma Public Library, Richards Collection, photo D43569-14)

grew, and by the early part of 1980 it was a question of when, not if. Not everyone took these concerns to heart. A feisty curmudgeon named Harry Truman was the proprietor of a lodge on Spirit Lake, located on the slopes of Mount Saint Helens. When the mountain began to rumble and emit steam—a precursor to a volcanic eruption—Truman shook it off and defiantly vowed to stay on the mountain near the burial site of his beloved wife. Perhaps egged on by a fascinated media, Truman continued his defiance as the rumbling intensified and an eruption seemed inevitable. Bad choice. On May 18, 1980, at 8:32 in the morning, a U.S. Geological Survey scientist named David Johnston shouted into his radio, "Vancouver, Vancouver—this is it!" It was to be his last transmission. At that moment, a massive earthquake and slide hit the mountain, shoving rocks down the side at five hundred miles per hour. As the face of the mountain disintegrated, the gasses trapped inside exploded vertically and horizontally, literally blowing the top off. Spirit Lake, Truman's home, was quickly buried under hundreds of feet of molten rock. A thick cloud of ash filled the sky, blotting out the sun in Eastern Washington as it drifted away. Downstream, toward the Columbia River, a twenty-foot wall of debris shooting down the channel wiped out more than twenty bridges. After the eruption and aftershocks were over, visitors described the scene as resembling a lunar landscape, devoid of vegetation and covered with a gray ash. That ash would, of course, find its way into thousands of souvenirs ("Hey, get your Mount Saint Helen's ash ashtray!"). By the late nineties, vegetation had returned to the sides of the mountain and several new visitors centers had opened, including one named for Johnston.

Myrtlewood

You can't drive along the southern Oregon coast without finding scads of stores offering myrtlewood bowls, clocks, plaques, and assorted geegaws. A member of the laurel family, the myrtlewood tree grows in small groves along southwestern Oregon rivers. A Northwest roadside treasure, to be added to your Mount Saint Helen's ash collection of oddball souvenirs.

Namu

During the summer of 1965, a two-ton killer whale was captured off the coast of British Columbia near a place called Namu. The curator of the Seattle Aquarium announced his intention to bring the whale back to Seattle before the fishermen killed it (killer whales destroyed their salmon runs). The city of Seattle became transfixed as the whale rescue mission developed. Local TV station KOMO set up a remote broadcast station on board the tugboat *Lorna Foss*, which was leading Namu back to Seattle. Local radio personality Bob Hardwick did his morning show on KVI from the rescue flotilla. Namu was a hit with aquarium visitors, but he tragically died in July 1966 after getting tangled in the netting of his pen. Ironically, the Northwest would see a reverse Namu situation more than thirty years later when Newport, Oregon, became the temporary home of Keiko the whale on his way back to freedom.

Northgate Shopping Center

While the Northwest loves to tout its livability, it also has the dubious distinction of being the birthplace of the modern shopping mall. While not the first shopping area to have a unified theme, Northgate (opened in 1950 and located in north Seattle) is generally recognized as the first shopping center built with anchor stores surrounding a central court and using a central heating plant. Seattle journalist David Brewster says, "Its bland uniformity soon obliterated alternative notions of colorful bazaars or cultural centers." Guess he didn't like it. By the 1990s, despite some periodic renovations, Northgate was down on its heels, eclipsed by newer, flashier malls. As a result, Northgate owners began plans for an "urban village" of sorts, incorporating offices, retail, entertainment, and housing on the site.

Oaks Park

The last surviving old-style amusement park in the Northwest, Oaks Park dates back to 1905. Located on the banks of the Willamette River south of downtown Portland, Oaks Park was originally built by the Oregon Water Power and Navigation Company. Ownership passed to the Bollinger family, who ultimately donated the Park to a nonprofit corporation. "The Oaks," which combines picnic facilities with amusement rides and a roller rink, remains a favorite Rose City summer family hangout.

Ⓜ Ocean Shores

When Ocean Shores was developed in 1960, it was marketed as the "Venice of the West"—thousands of homes surrounding a network of canals near the ocean. Over the next few years, it turned into the definition of a high-pressure real estate disaster, mired in scandal and litigation. One of the tools the promoters used to lure potential buyers was celebrity appearances, the pinnacle of which involved hiring Pat Boone to host a "celebrity" golf tourney for five years in the late sixties. The celebrities were fading stars such as Milton Berle and Joey Bishop, but for a region with a chip on its shoulder any celebrity was good enough, and the tourney became the summer promotional centerpiece. As it became clear to local residents that the developers were never going to make good on promised improvements, the situation unraveled. Ocean Shores eventually incorporated as a city and lawsuits abounded. Over time, however, the "Venice of the West" has maintained a long, slow climb toward respectability, gaining both population and tourists.

Ⓜ Oregon Country Fair

The Oregon Country Fair (OCF), located on a site near Eugene, has provided fun times and good vibes each summer for thirty years. A counterculture county fair, OCF features crafts, music, vaudeville, and more veggie burritos and tie-dye than you can shake a veggie burrito at. Originally a true "happening," the OCF has matured into a formal nonprofit organization with full-time employees.

Ⓜ Oregon Vortex

An exemplar of the "mystery spot," the Oregon Vortex is located in Gold Hill, near Medford. At a mysterious spot water appears to run uphill, people can walk on walls, and bodies appear to shrink and grow dramatically. The Oregon Vortex has been open since 1930 and is considered one of the granddaddies of roadside attractions in the entire country. Isn't it all just a fake caused by how they built the building? You'll just have to suspend your disbelief and find out.

Ⓜ Packy the Elephant

The first elephant to be born in a zoo, Packy remains the main draw at Portland's Washington Park Zoo. Packy was born on April 14, 1962, an event that set a zoo attendance record. Prior to Packy's birth, researchers did not have an accurate idea of elephant gestation periods. Using data from Packy, and almost thirty births that have followed, Portland researchers have gained a better understanding of elephant reproduction. The information is being used to help stem a precipitous decline in Asian elephant populations.

Ⓜ Paramount Theater

Opened in March 1928, Seattle's Paramount Theater has survived more makeovers than Madonna. Originally a premier "silent movie and vaudeville palace," the Paramount also hosted full-scale theatrical productions. As the movie business began to migrate to multiplexes, the Paramount struggled but never closed. It found a shot in the arm in the seventies and eighties as the main midsized rock concert hall in Seattle, known for good sound, excellent sight lines, and a perpetual smoky haze of illicit substances. Years of rock concert crowd abuse took their toll, and it was left to a "Microsoft Millionaire" to finance a complete remodel of the Paramount in the early nineties. The Paramount itself has been a movie star twice, in the 1982 movie *Frances* (the story of Seattle actress Frances Farmer), and in the 1991 River Phoenix movie *Dogfight*.

⚡ Pendleton Roundup

While the Northwest isn't exactly cowboy country, it does have its share of venerable rodeos. The Pendleton Roundup rodeo, which dates back to 1910, is the biggie—one of the ten largest in the world. Other rodeos of note occur in Ellensburg and Omak, where the annual "suicide race" down a steep hill into the river always draws a crowd of awed spectators and angry animal-rights advocates.

⚡ PNE (Pacific National Exhibition)

Western Canada's largest fair, the PNE (Pacific National Exhibition) has been held every August in Vancouver since 1910. More than one million visitors crowd the PNE grounds on Vancouver's east side for the agriculturally oriented event. PNE also boasts an extensive amusement park called Playland that remains open most of the year and includes an authentic wooden roller coaster. The PNE hosts hundreds of events annually: trade and consumer shows, conventions, concerts, meetings, rallies, banquets, film studio and commercial shoots, agricultural shows, and sporting events.

⚡ Portland Building

The Portland Building (home to city hall) set off a firestorm when it was built in 1982. Designed by Michael Graves, the Portland Building is an exemplar of postmodern architecture. Bold brown columns mix with huge medallions and triangular protuberances, over a cream-colored background punctuated with hundreds of tiny square windows. A typical staid govern-

ment building, it ain't. Among the kinder appel-lations hung on the building by early critics were "The Turkey" and "The Jukebox." Criticism appears to have softened over the years as people have gotten used to the most unusual-looking government building in America.

⚡ Puyallup Fair

Western Washington television viewers know it's September without looking at the calendar. Every year around Labor Day brings not only the return of school, but also the return of ubiquitous television ads featuring singing animals exhorting us to "Do the Puyallup." From humble beginnings in 1900, the Puyallup Fair (officially the Western Washington Fair) has grown into the sixth-largest fair in the United States. The fair begins after Labor Day and runs for seventeen days, drawing crowds that routinely top 1.2 million for the entire run. During World War II, the fair was suspended and the fairgrounds were turned into an internment camp for Japanese Americans. After the war, the fair resumed and began its modern era of expansion. Puyallup Fair traditions include greasy fair burgers, piled high with grilled onions, Fisher scones, and a ride on the vintage 1935 roller coaster. For your stomach's sake, we recommend the reverse order.

⚡ Rain Forests

In most of the Northwest it just *seems* like it rains all the time. On the Olympic Peninsula, it really does. The Hoh Rain Forest, in the coastal part of the Olympic National Park, is a good example. Annual precipitation ranges from 140 to 167 inches a year. Married with a temperate climate that doesn't fall below freezing or climb above 80 degrees, the rain produces a dense, lush, and moody forest permeated with moss.

Rajneeshpuram

In 1981, Indian Guru Bhagwan Shree Rajneesh moved his base of operations to the small eastern Oregon town of Antelope. Preaching a message that "sex is fun and materialism is good," Rajneesh attracted hundreds of followers who began building his "City of Rajneesh" or "Rajneeshpuram." The Guru—who had a fleet of ninety-three Rolls Royces at one point—would drive through his compound, surrounded by adoring disciples. Needless to say, the locals were not amused. They were less amused when the Rajneeshees tried to take over the town at the ballot box. Later it was discovered that Rajneesh's top lieutenant, Ma Anand Sheela, had masterminded a food-poisoning outbreak in the Dalles. Sheela was arrested and imprisoned, and the Guru was deported to India where he died in 1990.

Reedies

Reedies is the nickname for students at Reed College, Portland's very expensive, very prestigious, and very alternative college. The school held its first classes in 1911 and was named for Oregon pioneers Simeon and Amanda Reed. The college has hewed to an iconoclastic path since the beginning, shunning college traditions such as fraternities, intercollegiate sports, and social activities. Reed has loosened up some—the college hosts the annual Portland Juggling Festival—but the focus remains academics.

Rose Festival

Portland's annual civic blowout dates back to 1907. Following the Lewis & Clark Exhibition of 1905, city leaders wanted to establish an annual celebration. Since Portland's climate is perfectly suited to growing roses, the fragrant flower was chosen as the theme. The early Rose Festival featured a floral parade, still the highlight of what has grown into more than eighty events spread over two weeks.

Saturday Market

Inspired by the Eugene Saturday Market, Portland's version began in 1974, offering vendors a space to sell handcrafted items (aka stuff you don't really need but it looks cool). Originally located in a parking lot at N.W. First and Davis, Saturday Market now sprawls forth from a core location under the Burnside Bridge in Old Town Portland. Recognized as the largest continually operating open-air crafts market in the nation, Saturday Market sports a budget of more than four million dollars per year and operates weekends from spring to winter.

Sea Lion Caves

Sea Lion Caves is a classic roadside attraction of the Oregon Coast. It is known for the over-sized bumper stickers it affixes to visitors' cars. Billed as the largest natural sea cave in the world, the main chamber is more than an acre in size. The attraction dates back to the early thirties, when a person had to climb down to the caves via stairs. Today's visitors can descend in a long elevator to get to the twelve-story-tall cavern. There they are greeted by numerous large, loud, and fragrant sea lions.

Seafair

Dating back to 1949, Seafair is a blend of parades, community events, and—most important of all—the annual hydroplane races that take over Lake Washington every August (causing many neighbors to plan long vacations during that time). Besides the thunder boats, the most visible Seafair events are the Torchlight Parade that winds through downtown Seattle and the milk-carton boat races, which give amateur nautical engineers a chance to sink in Green Lake. The Seafair Pirates, who first terrorized the community in the early fifties, remain a joyful anachronism. The Pirates were an offshoot of the Ale and Quail Society (itself an offshoot of the Washington Press Club). Society members (no doubt fueled by Rainier Ale—aka Green Death) thought it would be peachy to get real drunk, dress up as pirates, and go about Seafair events menacing women and children with long swords and gruff talk. People loved it, and the Pirates prospered. While the Pirates have become a bit more community-minded over the years, they remain a refreshingly nonpolitically correct part of a sometimes painfully politically correct town.

⚒ Shake, Rattle, and Roll

While the Northwest waits for the really big one, memories are beginning to fade of the "big enough" one(s). On the morning of April 29, 1965, the Seattle area was shaken by a 6.5 magnitude earthquake centered about ten miles north of Tacoma. Seven people were killed, property damage ran into the millions, and the temblor sparked an increase in earthquake awareness and design. While the 1965 earthquake is the one most remembered, it is not the largest in recent history. In 1949, a 7.1 shaker was centered near Olympia, causing substantial damage throughout the South Sound. Recently, the Seattle area has had a number of short earthquakes measuring around 5 on the Richter scale, but seismologists warn of an 8+ quake in the next two decades.

⚒ Slinky Pull Toys

The first few dozen times you launch a Slinky spring toy down the stairs, it's interesting. Then the yawn begins to grow, and soon the Slinky takes up permanent residence in its box. A Seattle woman named Helen Malsed made a major breakthrough in Slinky technology. After her son got a Slinky for a present, Malsed began to experiment with putting wheels on the toy. Her son was delighted with the way the Slinky would lurch along, and Malsed approached James Industry (the maker of Slinky) with her idea. Eventually, Malsed's invention became the largest-selling pull toy of all time (in addition to landing a starring role in the hit movie Toy Story). Malsed continued inventing new toys, including oversized snap-together plastic beads that have delighted babies for decades.

⚒ Smith Tower

When it opened in 1914, the Smith Tower was taller than any building west of New York. The Smith family, of Smith-Corona typewriter fame, built the tower. The building was intended to promote the typewriter business; hence, the family decided to increase the size to forty-two stories (from an original eighteen). Costing $1.5 million, the Smith Tower defined elegance, especially the tower-topping Chinese Room. Recently restored, the Chinese Room features panels that tell the history of Seattle in Chinese characters. The Smith Tower was purchased in 1976 by local restaurateur and world-class promoter Ivar Haglund, who promptly stirred controversy by flying a giant fish-shaped wind sock from the top. After Haglund's health began to fail he sold the tower, which was renovated in 1986.

⚒ Snoqualmie Falls Lodge

Perched overlooking its namesake, the Snoqualmie Falls Lodge, which opened in 1919, was famous for its huge weekend breakfasts, a highlight of which was "mile high honey." To get "mile high honey," waiters were trained to pour honey from far above their heads, landing precisely on the food item of choice. The schtick made the lodge a prime special-occasion restaurant. Eventually, Puget Sound Energy (formerly Puget Power), which owns a hydroelectric facility at the site, bought the lodge and made it an upscale destination resort, changing the name to the "Salish Lodge." Old-timers, however, still fondly recall the original name, and a line of food products such as oatmeal and pancake mixes still carry on the Snoqualmie Falls Lodge tradition. The lodge also played a key role in the offbeat television series *Twin Peaks* as the Great Northern Lodge.

Space Needle

To the dismay of aesthetes and naturalists, the Space Needle is the icon of Seattle, a visual signature rising 607 feet in the sky, topped with a restaurant that rotates at one mile per hour. Recently named the city's youngest "historical landmark," the Needle is celebrated in song, picture, and those little globes that make snow when you turn them over. The Space Needle, built for the 1962 Seattle World's Fair, was inspired by a trip taken by Fair Chairman Eddie Carlson to Stuttgart, Germany. There, Carlson, with his friends Webb and Virgina Moffatt, dined in a restaurant perched high atop a television tower and was inspired to want a similar tower for the Seattle fair. The Space Needle was an instant sensation, with its elevators whisking passengers up to the restaurant and observation deck in a speedy forty-three seconds. Local broadcast personalities have used the Needle as a studio in the sky and numerous movies have used it as a backdrop, including *It Happened at the World's Fair* and *The Parallax View*. More recently, the Space Needle has been the focal point for Seattle's New Year's Eve celebrations, with fireworks being detonated

Seattle's landmark the Space Needle—it's kinda hip, kinda now.
(Photo Courtesy of the Museum of History and Industry)

from the top. The Needle was also the focus of Seattle's own take on Orson Welles's *War of the Worlds*. On April Fools' Day 1989, the local comedy show *Almost Live!* caused a panic when it broadcast a fake news report (complete with computer graphics) that the Space Needle had toppled. Gullible viewers panicked, flooding local emergency lines regardless of a flashing notice that the "news" report was a hoax. Despite threatened lawsuits, both the Needle and the show survived.

Spokane Carousel

One of the most beloved attractions in the city of Spokane, the Carousel has been a Lilac City fixture since it debuted in old Natatorium Park in 1909. Hand-carved by I. D. Looff, the Danish immigrant who introduced platform merry-go-rounds in the United States in 1876, the Carousel is the only one still in existence that was built by Looff himself. It holds fifty-four prancing horses, a tiger, a giraffe, and four Chinese dragons. In the spring of 1975, the Carousel was moved into a specially designed building in Riverfront Park where it continues to delight children of all ages today.

Springfield School Shooting

On May 21, 1998, student Kip Kinkel went to Thurston High School in Springfield, Oregon. Entering the cafeteria, he pulled a gun and opened fire. One student died at the scene, another died later at the hospital. Star wrestler Jake Ryker, despite serious gunshot wounds, wrestled the gun from Kinkel but not before twenty students were injured either by gunshots or in the resulting chaos. When the police went to Kinkel's home, they found both his parents dead of gunshot wounds. In the days that followed the shootings, Kinkel was described as a violent and unbalanced youth who had once been voted "most likely to start World War III" by his classmates. The day before the shooting, Kinkel had been suspended for bringing a gun to school. Kinkel ultimately pled guilty and went to prison.

Stanley Park

A greenspace luscious enough to make urban planners drool, Stanley Park's one thousand acres sit just west of Vancouver's downtown. Named for Governor General Lord Stanley, the park, a former military reserve, opened in 1888. The Vancouver Aquarium, with its popular killer whales, is located in the park, along with other activities including golf, lawn bowling, playgrounds, a miniature railroad, and a children's petting farm. Those preferring more solitude can choose from a variety of hiking paths as well as the seawall walkway, which wraps the entire outside perimeter. The "nine o'clock gun" sits in the harbor, near the park entrance. Originally, it was fired to signal the end of the legal weekend fishing period. Now, it is fired each night at nine, triggered by a remote electronic signal.

Sylvia Hotel

Located near Stanley Park, the Sylvia Hotel is a Vancouver landmark and a favorite of newlyweds and second honeymooners. It was built in 1912 and named after the owner's daughter. Until 1958, the Sylvia was the tallest building in Vancouver's fashionable West End. A "heritage" building since 1975, the Sylvia features distinctive "Virginia creeper" ivy-covered brick walls.

The Vancouver Aquarium is one of Stanley Park's most visited attractions. Calamari, anyone?

(Photo courtesy of the Vancouver Public Library, photo 80327)

Tacoma Aroma

Fueled by pulp mills located in the Commencement Bay industrial area, the Tacoma Aroma was a sinus-melting, sulfurous stench that became the butt of jokes for decades. Defenders were quick to point out that the smell meant jobs, but no doubt the aroma kept development away. The odor abated in the eighties as clean-air technologies and plant closures improved air quality, though one can still catch a periodic, eye-watering whiff.

Ted Murders

During the 1970s, the "Ted" murders frightened and captivated the Northwest and the nation. Ted Bundy was a handsome, articulate law student. In 1974, something snapped and he embarked on his murderous way. Authorities believe Bundy's first victims were Seattleites Lynda Ann Healy and Donna Manson. In the summer of 1974, Bundy frequented Lake Sammamish State Park, wearing his arm in a cast and asking potential victims for help loading gear into his VW bug. Two more women, Denise Naslund and Janice Ott, fell prey to Bundy at the lake. Bundy was captured in August 1974, but escaped twice, heading to Florida where he committed a number of murders in the Tallahassee area. Bundy was finally convicted and, after a decade of appeals, was executed in Florida's electric chair in February 1989. Throughout the decade, Bundy's charm and good looks led some to doubt that he could be guilty of such heinous crimes. When he first escaped, Bundy took on some "folk hero" trappings, a la Richard Kimble in *The Fugitive*. As the date of his execution neared, Bundy tried to trade information about murders for time. Ultimately, Bundy confessed to killing more than thirty women, blaming a fascination with pornography for his murderous rage.

Ted Murders: High-school yearbook photos don't always accurately predict one's future. Pictured is a young Ted Bundy.
(Photo courtesy of the Tacoma Public Library, Wilson High School Yearbook)

UFO Sighting

Forget Roswell—the granddaddy of UFO sightings occurred near Mount Rainier on June 24, 1947. A private pilot named Kenneth Arnold reported seeing nine flying objects about twenty-five miles from his plane. He reported his sighting to an Oregon newspaper, which reported about the "flying saucer" incident. Later government explanations speculated that research balloons could have been the cause of the sighting. Sure.

Underground Seattle

When Seattle rebuilt after a massive fire in 1889, portions of Pioneer Square near Yesler Way were raised up and new structures built on top of the old. A maze of streets, passageways, and buildings remained under the new construction, forgotten for decades. In 1964, a reader wrote to the *Seattle Times* "Troubleshooter" asking if tours of the underground area were available. A groundswell of interest followed and local author, entrepreneur, and public relations wizard Bill Speidel was more than happy to oblige. He started the popular Seattle Underground Tours, mixing a short walk through the old town with anecdotes about Seattle's early days. The Underground, which remains a popular attraction today, also served as a key location for the made-for-television movie *The Night Strangler*.

Wah Mee Massacre

Washington State's worst mass murder occurred February 19, 1983. Thirteen gamblers were found hog-tied and executed on the floor of the Wah Mee gambling club in Seattle's International District. Benjamin Ng, Tony Ng, and Kwan Fai "Willie" Mak were convicted of the killings, based on the testimony of the only survivor, card dealer Wai Chin. The Ngs received life sentences for the crime; Mak was sentenced to die on the grounds that he was more culpable in the killings. Mak's death sentence has since been overturned on legal grounds. Though the precise motive for the crime is not known, most speculation is that the killers belonged to one Chinese community gang (or tong), while the Wah Mee was operated by a rival faction.

Waterfront Blues Festival

A benefit for the Oregon Food Bank, Portland's Waterfront Blues Festival has grown over the past ten years to be the Northwest's premier blues showcase. Every year during the Fourth of July weekend, fans flock to Waterfront Park along the Willamette River. They are treated to a mix of national headliners and local favorites (such as Paul deLay) for cheap admission prices (three bucks and two cans of food as of 1999).

West Seattle Bridge Accident

The West Seattle Bridge over the Duwamish River is the only convenient connection between the core of the city and the thousands of people who live in its western end. Years ago, the bridge was a typical drawbridge that had to open frequently for ships. Drivers weren't happy, nor was the Port of Seattle, which saw the bridge as a hindrance to its plans to extend cargo docks up the Duwamish River. A serendipitous solution appeared on June 10, 1978, in the persona of Rolf Neslund, who at age eighty was the oldest boat pilot plying Puget Sound. While attempting to steer the freighter *Chavez* up the Duwamish, Neslund made a miscalculation and slammed into the bridge, knocking out half of the structure. Since the bridge was now a hazard to navigation, Senator Warren Magnuson could raid the Federal Bridge Replacement Fund. Construction of the new bridge was a scandal in itself as several government officials, including powerful State Legislator Bob Perry, were convicted of receiving kickbacks from bridge contractors. Neslund met a more bizarre end. In 1982, he disappeared without a trace from his home on San Juan Island. Parts of his dismembered body were later found under the house, and his wife was ultimately convicted of murder.

Whistler

A British Columbia gourmet ski resort and charming village, Whistler has attracted outdoor enthusiasts since the early 1900s. Whistler Mountain first opened for skiing in the mid-sixties after highway improvements made it easier for people to reach the area (located seventy-five miles north of Vancouver). In 1975, the name of the township was changed from Alta Lake to Whistler, and plans began in earnest to transform the area into a resort destination. Whistler Village, a carefully planned cluster of shops, restaurants, and lodging, was opened in the early eighties and the tourist boom began.

WPPSS (Whoops!)

The Washington Public Power Supply System has one of the all-time most appropriate acronyms. WPPSS (pronounced Whoops!) was a consortium of Washington utilities that embarked on an ill-fated venture to build a series of nuclear power plants in Washington State. In the mid-1960s, fear of an energy shortage began to grip the nation and the Northwest. Believing that the region's hydroelectric resources were tapped out, and not trusting conservation, public utilities bet the farm on a nuclear building program. They were spurred on by the Bonneville Power Adminstration (led by future Reagan cabinet member Don Hodel), which issued "notices of insufficiency" warning utilities that BPA might not be able to meet their future needs. What followed was characterized by journalist Daniel Jack Chasen as "Tom Swift with a multi-billion-dollar budget. Rube Goldberg backed by AAA-rated municipal bonds." Only one plant was ever completed, and WPPSS ultimately defaulted on its obligations—at the time the largest municipal bond default in American history. Since then, WPPSS has become shorthand for boondoggle and ineptitude, trotted out by opponents of every large public-spending program.

Ye Olde Curiosity Shoppe

Since 1899, the Ye Olde Curiosity Shoppe has successfully vacuumed money out of the pockets of Seattle waterfront tourists. An engaging mix of souvenirs and showmanship, the Shoppe is best known for its display of mummies, "merpeople," a freak pig in a jar, and an "African Voodoo Monkey." P. T. Barnum would be proud, though devotees of roadside Americana would point to the legendary "Jake the Alligator Man" display at Marsh's free museum on the Washington coast's Long Beach Peninsula as a worthy competitor.

Summertime visitors to the Pacific Northwest are often amazed to find day after day of warm sunshine, cloudless skies, and pleasant breezes. They are even more amazed when they venture over the Cascade Mountains into eastern Washington, Oregon, and British Columbia to find mile after mile of dry, sometimes high desert, conditions. They soon believe that the often lamented, grudgingly tolerated rain is a fiction invented by locals to discourage newcomers from staying in the region.

Certainly the image of the Northwest as relentlessly rainy is embedded in the national consciousness—and we do our best to reinforce it. Seattle's annual arts festival is called "Bumbershoot" (though real Northwesterners would rather wear a hooded parka from REI than carry an umbrella). In Portland, architect Tom Bender has proposed building a sort of Zen rain garden, where people can surround themselves with the sound of our most distinctive feature. Bumper stickers proudly proclaim that "Northwesterners don't tan—they rust."

It shouldn't come as a surprise that we embrace the rain, because the rest of our climate is so boring. We don't have hurricanes, we don't have tornadoes, and we don't disappear in periodic dust storms. It seldom gets really hot, and if it does, not for very long. It rarely drops into the deep freeze,

and again those spells pass quickly. That's not to say extreme weather is completely unknown—we've had our share of windstorms, for instance. It's just that most of the time weather in the Northwest is as bland as instant mashed potatoes.

Local civic boosters are always quick to point out that rainfall totals in the Northwest aren't that high compared to other regions in the country with sunnier reputations. Seattle, Portland, and Vancouver all average about forty inches of rain a year—not Palm Springs by any stretch of the imagination, but not a reason to build an ark either. It's more the nature of the rain than the amount that gives the Northwest its soggy stature. Where a city like New Orleans might see a torrential downpour measuring several inches in an hour or so, Northwest rain stretches out for months at a time in a seemingly endless gray drizzle.

When it comes to that endless gray drizzle, the winter of 1999 was world class. Throughout the region, records for consecutive days of rain were smashed. Between November 1, 1998, and February 28, 1999, Portland endured ninety-three days of rain and Seattle checked in with ninety. Rainfall totals also reached new heights, spurred on by the weather phenomena La Niña, which funneled moist tropical air to the Northwest. The *Seattle Times* quoted a University of Washington professor of atmospheric science as saying, "The saving grace about the rain is that it has come in a continuous, but moderate, stream." The newspaper went on to note, "That, of course, is the Northwest equivalent of pointing out that, sure it's hot in Death Valley, but it's a dry heat."

Not all the Northwest shares in the abundance of rain. Much of eastern Washington, Oregon, and British Columbia is dry and warm, with areas that average more than three hundred days of sunshine a year. On the west side of the mountains, small "rain shadows" exist near cities such as Victoria, Sequim, and Medford. These "rain shadows" are areas tucked behind mountains. As rain clouds sweep in from the ocean, they rise to clear the mountains, dropping their contents on the western slopes. Emptied, they pass over the rain shadow town before they can recharge to dump their contents again. The difference in rainfall totals this causes is spectacular. The west side of the Olympic Peninsula often gets 150 inches or more of rain a year, while Sequim averages less than 20 inches.

For people who suffer from Seasonal Affective Disorder (the "winter blues"), the Northwest can be a tough place to live. Sitting at a relatively high latitude, winter daylight is fleeting. Those with long commutes often find they rise and drive to work in the dark, spend all day inside, and then leave in darkness for the drive home. A month or two of that weighs heavily on the spirit. On the plus side, the constant drizzle is credited with helping spur the coffee and microbrew revolutions in the Northwest by creating a ready customer base for coffeehouses and pubs and the chemical therapy provided therein.

Through the years, many writers have celebrated or lamented Northwest weather. Canadian columnist Allan Fotheringham described Vancouver as the Canadian city with the best climate and the worst weather. In his epic novel *Sometimes A Great Notion*, Ken Kesey observed that the rain in the Northwest "falls on the just and unjust alike, falls all day long all winter long every winter every year, and you might just as well give up and admit that's the way it's gonna be, and go take a little snooze." In praising Timothy Egan's book on the changing Northwest (naturally titled *The Good Rain*), Tom Robbins described the Northwest as "this spectacularly mildewed corner of the American Linoleum."

Robbins himself made rain a central part of his breakthrough 1971 novel *Another Roadside Attraction*.

More recently, author David Laskin has published *Rains All the Time*, a book that manages to successfully mix scientific fact with lyrical prose. According to Laskin, "Perhaps it's because the weather out here has been the butt of so many jokes that it inspires such fascination—and clandestine pride. It's what we're known for, a regional specialty like Florida oranges or New York attitude, so we might as well revel in it." That and build up some frequent flyer miles so you can fly to Cabo in February.

ECOTOPIA AND CASCADIA ECOTOPIA ECOTOPIA AND CASCADIA

In 1975, writer Ernest Callenbach published a small book titled *Ecotopia*. Set just before the dawn of the twenty-first century, the book purported to be the diaries of William Weston, a newspaper reporter from the East sent to chronicle life in the former Pacific Northwest. Why was this necessary? Well, it seems that in 1980, the residents of Washington, Oregon, and Northern California had gotten more than a little fed up with the materialistic and militaristic culture of the United States, seceded from the union, and formed their own nation called "Ecotopia." After seceding, the Ecotopians cut off all communication with the United States, leading to wild rumors about what was happening in the new country. Weston's report would be the first comprehensive report on the state of Ecotopia since the secession.

And just what does Weston find in Ecotopia? Over the twenty years since secession, the entire region has turned into Eugene! Not really, but he does find a green haven, based on principles of sustainability. The economy of Ecotopia is deliberately "no growth," recycling is universal, and the energy system is based on solar power. The Ecotopians eat natural food, live in communal houses, and wear natural fibers. They don't drive cars, using the bike lanes, pedestrian walkways, and public transitways

that have replaced the roads. The mindless lust for possessions has been replaced by an interest in community activities and citizenship—good thing since Ecotopians work only twenty hours a week. Weston was obviously impressed since the book closes with him sending a note to his East Coast editors saying he is never coming back.

Not all institutions related to the United States were eliminated. Boeing stockholders will be pleased to note that the company fared well in Ecotopia. Before Ecotopia seceded, a recession and the failure of the ecologically controversial SST airplane wracked the company. The Ecotopian government decided to tap Boeing's excess manufacturing capacity to build the national high-speed rail system that ran the length of the country. On the political front, the Northwest didn't fare as well since the capital of Ecotopia is in San Francisco (not surprising since Callenbach hailed from Berkeley).

While critics slammed the writing in the book as clunky, the public loved it—especially in the Pacific Northwest. One reviewer said readers "regarded the novel not as good fiction but as a kind of wishful nonfiction, a forecast of how the future could or should evolve." Ecotopia also reflected (and inspired) a bit of civic isolationism, particularly in Oregon where Governor Tom McCall spoke of a "plywood curtain" to keep Californians out, and a famous (still sometimes seen) bumper sticker proclaimed "Don't Californicate Oregon." It's important to note the distinction that Ecotopia draws between mellow, green, Birkenstock-wearing, Jesse Colin Young-listening Northern Californians and those bad-driving, ostentatious, spandex-clad, mall-shopping Southern Californians. In the world of Ecotopia, Northern Californians aren't really Californians— they're just Northwesterners who fell a bit south.

Certainly Callenbach was on to something when he portrayed Ecotopia as a "bioregion." Political boundaries are always artificial—regions have more to do with biological, economic, and cultural similarities than they do with lines on a map. A few years after Callenbach published *Ecotopia*, Joel Garreau wrote *The Nine Nations of North America* in which he identified nine basic regional clusters. Ecotopia, defined a bit more broadly to include part of Alaska, was one of Garreau's "nations."

Over the past decade, another vision of the Northwest has been emerging. Dubbed "Cascadia," it focuses on the economic linkages in the region. Cascadia is usually defined as encompassing the I-5 corridor from Eugene, Oregon, to Vancouver, British Columbia. That dry stuff on the other side of the mountains doesn't count. Proponents of the Cascadian vision, led by people such as former *Seattle Weekly* Publisher David Brewster and Seattle Mayor Paul Schell, look to the European model where states still remain, but institutions exist to ensure cross-border cooperation. One of the first projects that Cascadia supporters have championed is improving transportation connections,

winning more frequent rail service from Eugene to Vancouver. Mayor Schell has even proposed renaming Puget Sound as the Salish Sea, to recognize native peoples.

Whereas many people supporting the notion of Cascadia have environmental reputations and motivations, it clearly doesn't equate to the Ecotopian vision. Cascadia supporters take care to note that environmental problems don't respect boundaries so that cooperation is essential. Still, their key focus is the economic power of the region.

Although Cascadia has the eye of policy makers and the media at the moment, there are still many people in the Northwest hewing to the Ecotopian vision. Environmental think tanks, such as Northwest Environment Watch, have sprung up declaring that the Northwest "remains—after two centuries of aggressive development—the most ecologically intact part of the industrial world. If the Northwest cannot achieve sustainability, probably no place can. If it can, it will lead the globe." There also is a substantial "simple living" movement, which preaches the virtues of working less and spending less—right in line with the Ecotopians.

Which will prevail? If the past twenty years is a guide, the smart betting would be on Cascadia, tempered by a bit of Ecotopian philosophy. One could call it "green greenbacks," except that funny-colored Canadian money messes everything up. It doesn't matter what they call it as long as we get those twenty-hour workweeks.

SPORTS AND RECREATION

the Mariners prevailed and Perry became the oldest baseball player to earn 300 career victories. One side note to the game was that a mere 27,369 Mariners fans showed up to see this bit of baseball history, while 36,716 would pack the Kingdome two nights later for a Funny Nose Glasses giveaway night. It would take thirteen more years for Seattle baseball fans to restore their credibility during the team's memorable 1995 divisional play-off series against the same Bronx Bombers.

〽 Akers, Michelle

One of the heroes of the U.S. Women's 1999 World Cup championship soccer team is a 1984 graduate of Shorecrest High School, just north of Seattle. Sometimes referred to as the "Pele" of women's soccer, Michelle Akers began playing the sport as an eight-year-old in Santa Clara, California, and by high school was one of the top female players in the nation. A four-time All-American at the University of Central Florida, Akers is a fourteen-year veteran of the U.S. National Team. An Olympic gold medalist in the 1996 Atlanta Games and World Cup champion in 1991 and 1999, Akers is the all-time leading scorer for the U.S. National Team programs (women's or men's). In 1999, Akers became the first professional soccer player to appear on the Wheaties box.

〽 Ancient Mariner, The (Gaylord Perry)

The Ancient Mariner nickname was given to baseball Hall of Fame pitcher Gaylord Perry during his short but historic stint with the Seattle Mariners baseball team in the early eighties. Perry began the 1982 season with the Mariners with 297 career victories and picked up wins 298 and 299 early in the season. On Thursday, May 13, 1982, Seattle scored five runs in the third and two more in the seventh against the New York Yankees, providing the forty-three-year-old "Ancient Mariner" with a comfortable cushion as

〽 Anthony, Earl

The greatest professional bowler of all time, Earl Anthony ("The Earl of Tacoma") got his start in the Puget Sound area. In the sixties, the

Tacoma's Earl Anthony was the "kingpin" of professional bowling during the 1970s and 1980s.
(Photo courtesy of the Tacoma Public Library, Bicentennial Collection)

crew-cut Anthony was a forklift driver for a local grocery wholesaler, spending his off hours perfecting his skills at local bowling lanes (up to five hours a day). In 1970, after his first stint on tour, Anthony told the *Tacoma News Tribune*, "I now feel that I belong. I'm not just an orphan, and I feel that I can bowl well enough to make a living." Always a master of understatement, Anthony went on from that point to dominate professional bowling the way Jack Nicklaus did professional golf. With his calm demeanor and good sportsmanship, Anthony was a role model who transcended his sport. Anthony still owns the record for most wins on the Professional Bowlers Association (PBA) Tour with forty-one regular tour victories and five on the senior circuit. He has been named Bowler of the Year six times and was the first bowler to earn $100,000 in a season and $1 million in a career. Anthony briefly came out of retirement in the mid-nineties at the Seattle Senior Open. He now makes his home near Portland.

Apple Cup

One of college football's best "rivalry" games, the annual Apple Cup contest pits the University of Washington Huskies against their cross-state rival, the Washington State University Cougars. This gridiron battle dates back to 1900 when the teams played to a 5-5 tie in Seattle, but only since 1962 has the winner been awarded the Apple Cup. Washington currently holds a sizable edge in the series. One of the greatest Apple Cup wins by the Huskies was in 1975 when the Dawgs came from a 27-14 deficit with 3:01 to go to win the game 28-27. A memorable Cougar victory occurred in 1992 when quarterback Drew Bledsoe shredded the Husky secondary in a driving snowstorm in Pullman for a 42-23 victory.

Baker, Terry

Oregon State University's (OSU) all-time greatest football player, southpaw quarterback Terry Baker won the Heisman Trophy in 1962—the first West Coast player to capture college football's top honor. During the 1962 season, Baker completed 112 of 203 passes for 1,738 yards and 15 touchdowns and led the Beavers in net yards, averaging 4.5 per carry. At the end of the season, he led OSU to a 6-0 Liberty Bowl victory over Villanova by running 99 yards for the game's only score. Baker was also honored that year with *Sports Illustrated*'s Sportsman of the

Beaver quarterback Terry Baker was the first West Coast player to win the Heisman Trophy.
(Photo courtesy of Oregon State University)

Year Award. After graduating in 1963 with a degree in mechanical engineering, Baker went on to play professional football for the National Football League's Los Angeles Rams and the Canadian Football League's Edmonton Eskimos. He earned his law degree in 1968 and today is a practicing attorney in Portland.

Baylor, Elgin

Named one of the fifty greatest players in National Basketball Association history, Elgin Baylor is also the greatest hoopster ever to play for the Seattle University Chieftains. Described as "the man with a thousand moves," the six-foot-five Baylor was an offensive scoring machine. During the 1957–58 season, Elgin scored 32.5 points per game and grabbed 559 rebounds—second and third in the nation, respectively. More importantly, he led the Chieftains to the National Collegiate Athletic Association (NCAA) title game. Although they lost to Kentucky, Baylor was named the tournament's most valuable player. Even though he was only a junior, Baylor decided to turn pro the next year and went on to a phenomenal fourteen-year career with the Minneapolis–L.A. Lakers.

B.C. Lions

A Canadian Football League (CFL) franchise since 1954, Vancouver's B.C. Lions have entertained millions of lower mainlanders, first in old Empire Stadium, and currently in the B.C. Place domed stadium. The Lions won CFL Grey Cup championships in 1964, 1985, and 1994, the last against the Baltimore Stallions in B.C. Place—the Lions' first title win before a home crowd. Memorable B.C. Lions players throughout the years include quarterbacks Joe Kapp, Doug Flutie, and Roy Dewalt; running backs By Bailey, Willie Fleming, Cory Philpot, and Larry Key; kickers Norm Fieldgate and Lui Passaglia; receivers

Mervyn Fernandez and Jim "Dirty 30" Young; and defensive standout Al Wilson.

B.C. Place Stadium

B.C. Place Stadium in Vancouver is the largest air-supported domed stadium in the world. Built in 1983, the stadium is covered with a fiberglass and Teflon roof which is only one-thirtieth of an inch thick but stronger than steel. B.C. Place is the home field for the B.C. Lions of the Canadian Football League and has also featured major league baseball games with the Seattle Mariners and Toronto Blue Jays. Musical acts that have performed at B.C. Place include the Rolling Stones, U2, Pink Floyd, the Who, and the Three Tenors. The largest crowd ever to fill the stadium was for Pope John Paul II. He had no opening act.

Beavers of Oregon State University

"OSU, our hats are off to you" is the first line of the Oregon State University fight song, which faithful alumni sing lustily as they cheer their Beaver teams to victory in Corvallis, Oregon. OSU athletes wear orange, black, and white colors and play in Reser Stadium (football) and Gill Coliseum (basketball). Under former OSU football coach W. H. "Bill" Hargiss (1918–19), the Beavers were the first team to use the forward pass and the huddle.

Beckey's Bibles

If you periodically haul your carcass up the mountains of Western Washington, you're probably packing a "bible" with you. Of course, we mean a "Beckey's bible," the popular name for the *Cascades Alpine Guide*, three books by Fred Beckey that identify every mountain in the Cascade Range from the Columbia River to the Fraser River Valley. They contain an immense collection of information on climbing routes, geology, and mountaineering history and are enjoyed by serious climbers as well as weekend hikers. If you prefer to sit at home in your recliner, you've probably never heard of these books.

⚡ Bostrom, Trish

University of Washington tennis star Trish Bostrom put Seattle and the Northwest on the worldwide tennis map in 1977, when she teamed with Mary Carillo to upset Billie Jean King and Karen Susman in an early qualifying match in the women's doubles at Wimbledon. Bostrom and Carillo progressed as far as the fourth round, but in future years never got back to Centre Court. Bostrom, who was the third-ranked women's doubles player in the United States in 1979, now produces tennis instructional materials and occasionally reports on tennis events for Seattle radio stations.

⚡ Bosworth, Brian

The most flamboyant and "hyped" player to ever don a Seattle Seahawks football uniform, Brian Bosworth was first a controversial star football player at the University of Oklahoma. Bosworth's on- and off-field antics resulted in the creation of "The Boz" persona, a larger-than-life antihero. Think professional wrestler "Stone Cold Steve Austin" with hair and you're in the ballpark. The Seahawks secured Bosworth in a special supplementary draft in 1987 and, after weeks of negotiation, signed him to a then unheard of ten-year $11 million contract. Despite his considerable football skills, Bosworth's biggest weapon was his mouth. In his autobiography written and published during the 1988 off-season, he boasted that he wanted to "shoot" Denver Broncos quarterback John Elway. He also thumbed his nose at National Football League Commissioner Pete Rozelle, who refused to let Bosworth wear his college

football number in the pros. A degenerative shoulder condition limited Bosworth's playing time during his first two seasons, and in 1990 he unceremoniously retired from football after playing only twenty-five undistinguished games. Today, Bosworth is an unassuming husband and father, churning out B-grade action movies.

⚡ Bowerman, Bill

What do actors Donald Sutherland and R. Lee Ermey have in common? They both portrayed legendary University of Oregon (UO) track coach Bill Bowerman in movies about the life of long-distance runner Steve Prefontaine. A lifetime Oregonian born in 1911, Bowerman is one of the most important figures in competitive and recreational running during the past fifty years. From 1949 to 1972, Bowerman's UO track teams won four national championships, set thirteen world and twenty-two American records, and produced twenty-three Olympic athletes. Bowerman was also a pioneer in the field of training and conditioning. The "hard/easy" system of runners' training (generally attributed to Bowerman and his UO successor Bill Bellinger) is a method that alternates hard workouts with recovery days. Bowerman is also credited with inventing the waffle outsole for running shoes. The first test model was actually made by pouring urethane on his wife's waffle maker, and the design became the best-selling shoe in America and helped launch the seventies jogging boom. Bowerman developed a business partnership with former UO track athlete Phil Knight in the early sixties that became the Nike company. Bowerman died in 1999.

Brown, Fred

One of the most popular players in Seattle Supersonics basketball history was Fred Brown, a six-foot-four guard from the University of Iowa who earned the nickname "Downtown" for his deadly long-range jump shots. Drafted by the Sonics in 1971 as the sixth overall pick, Brown made an immediate impact on the team, averaging 13.5 points per game in only his second season. During the mid-1970s, Brown started in the backcourt with Slick Watts and was the Sonics' leading scorer, netting a club record 58 points in a game against the Golden State Warriors in 1974. When Lenny Wilkins took over the team in 1977, Brown became a valuable "sixth man," coming off the bench to lend instant offensive firepower with his pure shooting ability and helping the Sonics win the National Basketball Association (NBA) championship in 1979. When the three-point shot became official during the 1979–80 season, Brown became the league's first ever percentage leader, hitting at a .443 clip. After thirteen seasons (the longest ever by a Supersonic), "Downtown" Freddie Brown retired in 1984 as the team's career leader in games played, points scored, field goals, and steals. His number 32 was retired in a special ceremony in 1986.

Canucks, Vancouver

The Pacific Northwest's only National Hockey League (NHL) team, the Vancouver Canucks were awarded their franchise in May 1970 and played their first game the following October, losing to the Los Angeles Kings 3-1. For several seasons the Canucks struggled like most expansion teams, but in 1982 the Canucks achieved near greatness with a remarkable play-off run against teams with better regular-season records. The Canucks made the Stanley Cup Finals, only to be swept in four games by the New York

Islanders. Twelve years later, the Canucks were back in the finals, again winning against heavily favored opponents. They stretched the New York Rangers to the limit before a heartbreaking 3-2 loss in game seven. Famous Canucks players through the years include Stan "The Steamer" Smyl, Kirk McLean, and Trevor Linden.

Carner, JoAnne

One of the greatest women amateur and professional golfers of all time hails from the Seattle suburb of Kirkland. JoAnne Carner was born in 1939 and learned the game of golf on Seattle-area public courses. As JoAnne Gunderson (her maiden name), the "Great Gundy" won five U.S. Amateur titles between 1957 and 1968 before turning pro in 1970. In her first year on the tour, Carner captured her first Ladies Professional Golf Association (LPGA) title and won Rookie of the Year honors. Since then, she has won forty-two LPGA events, three Rolex Player of the Year honors, and eight national titles. Elected to the LPGA Hall of Fame (one of the toughest in all of sports) in 1982, Carner now lives in Florida and is still active on the tour.

Chieftains of Seattle University

Once upon a time during the fifties, Seattle University (SU) basketball was the hottest ticket in town. In January 1952, the SU Chieftains (later renamed the Redhawks), led by twin brothers Johnny and Eddie O'Brien, upset the mighty Harlem Globetrotters. Six years later, the Chieftains made it to the National Collegiate Athletic Association (NCAA) championship game, led by future National Basketball Association (NBA) Hall of Famer Elgin Baylor. During their improbable run, SU beat the mighty University of San Francisco on Baylor's last-second jump shot, and then downed California in another buzzer-beater to make the Final Four. In the semifinals, the Chieftains easily handled Kansas State 73-51, setting up a marquee final match-up with the University of Kentucky and their legendary coach Adolph Rupp. Unfortunately, Baylor's ribs had been badly bruised during the Kansas State game and he was heavily taped for the finals. Seattle lost to Kentucky 84-72 as Baylor had one of the worst performances of his career. A month after losing the game, SU was hit with a two-year suspension for recruiting violations, and twenty-two years later SU dropped out of Division 1 to join the ranks of the lesser National Association of Intercollegiate Athletes (NAIA).

⚡ Civil War, The

The Civil War is the nickname for the annual football rivalry game between the University of Oregon Ducks and the Oregon State University Beavers. The inaugural Civil War game was played in 1894, making it one of the oldest Division I-A rivalry games in the nation. Oregon holds the series lead, winning twenty of twenty-five games between 1974 and 1998. Oregon State, however, may have turned the corner with a dramatic 44-41 double-overtime victory in the 1998 Civil War contest. Perhaps indicative of a trend in sports requiring every moment of every event to have a corporate host, the Civil War is now officially "sponsored" by your Northwest Dodge Dealers.

⚡ Commonwealth Games (Vancouver 1954)

The Commonwealth Games are modeled on the Olympic Games but include only countries that are or were at one time part of the British Empire. The first "British Empire Games" were held in 1930 in Hamilton, Ontario, and a quarter century later, Vancouver hosted the games. The main venue was twenty-five-thousand-seat Empire Stadium, which later became the home field of the B.C. Lions football team. The major

highlight of the 1954 games was England's Roger Bannister winning the gold medal in the mile with a time of 3:58.8. Bannister had broken the four-minute barrier only weeks earlier in Oxford, England.

⚡ Commonwealth Games (Victoria 1994)

British Columbia's second Commonwealth Games came four decades after Vancouver hosted the games in 1954. By the nineties, of course, marketing had entered the picture and the Victoria Commonwealth Games were heavily promoted. The official mascot of the games was "Klee Wyck," an orca whale (and the nickname that Vancouver Island's native peoples had given to famed British Columbia artist Emily Carr.) Australia won the games, earning 182 total medals, with Canada placing a distant second. Britain's Linford Christie electrified the crowd by winning the gold medal in the 100 meters with a time of 9.91 seconds, defeating favorite son Donovan Bailey.

⚡ Cougars of Washington State University

Pullman's Washington State University (or "Wazzu" as it's affectionately known to Cougar alumni) is located about eighty miles south of Spokane in the rolling wheatfields of southeastern Washington State known as "The Palouse." Often reviled by their city cousins at the University of Washington (UW) in Seattle, Cougar fans are passionate and proud of their sports teams (perhaps because there is nothing else to do in Pullman). Nothing brings out Husky hatred more than the annual Apple Cup football game between UW and WSU.

WSU home football games are played in Martin Stadium and basketball games are contested in Friel Court, both located on the Pullman campus. The school also has a proud tradition in track and field and baseball. Famous WSU athletes include football stars Jack Thompson and Mark Rypien, basketball great Steve Puidokas, and long-distance runners Gerry Lindgren and Henry Rono.

Davis, Alvin

Alvin Davis is often referred to as "Mr. Mariner" because of his longevity with the Seattle baseball club and the fact he was the first marquee player produced by the Mariners' farm system. Davis made his debut at first base with the Seattle Mariners in 1984. During that season, he batted .284 with 27 homers and 116 RBIs, earning a spot on the American League All-Star team as well as American League Rookie of the Year honors. For the remainder of the decade, Davis was one of the bright spots on a team that perennially underachieved. He was a club leader in batting average, RBIs, and walks, and was voted the team's most valuable player three times. Davis played eight seasons with the M's and was the first inductee into the Mariners Hall of Fame in June 1997.

Drexler, Clyde

One of the most popular players in Portland Trail Blazers basketball history, Clyde Drexler was a 1983 first-round draft pick who had been part of the University of Houston's legendary "Phi Slamma Jamma" National Collegiate Athletic Association (NCAA) Final Four teams. Nicknamed "The Glide" because of his ability to drive, swoop, and dunk, Drexler is considered second only to Michael Jordan as the best shooting guard of his generation. A perennial all-star, Drexler led the Trail Blazers into the National Basketball Association (NBA) Finals in 1990 and 1992, losing to the Detroit Pistons and Chicago Bulls, respectively. In 1992, he was a member of the original U.S. "Dream Team" that captured the gold medal in basketball at the Summer Olympics in Barcelona. Frustrated by contract negotiations and his inability to win a championship, Drexler asked to be traded, and in February 1995, he was sent to the Houston Rockets to reunite with his college teammate Hakeem Olajuwon. That spring, the Rockets beat the Orlando Magic in the finals and Drexler had his championship ring. Although he retired in 1998 after three years with the Rockets, he is still the Trail Blazers' career leader in games played (867), points (18,040), rebounds (5,339), and steals (1,795).

Ducks of the University of Oregon

While the image of an angry Donald Duck shaking his fist through a giant letter "O" is not the most intimidating of college mascots, the University of Oregon (UO) Ducks have enjoyed decades of athletic success in football, basketball, track and field, and other National Collegiate Athletic Association (NCAA) sports. Duck football teams play their home games near the Eugene campus in Autzen Stadium which is named for a prominent Portland lumberman. Oregon basketball is played on campus in MacArthur Court—a four-story ivy-covered pavilion known as "The Pit." Notable UO athletic alumni include Steve Prefontaine, Dan Fouts, Ahmad Rashad (formerly Bobby Moore), Mel Renfro, Norm Van Brocklin, and Alberto Salazar.

⚡ Fosbury, Dick

Medford High School and Oregon State University's Dick Fosbury won the 1968 Olympic high jump gold medal using his then-unorthodox "Fosbury Flop." Instead of using the traditional method of straddling the bar and crossing over facedown, Fosbury went over the bar by turning his back to it and going over shoulders first. The technique helped him shatter the previous Olympic high jump record by clearing the bar at 7' 4¼" and gave birth to a whole new way of jumping. Today the Fosbury Flop is the accepted method of high jumping and Fosbury himself was elected to the U.S. Olympic Hall of Fame in 1993. Fosbury came out of retirement at the 1998 Nike World Masters Games and placed third in the high jump.

Dick Fosbury: His "flop" was a big success.
(Photo courtesy of Oregon State University)

⚡ Fouts, Dan

Although the University of Oregon (UO) teams he played on were average at best, that didn't stop Dan Fouts from making his mark in Ducks football history as one of their greatest quarterbacks and most prolific passers. During his tenure as Oregon's starting signal caller (1970–72), Fouts teamed up with Bobby Moore (now Ahmad Rashad) to form one of the Pacific-8 Conference's most potent offensive duos. During his senior season, Fouts was named to the All-Conference team. He also served as a test subject for Nike's first waffle outsole shoe designed by legendary UO track and field coach Bill Bowerman. A third-round National Football League draft choice in 1973 (sixty-fourth pick overall), Fouts went on to become a Hall of Fame quarterback for the San Diego Chargers. Fouts lives in Sisters, Oregon, and currently broadcasts college football games for ABC Sports.

⚡ Fox, Terry

Canadian Terry Fox was born in the province of Manitoba but attended college at Simon Fraser University near Vancouver. In 1977, his right leg was amputated because of bone cancer, and during his recovery, Fox decided to raise funds for cancer research by running across Canada. After months of training to run on an artificial leg, Fox began his "Marathon of Hope" at St. John's, Newfoundland. For five months, Fox's run received constant media attention, but on September 1, he was forced to abandon the journey near Thunder Bay, Ontario, because the cancer had spread to his lungs. Terry Fox died a few months later just prior to his twenty-third birthday. His courage has inspired others to continue his work, and today, Terry Fox Runs for cancer research are held annually in Canada, the United States, and other countries.

⅏ Glickman, Harry

Oregon Sports Hall of Fame member Harry Glickman is the father of the Portland Trail Blazers National Basketball Association (NBA) franchise. A Portland native and sports impresario, Glickman founded Oregon Sports Attractions in 1952, which promoted National Football League (NFL) games and the Harlem Globetrotters. He also served as president and general manager of the Portland Buckaroos of the Western Hockey League. In 1970, Glickman succeeded in securing Portland's first major league sports franchise, the Portland Trail Blazers, which has been one of the league's most stable and successful teams. Glickman has also been involved in numerous civic projects, and each year the state of Oregon's top professional athlete is honored with the Harry Glickman Professional Athlete of the Year award at the Oregonian Banquet of Champions.

⅏ Gorman, Tom

A mainstay on the professional tennis circuit during the 1970s, Seattle's Tom Gorman won seven tennis tournaments starting in 1971 and had a .500 winning percentage as a doubles player, claiming ten victories during his professional career. For many years, Gorman was captain of the United States Davis Cup team and has posted more wins (eighteen) than any other captain. Gorman still competes in mixed doubles masters competitions. Gorman also led the Sea-Port Cascades franchise in the short-lived professional tennis league during the late 1970s.

⅏ Greene, Nancy

The most successful alpine skier in British Columbia history was a young woman from Rossland, B.C., deep in the heart of West Kootenay, about six hundred miles east of Vancouver. In the late sixties, Nancy Greene was considered the best skier in the world, and had the credentials to prove it. Nicknamed "Tiger" because of her fearless style of skiing, Greene won the World Cup in 1967 and 1968, and captured a gold medal in the giant slalom and a silver medal in the slalom at the 1968 Winter Olympics in Grenoble, France. Much of her success was attributed to her lack of fear and to her strength, since Greene was one of the first female skiers to do extensive weight training. Today, Greene operates a ski lodge in Sun Peaks, B.C. (near Vancouver) with her husband Al Raine, former Canadian national alpine ski coach.

⅏ Griffey Jr., Ken

The player who personifies the Seattle Mariners for millions of baseball fans around the world is shoo-in future Hall of Famer Ken Griffey Jr. Drafted number one by the M's in 1987, "Junior" spent less than two seasons in the minors before being called up to the big club in 1989 at the age of nineteen. In his first major league at-bat Griffey hit a double, and in his first appearance at the Kingdome he hit his first major league home run. In 1993, Griffey tied a major league record by swatting home runs in eight consecutive games, and he has hit more home runs before the age of thirty than all but a handful of baseball greats. Griffey is also one of baseball's best defensive center fielders and a perennial Gold Glove winner. An over-the-back catch in New York's Yankee Stadium several years ago still has baseball fans buzzing, and Griffey has stolen more than a dozen sure home run balls by scaling the outfield walls.

⅏ Hacky Sack

Since the Northwest is home to both Reed College in Portland and the Evergreen State College in Olympia, the hacky sack—a game often associated with students at alternative liberal arts colleges—just had to be invented here. In 1972, John Stalberger and Mike Marshall of Portland developed a refinement of old footbag games commonly called hacky sack. Originally, the game was little more than a way for Stalberger to rehabilitate an injured knee. Over time, the two developed a unique, durable bag that players would propel with their feet. After Marshall's untimely death, Stalberger continued to promote hacky sack, eventually selling the U.S. rights to the Wham-O Toy Company.

Ⓜ Hansen, Lars

The only British Columbia-born and schooled athlete (Husky great Bob Houbregs was born in the province but moved to Seattle at an early age) to play in the National Basketball Association (NBA) was Coquitlam, B.C., native Lars Hansen. A six-foot-ten center, Hansen led his high school to the British Columbia provincial title in 1972 and then went on to play four seasons for the University of Washington in Seattle. Although his NBA career never amounted to much, he did play fifteen games for the Seattle Supersonics during their 1978–79 championship season, averaging about five points per game.

Ⓜ Hansen, Rick

Champion wheelchair athlete Rick Hansen hails from Vancouver. When Hansen was fifteen years old, he was involved in an automobile accident that left him a paraplegic for life. Undeterred, Hansen decided to remain physically active, competing in a variety of sports and eventually becoming one of the top three wheelchair marathoners in the world. In 1986, Hansen conceived a world tour to raise awareness of the potential of disabled people and raise money for spinal cord research. During his "Man in Motion Tour," Hansen literally wheeled through thirty-four countries and four continents, leading to the creation of the Rick Hansen Institute at the University of British Columbia, which supports education for the disabled and funds spinal cord research.

Ⓜ Harding, Tonya

Portland's Tonya Harding will not be remembered for her two U.S. figure skating championships, but for the scandal resulting from an assault on her competitor that provided the world with an unprecedented Winter Olympics soap opera. On January 6, 1994, figure skating diva Nancy Kerrigan was struck on the knee after practice by an assailant hired by Harding's ex-husband Jeff Gillooly and loutish bodyguard Shawn Eckardt. Harding denied any involvement, and deployed a phalanx of lawyers to ensure she could compete at the 1994 Winter Olympics in Norway. Kerrigan recovered to take the silver medal at the Games, while Harding emotionally dissolved in front of the world. After the Olympics, Harding ultimately admitted conspiring to hinder prosecution, though she continues to deny prior knowledge of the assault on Kerrigan. Harding was stripped of her national title and banned for life from U.S. amateur figure skating competitions, but the greatest insult came when Gillooly, strapped for cash, sold an explicit videotape of their wedding night triple lutz to Penthouse magazine.

Ⓜ Harshman, Marv

A Northwest basketball icon, Marv Harshman had a forty-year run as coach at Pacific Lutheran University (PLU) in Tacoma, Washington State University (WSU) in Pullman, and the University of Washington (UW) in Seattle. Raised in Lake Stevens, Washington, Harshman was a four-sport star at PLU and began his coaching career there in 1945. Harshman's Lute teams made six appearances in National Association of Intercollegiate Athletes (NAIA) tournaments and this success earned him the head-coaching job at WSU in the late fifties. His greatest college success was at the UW where he was the head coach from 1971 to 1985. Harshman took three UW teams to National Collegiate Athletic Association (NCAA) postseason tournaments (1976, 1984, and 1985). His 1984 squad, which featured National Basketball Association (NBA) star Detlef Schrempf, made it to the Sweet Sixteen. A contemporary of University of California Los Angeles' legendary John Wooden, Harshman was the only coach to defeat Wooden the first time he met him and was the last coach to defeat him before Wooden retired. Harshman himself retired with 642 college victories and was the second-winningest coach in the history of UW next to "Hec" Edmundson. Harshman has been elected to the Naismith Basketball Hall of Fame.

Heinrich, Don

The University of Washington Huskies' first "superstar" football quarterback of the modern era was the late Don Heinrich. A two-time All-American, Heinrich twice led the nation in passing. While he teamed in the same backfield with Husky great Hugh McElhenny, injuries kept the two from playing more than one full season together and spoiled what surely would have been one or two Rose Bowl appearances. After college, Heinrich played and coached in the National Football League (NFL) for eighteen seasons. He also was a football broadcaster, including a stint with the Seattle Seahawks.

Holman, Marshall

Marshall Holman, the pride of Medford, Oregon, is a member of the Professional Bowlers Association (PBA) Hall of Fame and fourth on the PBA's all-time money list. Holman has more than twenty national tour titles to his credit and was named PBA Player of the Year in 1987. A fiery competitor, Holman's bad-boy image proved an effective counterpoint to the calm and conservative Earl Anthony from Tacoma, sparking increased interest in professional bowling. A mellower Holman now works as a television commentator for bowling events.

Houbregs, Bob

One of the greatest basketball players to suit up in the purple and gold of the University of Washington (UW), Bob Houbregs was born in 1932 in Vancouver, British Columbia. He attended Queen Anne High School in Seattle before moving on to the UW where in 1953 he became National Collegiate Athletic Association (NCAA) Player of the Year as he led the Huskies to a best ever 30-3 record. Houbregs ranks second in NCAA tournament history with a 34.8 scoring average. "Houby" (as he was known) was drafted by the then-Milwaukee Hawks in 1953 and played five years (1953–58) in the National Basketball Association (NBA) with Milwaukee, Baltimore, Boston, Fort Wayne, and Detroit. During his 1957–58 season with the Detroit Pistons, Houbregs suffered a career-ending back injury. He served as general manager of the Seattle Supersonics basketball team from 1970 to 1973 and was elected to the basketball Hall of Fame as a player in 1986.

Huskies of the University of Washington

The University of Washington (UW) is the Pacific Northwest's largest university and home to storied sports traditions in football, basketball, baseball, and rowing. Established in Seattle in 1861, the UW, or "U-Dub" as it's better known to locals, plays home football games in picturesque Husky Stadium, located on the beautiful shores of Lake Washington. Basketball games are contested in the nearby venerable Hec Edmundson Pavilion named after the Dawgs' longtime men's basketball coach. "Hec-Ed" is currently undergoing a multimillion-dollar remodeling project that will expand seating capacity and upgrade facilities. Given the school's proximity to water, it's no wonder that Husky men's and women's rowing teams have won numerous national and international titles. Races are conducted on the "Montlake Cut"—a narrow waterway that connects Lake Washington with Lake Union bordering the southern portion of the campus.

Hydroplanes

It just wouldn't be summer in the Pacific Northwest without hydroplane racing, especially with three stops on the annual Unlimited Hydroplane Racing Association tour—the Columbia River in the Tri-Cities (Richland, Kennewick, and Pasco), Lake Washington in Seattle as part of the annual Seafair celebration, and Okanagon Lake in Kelowna, B.C. Seattle's Anchor Jenson (a boatbuilder), Ted Jones (an engineer), and Stan Sayres (a wealthy car dealer) combined in the late forties to perfect the world's first hydroplane racing boat. In 1950, the Jensen-Jones-Sayres team built the historic "Slo-Mo-Shun IV" which set a world straightaway record at the Gold Cup championship in Detroit. The danger of the sport was immediately apparent—the following year, the Gold Cup was held on Seattle's Lake Washington and local sports broadcaster Bill O'Mara led the audience in the Lord's Prayer after the Quicksilver boat flipped, killing its two-man crew. During the sixties Bill Muncey dominated the sport, but Seattle's Chip Hanauer owns most of the unlimited hydroplane world records, many of which were set when he piloted the Miss Bud-

weiser in the early nineties. Hydros are such a big part of the Northwest sports psyche that thousands of Seattle Mariners baseball fans enjoy a computer-animated hydroplane race in the middle of the sixth inning during every home game at Safeco Field.

James, Don

The winningest-coach in University of Washington football history, Don James is a low-key, somewhat aloof chief executive officer who ran the football program with military precision and organization. James was the headman at Kent State when he was tapped to be the Huskies' new head coach after Jim Owens retired in 1974. The team hadn't been to a postseason bowl game since 1964 and attendance had declined. James's first two seasons were middling at best, and when the Huskies began the 1977 campaign at 1-3, calls for his ouster could be heard throughout

Don James is cerebral and reserved but the winningest coach in Husky football history.
(Photo courtesy of the University of Washington and Don James)

the local media. A 54-0 rout of the Oregon Ducks in week five started the Dawgs on a roll that would propel the Huskies into the Rose Bowl and a shocking 27-20 upset of the Michigan Wolverines. James's teams never looked back after that season as the Huskies began an impressive string of postseason appearances including a Rose Bowl triumph in 1982 and an Orange Bowl victory in 1984 when the team finished second in the national polls. After failing to go to a bowl game following the 1988 season, James revamped the team's traditional conservative play calling to emphasize offensive speed and a gambling aggressive defense. This led to three straight Rose Bowl appearances, including a share of the National Championship with the University of Miami following the 1991 season. Although he was not considered a "player's coach," James nevertheless earned players' respect from a distance. He resigned just before the start of the 1993 season in protest of heavy sanctions levied against the Huskies by the Pacific-10 Conference for recruiting violations.

Kamikaze Kids

In the early seventies, the University of Oregon (UO) hired a former marine named Dick Harter to resuscitate the school's basketball program with a mixture of fear, intensity, and intimidation. Harter's practices were brutal and the players who survived became known as the "Kamikaze Kids"—so named by Wichita State basketball coach Harry Miller, noting that on defense, the Duck players came after his team like World War II kamikaze pilots. Thus was born a memorable era in Duck basketball that stressed defense and hard-nosed play. UO fans of the Kamikaze Kids were more apt to lustily cheer a player taking a charge or scrambling for a loose ball than a slam dunk or long-range shot. Harter also borrowed a trick from legendary University of Kentucky basket-

ball coach Adolph Rupp, having his team stand at midcourt during pregame drills and stare at the opposition. Harter's best Kamikaze team comprised Ernie Kent (current UO head basketball coach), Mark Barwig, Greg Ballard, Stu Jackson, and Ronnie Lee. In 1996, the Kamikaze Kids were inducted into the UO Sports Hall of Fame.

Keller, Kasey

Kasey Keller, one of the world's best soccer goalkeepers, hails from the town of Lacey, Washington, near the state capital. The former North Thurston High School soccer star attended the University of Portland where he led his team to the National Collegiate Athletic Association (NCAA) Final Four in 1988 and was a first-team All-American in 1990. In his senior year, Keller joined Millwall in the English First Division, and despite their lowly status (the team eventually dropped to the Second Division), Keller was considered one of the top keepers in English soccer. Keller was also a member of the 1996 U.S. Olympic squad, the 1998 U.S. Men's National Team that beat Brazil 1-0, and the 1998 U.S. World Cup team. The 1997 U.S. Soccer Federation's Male Athlete of the Year, Keller currently plays for a professional soccer team in Spain.

Kingdome

Derisively referred to as "The Concrete Mushroom" or the "Con-Dome," the Kingdome opened in Seattle in March 1976 and has been home to four professional sport teams (the Seahawks, Mariners, Sounders, and Supersonics) as well as numerous special events, including the National Collegiate Athletic Association (NCAA) Final Four. One positive aspect of having a cement roof was that the reverberation it caused made the Kingdome one of the noisiest and most imposing places in the country for opposing teams. Built on time and under budget, the King-dome began to prematurely show signs of age in the early 1990s due to years of deferred main-tenance. Falling acoustical ceiling tiles during the 1994 baseball season led to increased calls from sports officials and the Seattle media for the Kingdome's demise. In October 1995, the Wash-ington State legislature passed a financing pack-age for a new baseball-only stadium. In June 1997, a statewide ballot measure passed calling for construction of a new professional football stadium on the Kingdome site.

⚡ Kirkland Little League Champs

Remember those old movies where the All-American kid with the curly blond hair wins the big baseball game with a bravura performance for the ages? Well, that fantasy actually hap-pened one summer to a big, golden-haired kid from the Seattle suburb of Kirkland, Washing-ton, and his Kirkland National little league base-ball team. In the 1982 Little League World Series at Williamsport, Pennsylvania, Cody Webster pitched a brilliant two-hitter and swatted a mam-moth home run to beat the Chinese Taipai team 6-0. More than forty thousand fans turned out to see the game, which was doubly exciting because it ended Taiwan's five-year winning streak. The Kirkland National team remains the only team from the Northwest to ever appear in the little league world series title game.

⚡ Kirkman, Boone ("Boom Boom")

Seattle's "Great White Hope" in the six-ties and seventies was a heavyweight boxer named Boone "Boom Boom" Kirkman, who hailed from the blue-collar burg of Renton. Kirkman was a strong, hard-hitting boxer in the style of Jerry Quarry. He won most of his early fights by knockouts and started getting a lot of buildup by the local media and the

national boxing press as a potential champi-onship contender. In 1970, Kirkman was given a shot at 1968 Olympic boxing gold medalist George Foreman in Madison Square Garden. The bout was a disaster for Boone who was clobbered by Foreman in just two rounds. Discouraged, Kirkman "retired" for a couple of years but by 1973 was mounting another comeback. Despite a string of victories (including a ten-round deci-sion over Jimmy Ellis), Kirkman failed to beat any big-name fighters, losing first to Ron Lyle and then Ken Norton. After a few more bouts against lesser opponents, "Boom Boom" hung up the gloves for good in 1979.

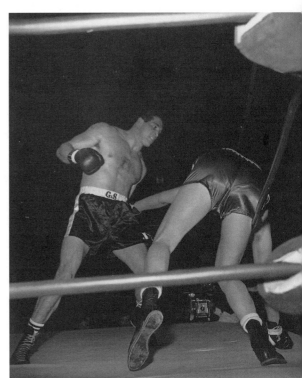

Boone Kirkman was Seattle's Great White Hope in the 1960s and 1970s.
(Photo from *Seattle Post-Intelligencer* Collection, Museum of History and Industry)

〽 Knox, Chuck

Chuck Knox, the most successful football coach in Seattle Seahawks history, took over as the Hawks' headman in 1983. Knox had previously served as head coach of the Los Angeles Rams (1973–77) and Buffalo Bills (1978–82), winning six National Football League (NFL) division championships. In his first season, Knox guided the Seahawks to the play-offs where they beat Denver and then upset Miami before losing to the Los Angeles Raiders in the American Football Conference (AFC) championship game. For the remainder of the decade, Knox's Seahawk teams were perennial play-off contenders featuring a ball-control possession offense and a hard-hitting defense. An AFC West division championship in 1988 would be the Seahawks' last hurrah under Knox as new owner Ken "I'm a California Real Estate Developer" Behring began to dismantle the team with a series of bizarre personnel and draft moves. Knox and the team mutually agreed to end his nine-year tenure as head coach in 1991. He left with an 80-63 regular-season record and four play-off appearances.

〽 Krieg, Dave

He played football at a college that doesn't exist anymore and wasn't drafted by any National Football League (NFL) team. Despite these handicaps, former Seattle Seahawks quarterback Dave Krieg ranks in the top ten in career statistics for passing attempts, completions, yards, and touchdown passes. Undrafted out of tiny and now-closed Milton College in Wisconsin, Krieg (or "Mudbone" as his teammates affectionately referred to him) became the full-time starter for the Seahawks in 1983 and led the team to the American Football Conference (AFC) title game. For the next seven seasons, Krieg was the Hawks'

main man at the quarterback position, setting club records in passing and making three Pro Bowl appearances. What's probably kept Krieg from being considered in the same league as his contemporaries Dan Marino, Jim Kelly, and John Elway is that he also holds the NFL quarterback record for most times sacked (492) and most fumbles (150). After being released by the Seahawks in 1992, Krieg played for the Kansas City Chiefs, Arizona Cardinals, Detroit Lions, Chicago Bears, and the Tennessee Oilers/Titans.

〽 Largent, Steve

The only Seattle Seahawks football player elected to the Professional Football Hall of Fame had an inauspicious start. In 1976, Steve Largent was an unheralded eighth-round draft pick by the Houston Oilers, who traded him to expansion Seattle just before the start of their inaugural season. Although Largent wasn't a speed burner, he ran incredibly precise routes and made the most of his quickness and sure hands. In the Seahawks' early years, Largent was most of Seattle's offense, catching ten touchdown passes in 1977 from quarterback Jim Zorn. As the Seahawks became a perennial playoff team in the eighties, Largent was a major key to their success and annually led the club in receptions, receiving yards, and touchdown catches. When he retired in 1989, Largent held six National Football League (NFL) records including most catches (819), receiving yards (13,089), and touchdown catches (100). He was also voted NFL Man of the Year in 1988. Largent was elected to the Hall of Fame in 1994 in his first year of eligibility—the same year he was elected to the U.S. Congress from his native state of Oklahoma.

〽 Lindgren, Gerry

Spokane's Gerry Lindgren is arguably America's all-time greatest high school runner. In

1964, as a junior, Lindgren shocked the racing world when he beat a heavily favored group of Soviet runners in a California track meet. His time in the race is still the national high school record for the 5,000 meters—13:44.000. Lindgren made the U.S. Olympic team that summer and went on to a spectacular college career at Washington State University, winning a number of National Collegiate Athletic Association (NCAA) titles from 1966 to 1969. In his last college race, fifth-year senior Lindgren defeated University of Oregon freshman Steve Prefontaine in the Pacific-8 Conference cross-country race—"Pre's" only NCAA loss. After decades of seclusion, Lindgren resurfaced in Hawaii and recently won the masters division in the state 15k championship.

⚡ Lucas, Maurice

Acquired by the Portland Trail Blazers when the old American Basketball Association (ABA) merged with the National Basketball Association (NBA) in 1976, the six-foot-nine Maurice Lucas was a classic "enforcer" power forward who didn't shy from throwing an elbow or three down in the paint. Although he played only four seasons with the Trail Blazers, his first was the most successful season in team history. An exceptional rebounder and defender, Lucas's toughness under the boards helped the team to the NBA title in his first season and the best record in the NBA the following year. After three seasons, Lucas was traded to the New Jersey Nets for Calvin Natt. He played again for the Blazers during the 1987–88 season. Lucas is a member of the NBA's All-Time Top 100 players and his number 20 has been retired by the Trail Blazers.

⚡ Magnuson, Karen

North Vancouver's Karen Magnuson was the toast of women's amateur figure skating in the early seventies. In 1971, she placed third in the world championships, was second the next year, and picked up a silver medal at the 1972 Winter Olympics in Sapporo, Japan. In 1973, Magnuson won the gold medal at the world championships in Bratislava with a solid performance over America's Janet Lynn. Magnuson turned pro with the Ice Capades and now resides in Boston.

⚡ Mahre, Phil and Steve

Twin brothers Phil and Steve Mahre are the most successful skiers in Northwest sports history. Born in Yakima, Washington, in 1957, the twins grew up skiing at White Pass in the Cascade Mountains and went on to become three-time Olympians (1976, 1980, and 1984). Phil won the silver medal in the slalom at Lake Placid in 1980 and took the gold in 1984. In 1981, 1982, and 1983, Phil won the overall title for the World Cup season—only the third man to win the title three consecutive times. During his career Phil compiled twenty-seven individual World Cup victories. He was inducted into the U.S. Olympic Hall of Fame in 1992, the first skier to earn the honor. Steve won the silver medal in the slalom at Sarajevo in 1984 and placed third in the overall World Cup standings in 1982. Both brothers still live in Yakima.

⚡ Mariners, Seattle

Long considered the definition of professional sports futility, the Seattle Mariners are currently one of the American League's model franchises with a new retractable roof stadium and some of the brightest stars in baseball on the team's roster. It wasn't always that way. The Mariners were born in 1977 and initially owned by a consortium that included Hollywood movie star Danny Kaye. Like most expansion teams, the "M's" struggled mightily, losing at least one hundred games in each of their first seven seasons. Many thought the team's fortunes would turn around in the mid-1980s as young players such as Alvin Davis, Harold Reynolds, Mark Langston, and Phil Bradley cracked the starting lineup. Although they did play better, it wasn't good enough and the team continued to lose. It wasn't until 1991 that the Mariners finally finished above .500 for the first time in team history, only to see then-owner Jeff Smulyan threaten to move the team to Tampa Bay. A new consortium of owners backed by the deep pockets of the Japanese-based Nintendo Corporation stepped in, bought the team, and hired Lou Piniella as manager. With all-star players like Ken Griffey Jr., Alex Rodriguez, Edgar Martinez, Jay Buhner, Dan Wilson, and Randy Johnson, the team won American League West Division titles in 1995 and 1997.

Mayes, Rueban

The Washington State University Cougars' all-time leading football rusher was a humble superstar from North Battleford, Saskatchewan, named Rueban Mayes. From 1982 to 1985, Mayes was the main man in the Cougar backfield, and one-third of the famous "RPM" offense that also featured quarterback Mark Rypien and wide receiver Kerry Porter. Mayes was a two-time All-American, a Top 10 finisher for the Heisman Trophy in 1984, and National Collegiate Athletic Association (NCAA) record-holder for most rushing yards in a single game (357). He went on to play professionally for the New Orleans Saints, earning Rookie of the Year honors and two Pro Bowl selections. Now retired from football, Mayes lives in the Seattle area and works with at-risk youth.

McElhenny, Hugh

Considered one of the greatest University of Washington (UW) college football players, Hugh McElhenny grew up in Los Angeles where he was a high school track star. After one season at Compton Junior College (where he scored twenty-three touchdowns), McElhenny was the subject of fierce recruiting from more than sixty major college football programs. He ended up choosing UW despite allegations of payoffs and special treatment. It didn't take long for Husky players and fans to realize that the California golden boy was in a class by himself as a running back—a superb athlete who could change pace and acceleration almost at will. Although his exploits on the gridiron are numerous, perhaps his greatest college performance was the 1950 Apple Cup when he rushed 296 yards for a school record and scored five touchdowns in a 52-21 rout of Washington State University. In his senior season in 1951, McElhenny was a consensus All-American and finished third in the Heisman Trophy balloting. He left UW holding almost every record possible for a running back and was drafted by the San Francisco 49'ers. In total, "The King" (as he was nicknamed in the pros) played thirteen years professionally and gained more than 11,000 yards. He was named to the Pro Football Hall of Fame in 1970.

McMillan, Nate

When Nate McMillan retired he was the Seattle Supersonics professional basketball team's all-time leader in assists and steals. The former six-foot-seven swingman was drafted out of North Carolina State in 1986. McMillan displayed his prowess in handing off to other players in his first season when he set a Supersonics franchise mark with twenty-five assists in a game against the Los Angeles Clippers. During his career, McMillan appeared in more playoff games (ninety-eight) than any other player in team history. He retired following the 1997–98 season after playing twelve seasons with Seattle. Only Fred Brown had a longer tenure (thirteen years) with the team. McMillan's number 10 jersey was retired in a special ceremony in March 1999.

⚡ Miller, Ralph

Once referred to as the "Curmudgeon of Corvallis" because of his irascible personality, former Oregon State University (OSU) hoops coach Ralph Miller was still well loved by players and fans who watched him work his basketball wizardry for almost forty years. A star football and basketball athlete at the University of Kansas, Miller began his college coaching career at Wichita State and then moved to the University of Iowa. He took over the reins of the flailing Beaver basketball program in 1971, and during the ensuing eighteen years, won four Pacific-10 Conference championships, made eight National Collegiate Athletic Association (NCAA) tournament appearances, and endured only two losing seasons. A two-time national coach of the year, Miller retired following the 1989 season as the sixth-winningest coach in NCAA history. All told, Miller accumulated a college mark of 674-370. He was elected to the Naismith Basketball Hall of Fame in 1988 and the floor at OSU's Gill Coliseum has been dedicated in his honor.

⚡ Moon, Warren

While Warren Moon played only two seasons as quarterback of the University of Washington football team, he secured a place in the hearts of all Husky fans by leading the team to a memorable Rose Bowl victory over the University of Michigan. Coach Don James was widely criticized for starting the Los Angeles junior college transfer over local favorite Chris Rowland during the 1976 season, and as Moon struggled,

the quarterback controversy heightened. After a 1-3 start in 1977, however, Moon led the team to six wins in their last seven games and the Pacific-8 Conference championship. In the Rose Bowl, although Michigan was a 14-point favorite, the Huskies jumped out to a 17-0 halftime lead and made it 24-0 in the third quarter on Moon's twenty-eight-yard touchdown pass to wide receiver Spider Gaines. Michigan staged a furious comeback, but the Dawgs held on and Moon was named the game's most valuable player. He has since gone on to a highly successful professional career in both the Canadian Football League (CFL) and the National Football League (NFL), including a short stint with the Seattle Seahawks.

⚡ O'Brien, Johnny and Eddie

These Seattle University All-American basketball brothers are best remembered for a historic victory over the Harlem Globetrotters. In 1952, when the Globetrotters were a legitimate touring squad that played the top college basketball teams, they took their road show to Seattle to play the Seattle University Chieftains in a benefit game for the U.S. Olympic Committee. At the time, the Globetrotters had amassed a .936 winning percentage in more than three thousand games. The Chieftains were led by the nation's top collegiate scorer Johnny O'Brien and his twin brother Eddie. With the five-foot-nine Johnny pouring in 43 points, the Chieftains shocked the Globetrotters 84-81. The twins went on to play major league baseball for the Pittsburgh Pirates. Johnny also served as a King County Commissioner and assistant manager of the Kingdome in Seattle. Eddie was an assistant coach with the Seattle

Pilots major league baseball team (where Jim Bouton derisively referred to him as "Mr. Small Stuff") and as athletic director for his alma mater.

⦿ Owens, Jim

Jim Owens re-instilled national respect and prominence to West Coast college football by returning the University of Washington Huskies to the Rose Bowl after a two-decade absence. A player on the great Bud Wilkinson University of Oklahoma football teams of the late forties and early fifties, Owens took over the Husky program in 1957 and instituted a fierce practice regimen called the "Death March"—a series of seemingly endless fifteen-yard sprints that gave the Dawgs a reputation as tenacious hitters. Although the team struggled at first, by 1959 Owens had the Huskies in the Rose Bowl against Big Ten power-house Wisconsin. Although the Dawgs were ranked number eight in the Associated Press poll, West Coast teams had dropped eleven of the past twelve Rose Bowls and the Huskies hadn't been to a Rose Bowl in twenty-two years. The oddsmakers barely gave them a chance. Owens shocked the media by leading the Huskies to a 44-8 whipping of the Badgers and beginning a reversal of trends. The Huskies beat the University of Minnesota 17-7 in the 1961 Rose Bowl, and Pacific-8 Conference teams went on to win eleven of the next seventeen games. Owens continued to coach the Huskies until 1974. While his tenure was marked by allegations of racism during the late sixties, Owens enjoyed a last hurrah during the Sonny Sixkiller years in the early seventies.

⦿ Owings, Larry

On a wintry night in Evanston, Illinois, in 1970, University of Washington wrestler Larry Owings shocked the sports world. In the 142-pound finals of the National Collegiate Athletic Association (NCAA) Championships at Northwestern University, Iowa State's Dan Gable (undefeated with a record of 181-0) lost 13-11 to a kid from Oregon wrestling for the Huskies. Owings had won the Pacific-8 Championship at 158 pounds but dropped two weight classes just so he could face Gable (confident, Owings told an interviewer from *Sports Illustrated* that he would beat the legendary Iowan). After the match, Gable was inconsolable as the enormity of the loss sank in. He would go on, however, to Olympic glory in 1972 and enjoy an unprecedented string of national championships as a coach for the University of Iowa wrestling team. Owings would never win another NCAA title and did not make the Olympic team.

⦿ Pacific Coast League

From the forties to the sixties, professional baseball in the Northwest meant the Triple A Pacific Coast League (PCL). While the teams were minor league, fan support was major league and the rivalries were fierce. For a time, the PCL was poised to become a new major league, but when professional baseball teams began moving to the West Coast (Dodgers, Giants, Athletics), it dropped back to minor league status. Key teams during the PCL's glory years included the Seattle Rainiers, San Francisco Seals, Los Angeles Stars, Vancouver Mounties/Canadians, and the Portland Beavers.

⦿ Patera, Jack

Jack Patera, the first head football coach of the Seattle Seahawks, had deep roots in the Pacific Northwest. Patera was a graduate of Washington High School in Portland and attended the University of Oregon where he was a four-year football letterman. He was chosen as the Seahawks' coach in January 1976 after much success as a National Football League (NFL) assistant coach with the Los Angeles Rams and Minnesota Vikings. In his second season, Patera led the Hawks to a record of 5-9—the best second-year expansion record in NFL history. In 1978, the team posted a winning record of 9-7 and repeated the feat the next year when Patera was named NFL Coach of the Year. During this time, the Hawks were a colorful and unconventional bunch, faking field goals and punts, calling trick plays and throwing long passes with reckless abandon. In 1980, however, the Seahawks' fortunes began to sour, in part due to the lack of a consistent running attack. Patera's tough-guy coaching style (he refused to allow water on the training camp practice field) was also beginning to wear thin, and an arrest for drunk driving didn't help improve his public image. When pro football players went on strike at the beginning of the 1982 season, Patera's strong anti-union stance combined with the team's lack of improvement resulted in his firing in October. Patera is now retired from coaching and lives in the Cle Elum, Washington.

Payton, Gary

The National Basketball Association's (NBA) premier point guard is Seattle Supersonics star Gary Payton. A product of the mean streets of Oakland, Payton played college ball for the Oregon State University (OSU) Beavers from 1986 to 1990. While at OSU, Payton became the team's all-time leading scorer, was a first-team All-American, and was named *Sports Illustrated*'s College Player of the Year in his senior season. Payton was the second overall pick in the NBA lottery draft in 1990 and as a rookie, was known more for his trash-talking mouth than overall ability. But under the tutelage of former Sonics coach George Karl (with whom he used to battle regularly), Payton emerged as a true superstar in the league. Always a fierce defender (his nickname is "The Glove" because of his ball-stealing prowess),

Payton has developed a strong offensive game that he often uses to single-handedly carry the Sonics to victory. A perennial NBA all-star and member of the U.S. Olympic "Dream Team" in 1996, Payton is virtually certain to hold most team records before he retires.

Petrie, Geoff

Hot-shooting guard Geoff Petrie was one of the most popular players in Portland Trail Blazers basketball history and the team's first bona fide star. Drafted in the first round in the Blazers' debut year of 1970, the six-foot-four Petrie was an immediate star as a rookie, leading the team in most offensive categories. He averaged almost 25 points a game (seventh best in the league) and shared National Basketball Association (NBA) Rookie of the Year honors with Dave Cowens of the Boston Celtics. As the expansion Blazers struggled in their first few seasons, Petrie was most of the Portland offense. He twice scored a team-record 51 points in games against the Houston Rockets in 1973 and was named to the NBA all-star team in 1971 and 1974. Prior to the 1976–77 season, the Blazers had to give up

Petrie to the Atlanta Hawks as compensation for their number-two pick in the ABA Dispersal Draft (when they acquired Maurice Lucas). After playing for six seasons with the struggling Blazers, Petrie would not be a part of Portland's first and only NBA championship in 1977. Petrie is currently vice president of basketball operations for the Sacramento Kings. He was named NBA Executive of the Year in 1999.

⚡ Pickle-Ball

In 1965, Western Washington residents Barney McCallum, Bill Bell, and Joel Pritchard (former U.S. Congressman and Washington State lieutenant governor) invented a new game called "pickle-ball" to liven up their vacation time. The game is a cross between badminton and tennis and emphasizes agility and quick reflexes over power and speed. With used badminton equipment and an old tennis court, they worked out the rules for pickle-ball over the course of several days. The game employs wooden paddles a little larger than Ping-Pong paddles, a whiffle ball, and a three-foot net and is played on a hard surface about half the size of a tennis court. Interest in pickle-ball spread quickly among their friends and slowly gained a following in the Puget Sound area and then nationally. Today, the U.S. Pickle-Ball Association is headquartered in Tacoma.

⚡ Pilots, Seattle

Today, the Seattle Pilots baseball team is mainly remembered as the answer to the trivia question, "What was the original name of the Milwaukee Brewers?" Entering major league baseball in 1969 along with the Montreal Expos, San Diego Padres, and Kansas City Royals, the Pilots were clearly the most underfinanced of the group and the owners were forced to sell the team after their first and only season in the Jet City. The Pilots' home opener in Seattle's Sicks Stadium (originally built in the 1930s by brewing magnate Emil Sick) was a fiasco. Hundreds of fans had to wait outside for an hour while work crews finished installing their seats. In addition, the antiquated plumbing couldn't handle the size of the crowd, and, as a result, there was little water pressure in the bathrooms. The team was a similar fiasco on the field. Led by their colorful (but inept) skipper Joe Schultz, the Pilots hung around third place in the West Division until the all-star break, and then collapsed in the second half to finish 64-98. Much of the Pilots season is chronicled in Jim Bouton's book *Ball Four*. Pilots broadcaster Rod Belcher's opening-day song was prophetic. "Go, Go You Pilots," he crooned, and they did the following spring, leaving Seattle without a major league baseball team until the Mariners arrived eight years later.

⚡ Piniella, Lou

The winningest manager in Seattle Mariners baseball history and the only skipper to take the M's to the postseason is former New York Yankees star Lou Piniella. Named Seattle's headman after a miserable 1992 campaign, Piniella led the Mariners to American League West Division titles in 1995 and 1997, and an American League Championship Series appearance in 1995 against the Cleveland Indians (they lost in six games). Although Piniella spent most of his playing days with the Yankees, as a rookie he was part of the Seattle Pilots' first and only spring training roster in 1969. Just before opening day, Piniella was traded to the Kansas City Royals. Piniella went on to win Rookie of the Year honors and played fifteen seasons, batting .291 and playing in four World Series.

⚡ Portland Wrasslin'

Back in the days before the World Wrestling Federation (WWF) and World Championship Wrestling (WCW) rode lucrative television contracts to national prominence, regional professional wrestling circuits thrived. One of the best operated out of Portland, where promoter Don Owen televised weekly matches from the dilapidated Portland Sports Arena. During the rest of the week, Owen's troupe would hit the small towns of the Pacific Northwest, bringing "Big Time Wrestling" to the people. The Owen promotion featured mainstays like perennial champion "Dutch" Savage and referee Sandy Barr, and served as the launchpad for some of the future stars of the WWF and WCW. Rowdy Roddy Piper perfected his Scottish wild-man routine in Portland, sometimes teaming up with a young future Minnesota governor—Jesse "The Body" Ventura. Ventura also was the tag-team partner of "Playboy" Buddy Rose and twice held the Northwest heavyweight title. "Superfly" Jimmy Snuka was a crowd favorite, launching himself from the top rope, and "Billy Jack" Haynes also had a large following. By the mid-eighties, competition from the better-heeled national promotions had reduced Portland wrestling to a shadow of its former self. When Portland-area appliance store mogul Tom Peterson filed for bankruptcy and had to stop his ubiquitous advertising, the television show was down for the count, with no one to come over the top rope to save it.

Prefontaine, Steve

One of the greatest American distance runners, Steve Prefontaine's flamboyant style, maniacal determination, and tragic end have made him an athletic icon. Born in Coos Bay, Oregon, in 1951, Prefontaine attended the University of Oregon, winning six national collegiate distance titles and two Amateur Athletic Union crowns. His races in Eugene, where he never lost when the distance was more than one mile, were like heavyweight prizefights where large crowds would show up to chant "Pre." After a disappointing finish at the 1972 Munich Olympics, Prefontaine returned to Eugene and continued to set American records. On May 30, 1975, a few hours after defeating famed runner Frank Shorter in a five-thousand-meter race, Prefontaine died in a car crash. The spot where he died remains marked with a simple inscription, "Pre 5/30/75 RIP." Since his death, Prefontaine's legend has grown. He was elected to

Steve Prefontaine was Oregon's most famous and beloved sports hero.
(Photo courtesy of the University of Oregon)

the U.S. Olympic Hall of Fame in 1991, and two biographical movies, *Prefontaine* and *Without Limits*, have been released.

Puidokas, Steve

Washington State University (WSU) basketball star Steve Puidokas was an unlikely candidate to move to the little town of Pullman, Washington, (as was his coach George Raveling—the first African American basketball coach in the Pacific-8 Conference.) A six-foot-eleven player from Chicago, Puidokas nevertheless became the Cougars' all-time career scoring leader (18.6) and rebounder (9.7) during his WSU playing days (1974–77). Puidokas was a tall, textbook-perfect player who could score from just about anywhere on the court. He scored almost 1,900 points during his career and ended up playing professionally in Europe. Puidokas died unexpectedly in March 1994 at the age of thirty-nine from a heart attack.

ᴟ Ramsey, Dr. Jack

The architect of the Portland Trail Blazers' first and only National Basketball Association (NBA) championship was Dr. Jack Ramsey. A former college coach at St. Joseph's, Ramsey became the general manager of the Philadelphia 76'ers in 1966 (the year they won the NBA championship) and then their coach in 1968, where he remained for four seasons. In 1977, he took over the reins of the Portland Trail Blazers and, with the help of Bill Walton and Maurice Lucas, shocked his former team by coming from an 0-2 deficit to win four straight games and capture the NBA title. Ramsey would continue to coach the Blazers for nine additional years, but could never match the magic of the 1976–77 season. He was let go by Portland after the 1985–86 campaign, having won 453 games as the team's coach. Ramsey's "number 77" (the year he won the championship) was retired by the Trail Blazers, and he was elected to the Naismith Basketball Hall of Fame in 1991.

ᴟ Randolph, Leo

Tacoma's Leo Randolph made a name for himself in the boxing field by winning five consecutive state Golden Gloves championships during the early seventies. Winning the national Golden Gloves flyweight championship convinced Randolph to try out for the Olympic team. Although he was given little chance of making the squad, Randolph won nine fights in a row to earn a spot in the Olympic trials box-off. He won that bout as well to make the U.S. team that competed in Montreal in 1976. Randolph won the gold medal by defeating

Ramon Duvalon of Cuba and turned pro two years later. In 1980, he won the World Boxing Association junior featherweight title, only to lose it a few months later and retire. Randolph later became a driver for Pierce County Transit in Tacoma and a volunteer worker at a local juvenile detention center.

ᴟ Rashad, Ahmad

Ahmad Rashad, then known as Bobby Moore, was a star running back and receiver for the University of Oregon (UO) in the early seventies. Rashad led the Pacific-8 Conference in receiving in 1969, rushing in 1971, and was named to the All-Conference team in 1969, 1970, and 1971. Rashad played professional football for a number of teams, including the Seattle Seahawks. After his professional career ended he went into broadcasting, including a short stint for the Seahawks doing preseason play-by-play. Rashad has been elected to both the Oregon Sports Hall of Fame and the University of Oregon Athletic Hall of Fame.

ᴟ Raveling, George

One of the first African Americans to lead a major college basketball program and the first in the Pacific-10 Conference was former Washington State University (WSU) head coach George Raveling. A college player at Villanova in the late fifties, Raveling began his coaching career at WSU in 1972. In eleven seasons in Pullman, Raveling led the "Cougs" to seven winning seasons and two National Collegiate Athletic Association (NCAA) tournament appearances in 1980 and 1983. After a successful 23-7 mark with WSU in 1983, Raveling was tapped to replace Lute Olson at Iowa where he stayed for three seasons before taking the head coaching position at the University of Southern California. A serious car accident forced Raveling to retire from coaching in 1994, but he still participates in summer basketball camps and is a color commentator for college telecasts on network television and radio.

⚡ Rebagliati, Ross

Whistler, B.C., native Ross Rebagliati made history and headlines at the 1998 Winter Olympics in Nagano, Japan, by becoming the first gold medalist in snowboarding and then being disqualified a few days later for testing positive for marijuana use. On February 8, 1998, the twenty-six-year-old Rebagliati won the gold in snowboarding. Three days later, the International Olympic Committee (IOC) voted to strip him of the medal when trace levels of THC, the chief intoxicant in marijuana, were found following a drug test. Rebagliati had admitted to having smoked marijuana in the past but claimed he had stopped about a year before (must have been some righteous stuff). One day later, an international arbitration board reversed the IOC decision and reinstated his gold medal. Rebagliati's situation was lampooned by Jay Leno, David Letterman, and *Saturday Night Live*, but he returned to a hero's welcome in Whistler. He's now busy preparing to defend his gold medal at the 2002 Winter Olympics in Salt Lake City, Utah.

⚡ Refuse to Lose

During the Seattle Mariners' improbable run toward the postseason in 1995, the chant "Refuse to Lose" became the most repeated phrase among baseball fans in the Pacific Northwest. On August 3, the team's fortunes looked bleak. Their star player Ken Griffey Jr. had been out for most of the season with a broken wrist, and the M's were languishing thirteen games behind the California Angels in the American League West Division. Over the course of the last thirty-four games, however, the M's with a healthy Griffey back in the lineup went on a tear, seizing victory from the jaws of defeat in game after game and literally "refusing to lose." Soon, the crowds picked up on the "Refuse to Lose" mantra and banners bearing the phrase appeared all over the Kingdome. The momentum carried the team through a one-game playoff win against the Angels to clinch the division title and a classic five-game series against the New York Yankees. In that contest, the M's came from an 0-2 deficit to win the last three games, taking game five in the bottom of the eleventh inning when Joey Cora and Griffey scored on an Edgar Martinez double to left field. As Mariners play-by-play announcer Dave Niehaus would say at the time, "My oh my, I don't believe it!"

⚡ Rollen, Rock'n

If you watched any major sporting event during the late 1970s and 1980s, you probably remember that weird guy sitting behind home plate or in the end zone wearing a rainbow-colored Afro wig and holding up a sign reading "John 3:16." And since the Pacific Northwest is populated by a large number of "free spirits," it should be no surprise that Mr. Rollen Stewart (aka "Rock'n Rollen" or "Rainbowhead") hails from Spokane. At a New Year's Eve party, Stewart wore a rainbow-colored Afro wig and was surprised by all of the attention he received. He then decided to wear the wig in public, first showing up at the 1977 National Basketball Association (NBA) finals dancing wildly and flashing thumbs-up signs. The cameras loved his antics and he loved the attention, so "Rock'n Rollen" began attending every major sporting event he could to try to get on television. In later years, Stewart became a born-again Christian and started holding up the John 3:16 Bible passage sign. When he decided to drop the rainbow wig and the antics, the cameras weren't interested anymore. By the late eighties, Stewart's money had run out and he began to deteriorate mentally. In 1992, he was arrested and later convicted of kidnapping and making terrorist threats. He is currently serving three consecutive life sentences in a California prison.

〽 Russell, Bill

The greatest defensive basketball center of all time really seemed like Seattle's ticket to a National Basketball Association (NBA) championship when he was named coach and general manager of the Supersonics in 1973. Bill Russell, whose NBA career spanned thirteen years and eleven titles with the Boston Celtics, had been a player-coach at Boston for three seasons, and fans hoped that his success would rub off on the Sonics. In Russell's second season, the team finished with a record of 43-39 and qualified for the play-offs for the first time in franchise history. During the next two seasons, however, Russell's teams failed to improve beyond the .500 mark. Remarks about his own team such as "We bring out the best in everybody" may have endeared him to the quote-happy press, but didn't do much to inspire the confidence of team management. Russell was replaced following the 1976–77 season. He continues to reside in the area.

〽 Schloredt, Bob

The leader of Jim Owens's famous "Purple Gang," Bob Schloredt quarterbacked the University of Washington (UW) to Rose Bowl victories over Wisconsin (44-8) in 1960 and Minnesota (17-7) in 1961, and was named most valuable player in both games. The Schloredt-led 1959 and 1960 Husky squads finished a combined 20-2 and sparked a Renaissance in West Coast football. Schloredt (who served as an assis-

tant coach at UW for eleven seasons) was named an Associated Press All-American in 1960 and was inducted into the Husky Hall of Fame in 1981. And if that isn't amazing enough, Bob Schloredt has only 10 percent vision in his left eye.

〽 Seahawks, Seattle

On June 4, 1974, the National Football League (NFL) awarded Seattle its twenty-eighth franchise to begin play two years later in the 65,000-seat-capacity Kingdome. The Seahawks logo draws on Northwest Coast Native American art and is one of the most distinctive emblems in professional sports. The team thrived for its first twelve years under the initial ownership group led by Seattle's Nordstrom family. In 1988, the Hawks were sold to much-reviled California real estate developer Ken Behring, who ran the team into the ground and in 1996 tried haplessly to relocate the franchise to Southern California. Microsoft cofounder Paul Allen purchased the team in 1997, and with a new stadium set to open in 2002 and former Green Bay Super Bowl coach Mike Holmgren at the helm, the Seattle Seahawks' fortunes appear to be back on the rise, and they made the playoffs in 1999.

⚡ Seales, "Sugar" Ray

An Olympic boxing champ from Tacoma, "Sugar" Ray Seales took the gold medal in the light welterweight division at the 1972 Summer Olympics the only U.S. gold medal in boxing at the Munich games. As an amateur, Seales won more than three hundred bouts. During his professional career, he amassed an overall record of fifty-six wins, eight losses, three draws, and thirty-three knockouts. He was the North American Boxing Federation Middleweight champion in 1979 and the United States Boxing Association Middleweight champion in 1980–81. Seales was forced to retire after suffering detached retinas in both eyes.

⚡ Sierawan, Yasser

Inspired by the famous Bobby Fischer–Boris Spassky chess duel of 1972, Yasser Sierawan, a young Syrian immigrant who moved to Seattle at the age of seven, decided to dedicate himself to becoming one of the world's best chess players. For the past two decades, Sierawan has been a force on the U.S. chess scene and one of the top twenty players in the world on several occasions. Sierawan has also defeated both Garry Kasparov and Anatoly Karpov in tournament play. The author of several books on chess for Microsoft Press and others, international grandmaster Sierawan is the founder of Seattle's International Chess Enterprises and publisher of the now defunct *Inside Chess* magazine.

⚡ Sikma, Jack

Jack Sikma, the pride of Illinois Wesleyan University, was a key member of the Seattle Supersonics basketball team during the late 1970s and early 1980s. Drafted by the Sonics in 1977, the six-foot-eleven Sikma made a great first impression at power forward with his rebounding skills and ability to score outside the low post. He was named to the National Basketball Association's (NBA) All-Rookie team as the Supersonics took the Washington Bullets to game seven of the finals before losing 105-99. The next season, Sikma moved to the center position after Marvin Webster signed with the New York Knicks, and Sikma helped lead the way with his relentless rebounding. In the 1979 NBA finals, Sikma had seventeen rebounds in each of the last three games against the Bullets as Seattle won the championship 4-1. A perennial all-star, Sikma continued to play with Seattle through the lean years of the early eighties. At his request, he was traded to the Milwaukee Bucks after the 1985–86 season where he played for five more seasons. Sikma's number

Tacoma's Sugar Ray Seales was the only U.S. boxer to win the gold in Munich.

(Photo courtesy of the Tacoma Public Library, Richards Collection, photo D164368-216)

2/2

43 was retired by the Supersonics, and he continues to live in the Seattle area where he is president of Sikma Enterprises, a golf course management company.

⚡ Sixkiller, Sonny

The most popular and celebrated quarterback in the history of University of Washington (UW) football is Sonny Sixkiller, a Cherokee who played high school football in Ashland, Oregon. In his Husky debut, Sixkiller completed sixteen of thirty-five passes for 277 yards and three touchdowns as UW upset Michigan State 42-16 in the 1970 home opener. Sonny was not only a great quarterback but also charismatic and admired by adults and children who bought "6-Killer" T-shirts, postcards, and headbands by the truckload. Sixkiller became only the second Husky player to appear on the cover of *Sports Illustrated* (October 4, 1971), and he was so popular that a record was made about him called "The Ballad of Sonny Sixkiller." In his sophomore season, he won the national passing championship. Although his short stature limited his success in professional football, Sixkiller still owns more individual Husky passing records than any other purple and gold quarterback. Today, Sixkiller provides color commentary for Husky home football games for a Northwest sports cable channel.

⚡ Six-Way Shaw

Sports Illustrated gave the nickname "Six-Way Shaw" to University of Oregon's (UO) versatile football star George Shaw—a quarterback and defensive back who sometimes played halfback/flanker, kicker, punter, and punt returner. Shaw was a graduate of Grant High School in Portland, where one of his classmates was future U.S. Senator Bob Packwood, now known more for making passes than receiving them. Shaw was a four-sport star for

Sonny Sixkiller is the greatest quarterback in Husky football history. Period.
(Photo courtesy of the University of Washington and Sonny Sixkiller)

the Grant Generals and led them to two state football championships. While at UO in the early fifties, Shaw earned All-America honors, and his thirteen interceptions as a freshman is still the single-season Duck record. He went on to play pro football for the Baltimore Colts and started for the team in his rookie season. An injury the next year allowed Johnny Unitas to move into the starting role he never relinquished. Shaw passed away in 1997 at the age of sixty-four.

⚡ Slaney, Mary Decker

Oregon's Mary Decker Slaney is considered America's greatest female middle distance runner. Slaney set seventeen world and more than thirty U.S. records in a career that goes back to the Nixon administration. Despite this impressive list of accomplishments, Slaney has been seemingly jinxed in her pursuit of Olympic glory.

Injuries kept her out of the 1976 and 1992 Olympics, and she performed poorly in Seoul in 1988. In 1980, the United States boycotted the summer games in Moscow, and 1984 featured her infamous collision with South Africa's barefooted Zola Budd in the L.A. Coliseum. At the age of thirty-seven, Slaney pulled off a remarkable performance at the Olympic qualifying trials in Atlanta by coming from fifth to second place and earning a spot on the 1996 U.S. squad in the five thousand meters.

Slew, Seattle

One of the most famous and successful Triple Crown winning horses of all time was bought by Washington State businessman Mickey Taylor and some friends at a yearling auction for a mere $17,500. Nicknamed "Seattle Slew," the horse went on to prove almost as good an investment as Microsoft stock. Seattle Slew is the only thoroughbred in history to capture the Triple Crown with an unbeaten record. During his entire racing career, Seattle Slew lost only three of seventeen starts and has career earnings of more than $1 million. He retired to a career of carousing with fillies, with much success. Some of Slew's famous progeny include 1984 Derby winner Swale, Slew o' Gold, and Landulace.

Smyl, Stan

The greatest player ever to skate in the uniform of the Vancouver Canucks hockey team, Stan "The Steamer" Smyl was often described as the "heart and soul" of the Canucks during his thirteen-year playing career. During this period, Smyl established team records for games played (896), goals (262), assists (411), and points (673). He combined all of this with a feisty, hard-nosed style of play which saw him lead Vancouver in goals (31), assists (47), points (78), and penalty minutes (204) during the 1979–80 season—the last time any National Hockey League (NHL) player led his club in all four categories. Named the Canucks'

most valuable player on three separate occasions, Smyl served the longest time as team captain (1982–90). He received the ultimate honor on November 3, 1991, when the Canucks retired his number 12 jersey.

Sneva, Tom

Tom Sneva is the most successful Indy car driver from the Northwest. A one-time schoolteacher, Sneva had raced in the Northwest in the late1960s and early 1970s, but it wasn't until

Canucks fans loved Stan Smyl, the "Steamer."
(Photo courtesy of Vancouver Canucks Archives)

he got the chance to drive at the Indianapolis 500 in 1974 that he decided to turn pro full time. Sneva was nearly killed in a fiery crash at Indianapolis in 1975, but in 1977 made racing history when he became the first driver to turn in a qualifying run above 200 mph (200.535). That same year, he won the first of two Indy Car Series Championships. After finishing second three times at the Indy 500 (1977, 1978, and 1980), he finally took racing's biggest prize in 1983, beating Al Unser Sr.

▧ Sounders, Seattle

An original member franchise of the now-defunct North American Soccer League (NASL), the Seattle Sounders were a popular attraction from 1974 to 1983 when the team folded. Before the Seahawks and Mariners hit town, the Sounders were Seattle's "other" professional sports team, and local interest for the sport in general gave the Sounders a strong and enthusiastic fan base. Led by head coach Alan Hinton (1980 NASL coach of the year), the Sounders were Soccer Bowl participants in 1977 and 1982. In both instances, the team lost the championship to their arch nemesis, the New York Cosmos. Notable Sounders players included Jimmy Gabriel, Mike England, Adrian Webster, Tony Chursky, Pepe Fernandez, Roger Davies (1980 NASL player of the year), and Jimmy McAlister. The Sounders were re-formed in 1994 as part of the American Professional Soccer League with Alan Hinton returning as head coach, and in 1995 they beat Atlanta to win the 1995 A-League championship.

▧ Storm, Thunder, and Breakers, Portland

Portland must not be destined to have a pro football team. In 1974, the World Football League (WFL) debuted as an alternative to the National Football League (NFL), and Portland was awarded a franchise called the Storm. Financial problems plagued the league all season, and the WFL was reconstituted the following year. Portland's team name was changed to the Thunder, and a new owner and coach were brought in. Fan apathy and a lack of resources continued, and the entire league folded in mid-October. Seven years later, the United States Football League (USFL) was formed with an ABC television contract and a spring/summer schedule that would not conflict with the NFL. While Portland was not awarded an initial franchise, by the USFL's third season the Breakers football team (which was in Boston in year one and New Orleans in year two) arrived in the Rose City. Interestingly enough, the Breakers' head coach Dick Coury had also been the head coach of the Portland Storm. Such inter-league cross-pollination, however, was not enough to keep the new Breakers afloat and when the league lost its antitrust suit against the NFL, the USFL and Portland's professional football history faded into oblivion.

▧ STP (Seattle to Portland)

Mass bicycle insanity reigns every spring when the Seattle to Portland (STP) race begins. The STP began as a race in 1979, when 179 hardy souls pedaled from the Seattle Municipal Building to Portland's City Hall. The ride is designed to take two days, though a select few manage to finish in one. After a one-year cancellation due to the eruption of Mount Saint Helens, STP began to grow dramatically. Insurance problems caused the race to be converted into a ride, and today ten thousand cyclists participate.

▧ Sumners, Rosalynn

An American women's figure skating champion from the north Seattle suburb of Edmonds, Rosalynn Sumners burst onto the international scene by winning the junior world championship when she was fifteen years old. Two years later Sumners captured the U.S. women's figure skating title, and at age eighteen, she was the world champion. She entered the 1984 Winter Olympics at Sarajevo as a favorite to win the gold medal, but a less-than-spectacular short program put her behind East Germany's Katarina Witt going into the finals. Despite skating a brilliant long program, it wasn't quite enough to beat Witt, and Sumners had to settle for the silver medal. To honor her Olympic success, the main street leading into her hometown of Edmonds was renamed Rosalyn Sumners Boulevard.

Supersonics, Seattle

Seattle was awarded a National Basketball Association (NBA) franchise in December 1966—the Jet City's first professional sports team. Los Angeles financier Sam Schulman was the Supersonics' first owner, named in honor of the planes built by the area's most prominent employer. The team has appeared in the NBA finals three times, capturing the title once in 1979 in five games over the Washington Bullets. Schulman sold the team before the 1983–84 season to Seattle billboard magnate Barry Ackerley, who persuaded the city to pour millions into renovating the old Seattle Coliseum (since renamed the Key Arena). While the Los Angeles Lakers may have their number-one fan Jack Nicholson, Microsoft's Bill Gates is a frequent Supersonics courtside visitor.

Synchronized Swimming

Admit it, you considered this whole sport a big joke when it debuted at the 1984 Los Angeles Summer Olympics (as did *Saturday Night Live*, which concocted a savage parody). But when two young women from the Puget Sound area became the first gold medalists in the history of synchronized swimming, we all jumped right on the

Esther Williams "Million-Dollar Mermaid" bandwagon. Candy Costie and Tracy Ruiz grew up in the Seattle suburb of Bothell and paired up for the first time as eleven-year-olds when their two swimming clubs merged into the Seattle Aqua Club. International success in the sport while they were teenagers led both to receive an athletic scholarship to attend the University of Arizona and join its synchronized swimming team. At the 1984 Summer Olympics in Los Angeles, they took the gold medal in pairs synchronized swimming and Ruiz won the gold in the individual competition. At the 1988 Summer Olympics in Seoul, Korea, Ruiz took the silver in individual competition. A pool in Bothell was subsequently named in their honor.

Thompson, Jack

Jack Thompson, the fabled "Throwin' Samoan," single-handedly revived interest in the Washington State University (WSU) football program during his college career. From 1975 to 1978, Thompson was the entire Cougar offense during a period when the team managed only one winning season. He led the conference in total offense and passing in 1976, was a first-team all-conference selection in 1977 and 1978, and a *Sporting News* first-team All-America selection in 1978. He finished his collegiate career as the most prolific passer in National Collegiate Athletic Association (NCAA) history, throwing for a then-record 7,818 yards and becoming only the fourth quarterback in NCAA history to throw for more than two thousand yards in three straight seasons. Despite the impressive list of Cougar quarterbacks who have come

WSU's Jack Thompson, "Throwin' Samoan," was the most prolific passer in NCAA history.
(Photograph courtesy of Washington State University Athletics)

after him (Mark Rypien, Timm Rosenbach, Drew Bledsoe, and Ryan Leaf), the Throwin' Samoan still owns half of the ten major career passing and total offense records at WSU. Thompson played professional football with the Cincinnati Bengals and Tampa Bay Buccaneers and now lives in Seattle. He is only the second football player in school history to have his jersey (number 14) retired.

⚡ Timbers, Portland

The Portland Timbers were formed in 1975 as part of the now-defunct North American Soccer League (NASL). In only their first season, the Timbers made it all the way to the NASL Soccer Bowl, losing to Tampa Bay 2-0. During

the next several years, Portland was dubbed "Soccer City USA," as the Timbers were one of the most successful franchises in the NASL. Every time the Timbers scored, "Timber Jim" would climb up a pole and cut off a piece with his chain saw. Portland played host to the 1977 Soccer Bowl when a record sellout crowd of 35,548 saw the New York Cosmos defeat the Seattle Sounders 2-1 at Portland's Civic Stadium. The Timbers folded in 1982, but were reborn (albeit for one year only) in 1990 with the creation of the American Professional Soccer League.

⚡ Trail Blazers, Portland

Established in 1970, the National Basketball Association's (NBA) Portland Trail Blazers were named in honor of Meriwether Lewis and William Clark who had "blazed" a trail across the United States to the Pacific Northwest as part of their "Corps of Discovery" (yeah, we watched that Ken Burns special too). In only their seventh season the Blazers captured the 1977 NBA championship, storming back from an 0-2 deficit to beat the Philadelphia 76'ers in six games. It would be fifteen seasons before the Blazers returned to the finals, losing to the Detroit Pistons in 1991 and again in 1992 at the hands of the Chicago Bulls. David Halberstam's landmark sports book *The Breaks of the Game* chronicles the ups and downs of an NBA season with the Portland Trail Blazers.

⚡ Walton, Bill

Named one of the fifty greatest National Basketball Association (NBA) players of all time, Bill Walton was also a world-class eccentric during his days as the center for the Portland Trail Blazers. Looking like a "mountain man" and spouting leftist philosophy, Walton led the Trail Blazers to their first and only NBA championship in the 1976–77 season. During his Trail

Blazers days, Walton was named the NBA's most valuable player, led the league in rebounds and blocked shots, and played in two all-star games. Injuries plagued Walton, whose Trail Blazers career ended in a flurry of litigation over allegedly improper medical treatment. While his playing was "all-league," Walton's persona while in Portland was "all-weird." The definitive Trail Blazers history *Rip City* quotes longtime team announcer Bill Schonely on Walton: "You could find him sitting cross-legged on the floor in airports, burning incense, drinking out of a goatskin pouch. Sometimes he'd carry around a paper sack with some kind of container of carrot juice. Put that with the beard, the weird clothes—I don't think he had more than two shirts—and the whole mountain-man look and the entire scene was just incredible." Walton also found controversy through his friendship with radical journalist Jack Scott who, with his wife Micki, was falsely accused of harboring fugitive Patty Hearst. Today, Walton has reincarnated as a clean-shaven, neatly coifed, suit-wearing television color commentator. Hey, it beats working!

Warner, Curt

The Seattle Seahawks' first "marquee" running back was Curt Warner, an All-American first-round draft choice from 1982 National Champion Penn State University. In Warner's very first game, he raced around left tackle for a sixty-yard gain. He finished his rookie season by leading the American Football Conference (AFC) in rushing with 1,449 yards and thirteen touchdowns as the Seahawks made it all the way to the conference title game before losing 30-13 to the Los Angeles Raiders. Despite a season-ending injury in 1984, Warner had strong years from 1985 to 1988, leading the team in rushing. By 1989, Warner's knees had begun to fail and the team released him after the season. He retired the following season as the Seahawks' all-time leading rusher (since surpassed by Chris Warren). Warner now owns and operates a car dealership in the Seattle suburb of Bellevue.

Waterskiing

In the late twenties, local Seattle high school graduate Don Ibsen began experimenting on Lake Washington with the crude ancestors of today's water skis. At first, Ibsen tried making skis out of wooden boxes and then used regular snow skis, neither of which worked. Finally, he nailed an old pair of tennis shoes to two slabs of cedar which provided the necessary buoyancy and support. Ibsen sold his first pair of water skis in 1934 for $19.95 and spent the next several decades promoting the new sport of waterskiing around the country.

Watts, Slick

Before Michael Jordan made the Yul Brenner-look part of his National Basketball Association (NBA) fashion statement, the mid-seventies version of the Seattle Supersonics featured a backcourt player who wrapped a sweatband around the top of his shiny, shaved head. Donald "Slick" Watts was so unheralded that no NBA team drafted him out of college, and he made the Sonics squad as a free agent at the beginning of the 1973 season. His nickname not only aptly described his bald head but also his uncanny ability to pass and steal on the court. In 1976, he became the first NBA player to lead the league in assists and steals. A crowd favorite who tempted fate by wearing number 13, Watts was traded by the Sonics when Lenny Wilkins returned to lead the club in 1977.

Watts remained in the Seattle area after his playing days and his son Donald helped lead the Washington Huskies to back-to-back appearances in the National Collegiate Athletic Association (NCAA) postseason tournament in 1998 and 1999.

Wave, The

Although hundreds of sports venues claim to be its birthplace, the true home of the most famous fan cheer in the world is Husky Stadium in Seattle. On October 31, 1981, University of Washington Marching Band director Bill Bissell and yell leader Rob Weller created the Wave. For a couple of years, the two had experimented with a version that moved horizontally from the bottom row of the stands to the top. Although it worked well, only part of the stadium could be involved at any one time. During the Halloween game with Stanford, however, they got the idea of moving the Wave section by section in a circular fashion throughout the stadium, and the thing just took off. Band director Bissell recalled that the players stood in awe of what the fans were doing and that Stanford almost didn't get its plays off. Today, the Wave is internationally popular and as much a part of outdoor sporting events as halftime shows and tailgate parties.

Western Hockey League

If you loved hockey in the Northwest from 1950 to 1970, you were probably a Western Hockey League (WHL) fan. One of the best "minor leagues" in the sport, the WHL had franchises throughout the Northwest, including the Portland Buckaroos (whose General Manager Harry Glickman would bring the city the Trail Blazers professional basketball team), the Seattle Totems, and the

Vancouver Canucks (which in 1970 made way for the National Hockey League (NHL) team of the same name).

Wethering, Frosty

A member of the National Association of Intercollegiate Athletics (NAIA) Hall of Fame and one of a handful of college football coaches who have won at least 250 games, Frosty Wethering has been the head coach at Pacific Lutheran University (PLU) in Tacoma since 1972. Since Wethering's arrival, the PLU Lutes have won NAIA Division II national football titles in 1980, 1987, and 1993, and finished as national runner-up in 1983, 1985, 1991, and 1994. In only their second season in NCAA Division III in 1999, the Lutes crushed Rowan University of New Jersey to win the Amos Alonzo Stagg Bowl 42-13, giving Wethering and his Lutes their fourth national title in twenty years. No Lutes team under Wethering has ever had a losing season and his winning percentage is a staggering .789. A former marine drill sergeant, Wethering's football philosophy matches his overall life philosophy of pride, hustle, desire, and the importance of playing to your personal potential. A full professor with a doctorate in education, he is also the author of the book *Make The Big Time Where You Are*.

Whitecaps, Vancouver

Now-defunct North American Soccer League (NASL) franchise the Vancouver Whitecaps was established in 1973 under the ownership of local B.C. sports and political celebrity Herb Capozzi. With such star players as Carl Valentine, Willie Johnson, and Trevor Whymark, the Whitecaps won the NASL championship in 1979 with a 2-1 victory over Tampa Bay in Giants Stadium in East Rutherford, New Jersey. The Whitecaps returned home to the biggest welcome ever accorded any Vancouver team in any sport, as one hundred thousand people crowded into downtown Robson Square for the celebration. While the Whitecaps would continue their winning ways, they never again succeeded as well in the play-offs. As the NASL declined, so did the franchise, and the Whitecaps folded after the 1984 season.

⚆ Whittaker, Jim and Lou

Twin brothers Jim and Lou Whittaker from Seattle may be the most famous American mountain climbers of the twentieth century. In 1963, Jim Whittaker became the first American to climb Mount Everest. Almost twenty years later, Lou Whittaker led the first American expedition up Mount Everest's perilous north side and returned two years later for a second attempt. Jim was the first full-time employee and later president of REI (Recreational Equipment, Incorporated), one of the largest outdoor equipment stores in the world. In 1997, Jim and his family sold their home in Seattle to sail around the world. Now in his seventh decade, Lou continues to run Rainier Mountaineering Guide Services, which leads hundreds of climbers up Washington's Mount Rainier every summer.

⚆ Wilkins, Lenny

The player and coach most closely identified with the glory days of Seattle Supersonics basketball is Hall of Fame member Lenny Wilkins. Wilkins was already an established National Basketball Association (NBA) star in 1969 when he arrived in the Jet City in a trade for Walt Hazzard and was named the Sonics' player-coach. In 1971, Wilkins was named to his third straight all-star game as a Sonic and won the MVP award. Seattle shocked its fans the next year by trading

Wilkins to the Cleveland Cavaliers for Butch Beard. Wilkins retired in 1975 and was hired to coach the Portland Trail Blazers. He was let go after one season, but was given another chance with the Supersonics early in the 1977 season when Bob Hopkins was dismissed after a miserable 5-17 start. With Wilkins in control, the Sonics stormed through the rest of the season, making it all the way to the NBA finals where they lost in seven games to the Washington Bullets. The next season, Seattle avenged the loss and defeated the Bullets in five games to claim their first and only NBA championship. Wilkins continued to coach Seattle through the 1985–86 season when he was "bumped" to the front office. He would go on to coach Cleveland and the Atlanta Hawks, becoming the winningest coach in NBA history.

⚆ Windsurfing

In the sixties, *Seattle Times* reporter Archie Satterfield was called by printing executive Bert Salisbury who wanted to report on a new sport he had discovered in California. Satterfield and his photographer went out to West Seattle's Alki Point where they found Salisbury riding a small surfboard with a sail attached. Salisbury called the sport "windsurfing," and the name stuck. The Columbia River Gorge on the east of Portland is considered one of the finest windsurfing spots in North America.

⚆ Zorn, Jim

During the Seattle Seahawks' first few seasons of futility, southpaw quarterback Jim Zorn personified the team's youthful exuberance and unpredictable nature. A scrambler out of habit and necessity (the expansion awks didn't have much of an offensive line), orn was at his best when the play had broken down and he was forced to improvise. His favorite target was Hall of Fame receiver Steve Largent, and together they formed most of the Seahawks offense early on. Zorn played college at little-known Cal-Poly Pomona but was good enough to gain the attention of the Dallas Cowboys on draft day. When he was cut, the Hawks picked him up, and he was their starter from 1976 to 1983, when Chuck Knox's "ball-control" style of play demanded a more "disciplined" quarterback. In 1991, Zorn was the second player inducted into the Seahawks Ring of Honor.

Mariners, Huskies, Beavers, and Seahawks—nicknames of Northwest sports teams that are instantly recognizable to fans throughout North America. But did you know this list of names might have been Green Sox, Sun Dodgers, Aggies, and Kings? Here's how some of our most popular teams got their monikers.

The oldest sports nicknames belong to Northwest colleges and universities, and animals associated with the region inspired the mascots. The Washington State University (WSU) Cougars were christened in 1927 when Washington Governor Roland Hartley presented a cougar cub to the school's students. The first cougar mascot was named Butch in honor of Herbert "Butch" Meeker of Spokane, who was WSU's gridiron football star at the time. The cougar is also the mascot of Vancouver's Canadian Football League (CFL) franchise the B.C. Lions as well as the Prince George Cougars of the Western Hockey League (WHL).

Up until the early twenties, University of Washington (UW) fans cheered for the Sun Dodgers, also the name of the school's humor magazine which had been banned from the campus. In protest of the ban, the students adopted the nickname for the school's sports teams. Since Sun Dodgers didn't do much to promote a posi-

tive image of the Northwest, a committee was formed in 1921 to select a new nickname. The contest came down to Malamutes and Huskies because of the school's proximity to the Alaskan frontier, and the nickname Huskies was officially adopted in 1923.

The University of Oregon (UO) and Oregon State University (OSU) both adopted animal mascots, but somewhat less fierce than their northern neighbors. OSU teams are named for the state animal, the beaver; although OSU teams had once been known as the Aggies (OSU was a "land grant" agricultural school) and the Orangemen (the school color) before the nickname Beaver was adopted in 1916. The UO mascot is the duck—the legendary killer mallard of Northwest waters which strikes terror into the hearts of all living creatures (well, at least Beavers, Huskies, and Cougars). The school's emblem features a green and yellow clad Donald Duck shaking his fists through a big green "O."

The strangest Northwest sports nickname is the Evergreen State College Geoducks. The geoduck, the world's largest-known burrowing mollusk, became the official mascot of the college during the 1970–71 academic year when Evergreen was still in its embryonic state. The idea snowballed during planning sessions that year when campus facilities were still under construction. Pictures of geoducks were tacked to trailers used as makeshift faculty offices and the idea of the geoduck as mascot became intertwined with the new college's Latin motto *Omnia Extares* which, loosely translated, means "let it all hang out." While no official action was taken to make the geoduck the school mascot, the college bookstore picked up on the idea and began selling geoduck T-shirts that became widely popular.

The University of British Columbia's (UBC) nickname is the mysterious Thunderbird of North Pacific Coast Native American lore, a creature able to grant supernatural blessings or engage in warfare with the Earth's most fierce beasts. Before the early thirties, UBC teams were known simply as Varsity or the Blue and Gold. In 1933, the sports department decided a popular nickname was needed, and the campus paper held a contest to select a name. After two attempts, the winning name chosen was Seagulls, which did not amuse university officials, who selected the name Thunderbirds themselves in 1934.

Northwest Coast Native American mythology also figured prominently in the naming of Seattle's NFL franchise the Seahawks. In the early seventies, former Husky and NFL football star Hugh McElhenny was involved with one of two groups vying for control of the new team. He wanted the nickname to be

Geoduck: My, it's so big! I just know it would make a wonderful college mascot.
(The Geoduck Derby Girls, 1946, by Vibert Jeffers, © Shadow Catchers, Olympia, WA)

Kings, after King County and the King Salmon. The "King" had also been McElhenny's nickname during his football career, and he was not shy about the notion of having the team named in his honor as well. McElhenny's group lost out, however, to the Nordstrom family. Of the more than 20,000 names submitted in a contest for naming the team, 151 people chose Seahawk—a powerful bird in Northwest Native American lore.

During the sixties, the entire Puget Sound area was obsessed with air travel, and the Boeing Company embarked on building a "Supersonic Transport," or SST. Such enthusiasm influenced the naming of Seattle's first professional sports team, the National Basketball Association's (NBA) Seattle Supersonics. Air travel also played a major part in the nickname of the city's ill-fated Major League Baseball (MLB) franchise, the Seattle Pilots.

Although Portland's NBA franchise was formed three years after the Supersonics, the owners looked to the past for their nickname, choosing to honor the Lewis and Clark expedition with the name Trail Blazers. During his playing days with the Blazers, Bill Walton did his best to live up to the team's rugged "mountain man" image, sporting long hair and a scraggly beard. The now-defunct Portland Timbers of the North American Soccer League were also part of the same "Great Woods" vibe.

Because of the Northwest's proximity to the Pacific Ocean and the millions who live near Puget Sound, nautical themes have been chosen for several regional sports teams. When Seattle was granted another MLB franchise after the Pilots left for Milwaukee, a number of names were suggested for the new team. Some wanted to invoke the past by naming the team the Seattle Rainiers, after the longtime Pacific Coast League Triple A team. Others preferred a more traditional baseball name like the Seattle Green Sox, evergreen trees being rather abundant in the Northwest.

The name Mariners was adopted after a naming contest and the team's first logo was a large letter M drawn in the shape of a trident. The nautical theme was taken so far that during the team's first three seasons, outfield distances were marked on the Kingdome fences in both feet and fathoms (one fathom equals six feet). Other nautically themed Northwest sports teams included the Seattle Sounders and Vancouver Whitecaps soccer franchises, both of which sank in the early eighties.

The Northwest may be best known for its generally miserable weather which has been used four times as the inspiration for a nickname. In the mid-1970s, Portland fielded two teams which were part of the disastrous World Football League. The Portland Storm debuted in 1974, followed the next year by the Portland Thunder. Storm? Thunder? It was really just a drizzle as the team failed to post a winning margin in

either year and the league folded midway through the second season. Wet weather also played a role in the naming of Seattle's first women's professional basketball team. The Seattle Reign was part of the now-defunct American Basketball League that folded in December 1998. Fittingly, the new Seattle team in the Women's National Basketball Association is the Storm.

During the next century, new Northwest sports teams will be formed while others will fold. The naming game, however, will continue. Whereas many of the Northwest's twentieth-century sports teams were inspired by the historical traditions and animals of the region, the teams of the future may be named after the regional icons of the late twentieth century. Seattle Java, Portland Ales, and the Vancouver Stars, anyone?

No professional sport is analyzed and mythologized more than baseball. While that's usually not a bad thing, some sports traditionalists (aka snobs) define the sophistication of their cities and regions by the age of their baseball teams. The longer the team has been around, the more lore and legend there is, allowing part-time baseball aficionados such as Doris Kearns Goodwin and George Will to write goopy articles that use baseball metaphors to describe the state of the economy or society's bias against left-handed clowns. Actually, we're just jealous because no one ever asked us to write a story about what we learned about life from going to ball games with our fathers.

Now, since the first major league baseball team didn't arrive in the Northwest until 1969 (and left after only one year), some of those dastardly East Coast columnists might try to fool you into believing the Northwest has no colorful baseball past. Perish the thought! While we'll admit that you can't get a real Philly cheese steak sandwich anywhere in Washington, Oregon, or British Columbia, there's still plenty of rich baseball tradition waiting to be told that rivals the best that Boston, New York, and Chicago have to offer.

The Northwest has certainly had its share of colorful baseball players over the years. In a Kingdome contest in 1981, Seattle Mariners infielder Lenny Randle actually got down on his hands and knees and tried to blow foul a slow-rolling grounder down the third baseline. Always the comic, Randle also once mimicked Richard Nixon's famous "V for Victory" salute the night the ex-president made a visit to the Mariners' locker room.

Speaking of comedians, former Mariners relief pitcher Bill Caudill often showed up in the dugout with a Sherlock Holmes hat and carrying a large magnifying glass, leading his teammates to call him "The Inspector." The Kingdome organist even got into the act by playing the theme from The Pink Panther as Caudill walked to the mound. "Cuffs," as he was known in the clubhouse, also once filled manager Rene Lachemann's hotel toilet with Jell-O.

Not all Northwest baseball players have been comedians. Portland has produced two of major league baseball's finest players. Former Atlanta Braves star Dale Murphy is a graduate of

Portland's Wilson High School and the only baseball player from Oregon to win baseball's Most Valuable Player Award twice, in 1982 and 1983. Detroit Tigers pitcher Mickey Lolich graduated from Portland's Lincoln High School where he led the Cardinals to the Oregon State High School title by striking out eighteen batters. And Vancouver Canadians pitcher Tom Drees once threw three no-hitters during the team's 1989 Pacific Coast League championship season. The first two were on consecutive starts on May 23 and May 29. The last was on August 16. Despite this incredible accomplishment, Drees never amounted to much beyond the minor leagues.

Unfortunately, a number of Northwest players are better known for their futility and foibles. Mario Mendoza was a journeyman infielder who played a couple of seasons with the Seattle Mariners. A lifetime .215 hitter, Mendoza finished five seasons batting under .200. His pathetic hitting skills prompted former Kansas City Royals great George Brett to once say, "The first thing I look for in the Sunday papers is to see who's below the 'Mendoza' line." To hit below .200 is now regularly referred to in baseball jargon as the "Mendoza Line."

In August 1991, Mariners catcher Dave Valle's hitting was so bad that two drinking establishments near the Kingdome announced that they would adjust the price of well drinks and beer in accordance with his batting average. For a while, it was a good deal for drinkers, with the price of amber ale pegged at $1.27 when the stunt began. Valle was not amused.

On September 30, 1980, Seattle Mariners pitcher Rick Honeycutt was pitching against the Kansas City Royals when the home plate umpire caught him in an illegal act. Hidden under a flesh-colored Band-Aid on the forefinger of Honeycutt's glove hand was a thumbtack and a piece of sandpaper which he was using to scratch the ball. According to Honeycutt, only three balls were scratched that night and none of them did anything strange. He was simply looking for something to help turn around a 10-17 season that had started so promisingly at 6-0. It didn't matter. Honeycutt was fined $250 and suspended for ten days. To top it off, on the way back to the dugout after getting tossed, Honeycutt wiped his hand across his brow and left a deep scratch mark on his forehead from the tack still taped to his finger.

Northwest baseball managers have also added to the region's hardball lore. During a game against the Milwaukee Brewers, former Mariners skipper Maury Wills casually walked to the pitchers mound and beckoned for a relief pitcher to come in. One problem. Wills had never told any pitchers to warm up. When the Texas Rangers played the Seattle Mariners in a game at the end of the 1980 season, it was the first time a father (Maury Wills) had managed against his son (Bump Wills) in the big leagues. Too bad father and son weren't on speaking terms due to an incident several years before in which Maury had caught his son having sex with Dad's girlfriend. When he was tapped to be Mariners manager in 1980, Wills was also quoted as saying, "Playing .500 baseball will be easy," even though the Mariners had never had a winning season. Wills ended his short reign of error with a record of 26-56.

Current Seattle Mariners manager Lou Piniella was briefly on the spring training roster of the Seattle Pilots. He was traded before the start of the regular season to the Kansas City Royals for outfielder Steve Whitaker and pitcher John Gelnar. "Sweet Lou" also spent some time in the minor leagues with the Portland Beavers, and one night his legendary temper got the best of him. After striking out with the bases loaded, Lou took out his frustration on the outfield fence only to have a fifteen-foot section collapse on top of him. It took the Civic Stadium grounds crew several embarrassing minutes to unpin him.

Perhaps the most colorful Northwest baseball manager was Joe Schultz of the Seattle Pilots. A former third base coach for the St. Louis Cardinals, Schultz was portrayed as a bit of a buffoon in Jim Bouton's *Ball Four*, particularly when it came to his "motivational" one-liners. "Attaway to go boys. Pound that old Budweiser into you and go get them tomorrow" was a favorite "Schultzism" that kept Pilots players in stitches (and beer) during the summer of 1969.

Players and managers always agree on one thing: baseball would be a lot easier without interference from the owners. Former Seattle Mariners promotions director Bill Long once had a miniature tugboat constructed to bring relief pitchers from the bullpen to the mound during the 1982 season. The players hated the spectacle and the idea only lasted one season. Long also created The Good Ship Mariner, which would rise from behind the centerfield wall to fire a cannon after every Mariners home run during the 1980s.

The Seattle Steelheads and the Portland Rosebuds were part of the six-team West Coast Baseball Association that was formed by several African American businessmen in 1946. The all-black-players league folded after three months. Other notable Northwest baseball owners include British Columbia premier W. A. C. Bennett, who was an original shareholder in the Vancouver Mounties Pacific Coast League club, and Danny Kaye (1976–1981) and David Letterman (1989–1992), who were both minority owners of the Seattle Mariners.

And then there are those Northwest baseball incidents that are just plain weird. On July 19, 1994, falling acoustical tiles shut down the King-

dome, forcing the Seattle Mariners to play their final games on the road until the baseball strike canceled play for the season. Two years later, a 5.4 magnitude earthquake caused the suspension of a ball game in the Kingdome between the Mariners and the Cleveland Indians.

Legendary Negro League pitcher Satchel Paige appeared in a game with the Portland Beavers as a promotional stunt in 1961. For a couple of innings, the fifty-five-year-old Paige threw his patented "two-hump blooper" and "hesitation pitch." In another Rose City Pacific Coast League contest in 1984, female umpire Pam Postema tossed Portland Beavers skipper Lee Elia and most of his players from a game. She even threw out the batboy who refused to retrieve a chair that Elia had thrown out on the field.

Although it may not be the stuff of the Cubbies, the Yankees, and the Red Sox, the Northwest is slowly building up its own stash of baseball lore. Now all we need is a World Series.